Clearing a Path

THEORIZING THE PAST IN NATIVE AMERICAN STUDIES

EDITED BY *Nancy Shoemaker*

ROUTLEDGE
New York London

Published in 2002 by
Routledge
29 West 35th Street
New York, NY 10001

Published in Great Britain by
Routledge
11 New Fetter Lane
London EC4P 4EE

Routledge is an imprint of the Taylor & Francis Group.

10   9   8   7   6   5   4   3   2   1

Library of Congress Cataloging-in-Publication Data

Shoemaker, Nancy, 1958–
Clearing a path: theorizing the past in Native American studies / edited by Nancy Shoemaker.
p. cm.
Includes bibliographical references and index.
ISBN 0-415-92674-2 — ISBN 0-415-92675-0 (pbk.)
1. Indians of North America—Historiography.   2. Indians of North America—Study and teaching.
I. Shoemaker, Nancy, 1958–
E76.8 C54 2001
970'.00497'0072—dc21   2001019493

Clearing
a Path

CONTENTS

INTRODUCTION

Nancy Shoemaker

"Clearing a path" is a metaphor appropriated from American Indian ritual and diplomacy. When northeastern Indians met other Indians or Europeans in council in the 17th and 18th centuries, they talked about "clearing the path" of brambles, fallen logs, and other obstacles so that trade and travel between their respective nations could flourish. As the title for this volume of essays, "clearing a path" has a different meaning, for it intends to suggest a clarifying or opening up of ways to see the past. There are eight paths in this volume, eight essays exploring ways to understand or conceptualize Native American history.

The subtitle for this volume further defines its subject as "theorizing," a choice of phrasing requiring explanation. Some fields of study, the social sciences especially, make theory a requisite for scholarly research and writing. In other fields of study, among many historians, for example, theory has about the same standing as certain four-letter words. Few historians ever mention the word *theory*, and only rarely do historians ask each other questions like "What theory are you using?" And even though anthropology in general, as a social science, mandates that research be grounded in theory, works in American Indian anthropology, and in ethnohistory in particular, can be purely descriptive without others challenging them for lack of a theoretical framework.

To some, theory has positivist connotations and conjures up images of scientific laboratories and computer spreadsheets. Or, in its most recent incarnation as a tool for postmodern humanists, theory can seem a cacophony of incomprehensible jargon. In his introduction to *The Blackwell Companion to Social Theory*, Bryan S. Turner (2000:6–7) provides a useful overview of the role of theory in scholarship that makes clear how theory can mean different things to different people. Theory can be an empirically based "causal explanation," "an interpretation of social reality which leads to understanding via adequate description," or even "a form of fictional writing which imaginatively reconstructs meaning." All those possible roles for theory apply here. If you do not care for the word theory, then think instead of these essays as dealing with models, paradigms, perspectives, ideas, narratives, research questions, or analytical frameworks. At best, theories are devices for articulating research questions and zeroing in on important issues. Theories trim away excess information and coagulate details to form meaningful explanations. To fall back on a handy cliché, theories make it possible for us to see the forest through the trees. Even misguided, mistaken, and abandoned theories have done some service by raising questions to ask about the past or by presenting us with different possibilities for how best to portray what happened in the past.

Despite the benefits of thinking theoretically, theory has not figured prominently in discussions of research, writing, and teaching about the past in American Indian studies. There have been efforts to describe and label a coherent body of rules and practices, but I doubt anyone thinks of these efforts as constituting theorizing. The most enduring of such attempts is *ethnohistory*, a term commonly employed by anthropologists and historians but one that still engenders debate (Axtell 1979; Trigger 1982; Meyer and Klein 1998). For anthropologists, ethnohistory usually means incorporating written, historical documents as sources of information and highlighting changes over time. Since such a definition would not distinguish what historians of Indian history do from what historians do generally, ethnohistory in history circles often signals an emphasis on culture as a force in explaining or influencing changes over time. Ethnohistory's origins among anthropologists hired to research Indian land claims in the post–World War II period has endowed it with the additional, awkward legacy of appearing to focus first on North American Indians, then colonial Latin America, and sometimes Africa and parts of Asia—the peoples Europeans colonized or, as Eric Wolf (1982) termed it, "people without history." Ethnohistory survives in the American Society for Ethnohistory and its journal, *Ethnohistory*. However, it is not generally considered a theory. Some might call it a methodology. Most of us prefer not to call it anything at all. As with *culture*, we prefer the luxury of using the word without having to state precisely what we mean by it.

Another effort to conceptualize the field under a rubric was the "New Indian History" proposed by Robert Berkhofer in the early 1970s. Directing his critique at other historians in Indian studies whose work concentrated on Indian-white relations, Berkhofer (1971:357) recommended instead that scholars put "more of the Indians into it" and consider investigating such topics as Indian-Indian relations and internal divisions within Indian tribes. Of course, any initiative claiming to be "new" cannot go on for 20 or 30 years and still be thought of as new. In this case, Berkhofer's propositions became the accepted standard by which much of Indian history would be judged; like ethnohistory, with which it was compatible, the "new Indian history" summed up a perspective and advocated new topics for research.

Neither ethnohistory nor the new Indian history provided models or overarching interpretations of past events. However, scholars avowing allegiance to either of these schools have indeed engaged with theory, often without saying so explicitly. For example, among historians in the 1990s, two influential theories have predominated and given titles to books: Richard White's (1991) *The Middle Ground* and James H. Merrell's (1989) *The Indians' New World*. Both authors, Merrell especially, might shudder at my claim that their books each center around a theory, but the utility and adaptability of their main arguments to other scholars' projects earn them that label. Both White and Merrell wrote about the effects of European trade and settlement on Native communities in two different regions, with White focusing on the Great Lakes and Merrell on the Carolina Piedmont. Richard White described the Middle Ground as arising at certain places and in certain times to form a kind of bridge between peoples, where each party accommodated elements of the other's cultural practices and forms but as a transitory mechanism designed to promote immediate objectives. Part of the appeal of Merrell's *The Indians' New World* lay in its articulation of a counterexplanation, a different story line for tracking the course of Indian-European relations. In his account, Merrell placed the burden of accommodation on Native peoples by arguing that Carolina Indians continually found new ways to adapt to the intrusive and expanding European presence. Both these books had a tremendous impact on Native, frontier, and borderlands scholarship in the 1990s as Middle Grounds and New Worlds sprung up all over North America.

The Middle Ground and The Indians' New World are models of the past that originated within the study of North American Native history. Other theories scholars in Indian studies employ often emerge from the same theoretical impulses wafting through other areas of academic inquiry. Thus in the 1970s, Marxism became a popular locus for the ideas behind research in Indian studies (see Albers's essay in this collection), just as Marxism was influential in informing the New Social History. The 1980s saw a wave of monographs organized around one of several Marxist-influenced dependency or world-systems theories (Wolf 1982; White 1983; Hall 1989). And by the 1990s, scholars in Indian studies were reading and responding to theoretical literature designated as postmodern, postcolonial, deconstructive, and/or self-reflexive (Strong 1996; Richter 1993; Brown and Vibert, 1996).

There are, therefore, plenty of theories within and outside of Native history that have been called upon in the act of research and writing to provide questions, possible explanations, and an understanding of complex historical processes. Admittedly, however, Indian studies—and not just the history wing of Indian studies—is a field tending toward skepticism about theory, and for a good reason. The individuals who come to mind as the world's most significant theorists are almost all European (Marx, Freud) and usually French (Foucault, Derrida, Lacan, Bourdieu). Even those theorists (Said, Fanon, Spivak, Bhabha) writing from the perspective of the colonized, or postcolonized, seem foreign and distant from North American Indian studies. The possibility of something called "indigenous theory" is in the air, but at the moment it is not clear what shape these discussions will take or what impact they will have (Smith 1999).

Another obstacle to recognizing a place for theory within American Indian studies is that theory generalizes whereas Indian studies for most of the 20th century has emphasized particularity. Franz Boas's early-20th-century promotion of cultural relativism as an ideal established a set of values within Indian studies that encourages us to look for differences and uniqueness and not to position a research study within part of a larger global pattern or phenomena. Moreover, the history of colonialism has constructed a perception of a world divided into two types of people: the colonizers and the colonized, Western and non-Western, advanced and primitive, civilized and savage, indigenous and nonindigenous, industrial and nonindustrial, literate and nonliterate. Ideally, theory should help us break away from such facile categorizations, but it is precisely these types of oppositions that underlie colonial power struggles. Ideas in the 19th century about human societies and culture, which drew heavily on evolutionary theory, found such categorizations useful in justifying an unequal distribution of power and wealth among the world's peoples. At the same time, the struggle of colonial peoples around the world for sovereignty and independence could not challenge such constructs without drawing further attention to them. Asserting grievances, demanding recompense, and protecting sovereignty lead to political acts, motivations, and strategies undergirded by a sense of difference, not a sense of commonality (Churchill 1983).

This collection of essays intends to bring all of these issues in under the light for full scrutiny and consideration. Although this volume is unique in what it offers, it also fits within a larger tradition of books that survey American Indian studies historiography (Swagerty 1984; Calloway 1988), provide a multidisciplinary assessment of the state of Indian studies as a field (Thornton 1998), address the politics of research and writing in Indian studies (Mihesuah 1998; Martin 1987; Biolsi and Zimmerman 1997), or manage some combination of all the above (Fixico 1997). The distinctive contribution *Clearing a Path* makes is its evaluation of the role of theory in American Indian historical studies while keeping one eye on the fruitful possibilities and the other eye on the limitations. These essays are more suggestive than they are exhaustive.

The eight essays are paired so as to cover four general topics: narrative and storytelling, social and cultural categories, political economy, and a section dealing with frames of reference, the micro and the macro, tribal histories and indigenous histories. By pairing the essays, I do not intend that they should be seen as promoting opposing views; instead, they complement each other. Thus, the anthropologist Julie Cruikshank and the creative writer LeAnne Howe both regard narrative as a form of theorizing, a way to make meaningful sense out of past events. Cruikshank describes how academic scholars and the Native women in the Yukon who told her their stories influenced her thinking on what narrative means and how people use stories to give shape to their individual and collective histories. In the same vein, LeAnne Howe argues that narratives—whether classified as mythological, scientific, historical, or fictional—all share in their power to create truths to live by and through which to see the world, as she says, in the past, present, and future.

Next, Gunlög Fur and I discuss the importance of social and cultural categories in understanding the past. My essay deals with categories in general and reviews how anthropologists and linguists have tried to explain the inner workings of categorization and whether these ideas have been and could be useful to those of us studying American Indian history. Fur's essay focuses on gender as a category of analysis, but she also emphasizes that limiting any study to gender alone will miss the significance of age and individuality, gaps between the ideal and the real, and other complexities.

The third section of the book, on political economy, has essays by Patricia C. Albers and Jacki Thompson Rand. Albers weighs the pros and cons of the two schools of thought that have prevailed in the last few decades: materialist theories heavily influenced by Marx and Engels and the more recent postmodern relativism. Albers articulates a necessary, sensible compromise between the two perspectives. Jacki Rand applies a different body of economic theory—dealing with the social and cultural meanings of economic exchange under colonialism—to provide an alternative vision of the political economy of reservations.

Finally, the last two essays take us out of our familiar boxes. Craig Howe liberates us from the written form and argues that other media—hypertext technology and museum exhibits—have the potential to recreate more fully the experience and effect of Native ways of telling history. James F. Brooks positions his previous research on Indian-Spanish relations in the southwestern borderlands within a comparative framework. He alerts us to how cultural mixing and the emergence of new, fixed identities are recurring processes accompanying the expansion and migration of peoples. Craig Howe emphasizes tribalism, the local and communal aspects of history. Brooks places American Indian history in a global perspective.

Although appearing within one of these four broad groupings, each of the eight essays crosses those boundaries to speak to issues raised elsewhere in the collection. Themes that emerge throughout the eight chapters are ideas about how to discern what events meant to the people who lived through them, how to make use of different types of historical sources, how to be open to all possible interpretations, and the importance of trying to understand American Indian history through the social and cultural forms of the peoples whose history is being told. Clearing a path of brambles and logs is a job requiring constant maintenance, and ideally this book will serve as a starting point for further discussion of what role theories should have in studies of the past.

REFERENCES

Axtell, James
    1979   Ethnohistory: An Historian's Viewpoint. Ethnohistory 26:1–13.
Berkhofer, Robert F., Jr.
    1971   The Political Context of a New Indian History. Pacific Historical Review 40:
            357–382.
Biolsi, Thomas, and Larry J. Zimmerman, eds.
    1997   Indians and Anthropologists: Vine Deloria, Jr., and the Critique of Anthropology. Tucson: University of Arizona Press.
Brown, Jennifer S. H., and Elizabeth Vibert, eds.
    1996   Reading Beyond Words: Contexts for Native History. Peterborough, Ontario:
            Broadview Press.
Calloway, Colin G., ed.
    1988   New Directions in American Indian History. Norman: University of Oklahoma
            Press.
Churchill, Ward, ed.
    1983   Marxism and Native Americans. Boston: South End Press.
Fixico, Donald L., ed.
    1997   Rethinking American Indian History. Albuquerque: University of New Mexico
            Press.
Hall, Thomas D.
    1989   Social Change in the Southwest, 1350–1880. Lawrence: University Press of
            Kansas.
Martin, Calvin H., ed.
    1987   The American Indian and the Problem of History. New York: Oxford University Press.

Merrell, James H.
    1989   The Indians' New World: Catawbas and Their Neighbors from European Con-
            tact through the Era of Removal. Chapel Hill: University of North Carolina
            Press for the Institute of Early American History and Culture.
Meyer, Melissa L., and Kerwin Lee Klein
    1998   Native American Studies and the End of Ethnohistory. *In* Studying Native
            America: Problems and Prospects. Russell Thornton, ed. Pp. 182–216. Madi-
            son: University of Wisconsin Press.
Mihesuah, Devon A., ed.
    1998   Natives and Academics: Researching and Writing about American Indians.
            Lincoln: University of Nebraska Press.
Richter, Daniel K.
    1993   Whose Indian History? William and Mary Quarterly 50:379–393.
Smith, Linda Tuhiwai
    1999   Decolonizing Methodologies: Research and Indigenous Peoples. New York:
            Zed Books.
Strong, Pauline Turner
    1996   Feminist Theory and the "Invasion of the Heart" in North America. Ethnohis-
            tory 43:683–712.
Swagerty, W. R., ed.
    1984   Scholars and the Indian Experience: Critical Reviews of Recent Writing in the
            Social Sciences. Bloomington: Indiana University Press.
Thornton, Russell, ed.
    1998   Studying Native America: Problems and Prospects. Madison: University of
            Wisconsin Press.
Trigger, Bruce G.
    1982   Ethnohistory: Problems and Prospects. Ethnohistory 29:1–19.
Turner, Bryan S, ed.
    2000   The Blackwell Companion to Social Theory. 2nd. ed. Malden, MA: Blackwell.
White, Richard
    1983   The Roots of Dependency: Subsistence, Environment, and Social Change
            among the Choctaws, Pawnees, and Navajos. Lincoln: University of Nebraska
            Press.
    1991   The Middle Ground: Indians, Empires, and Republics in the Great Lakes
            Region, 1650–1815. New York: Cambridge University Press.
Wolf, Eric R.
    1982   Europe and the People without History. Berkeley: University of California
            Press.

Stories

Oral History, Narrative Strategies, and Native American Historiography: Perspectives from the Yukon Territory, Canada

Julie Cruikshank

The place and meaning of stories and their contribution to how we think about the past are receiving fresh attention in humanities and human sciences (Cronon 1992; Cohen 1994; Hinchman and Hinchman 1998). In North America, as elsewhere, this development has consequences for oral histories, once evaluated by historians and anthropologists primarily with reference to questions about accuracy, objectivity, reliability, and verifiability (Lowie 1917; Malinowski 1926; Vansina 1985). A richer vein concerns how oral narratives intersect with social practice, how they continue to provide a framework for understanding contemporary issues, and how stories are inevitably part of larger social, historical, and political processes. Viewed from this perspective, narrative authorizes ways of seeing and interpreting the world (de Certeau 1984:123), invokes a social system (White 1987:14), and provides a moral education (McIntyre 1981:114). Oral transmission of stories is a panhuman activity, probably the oldest form of history making, and in many parts of the world has a continuing role in the production and reproduction of history.

Theoretical attention to the actual work narrative accomplishes destabilizes any simple idea that stories passed on as oral tradition transparently "speak for themselves" or that there is *a* prescriptive, cross-culturally valid method for evaluating their historical value. Facts, as Eric Wolf points out, cannot find their voice without some help from a theoretical scheme (1999:16). The notion that oral traditions from the North American continent can be viewed as broadly homogeneous data from which facts about "what really happened" can be extruded ignores substantial research on memory and forgetting now emerging from post-Stalinist Russia (Khubova et al. 1992), sub-Saharan Africa (Hofmeyer 1993), Kentucky coal mining communities (Portelli 1997), post-Fascist Italy (Passerini 1987), and elsewhere (Passerini 1992; Watson 1994; Leydesdorff et al. 1996). Oral histories from indigenous North America are too frequently evaluated with reference only to one another, and while the reasons are understandable, encapsulating them within a continental tradition sometimes partitions these narratives from international debates to which they might contribute.

Storytelling may be a universal human activity, but the concepts communicated in stories depend on close attention to local metaphor and local narrative conventions. The Modoc writer and scholar Michael Dorris pointed out years ago that national literatures (like national histories) come from coherent aggregations of people who share an identifiable language and worldview; terms like "American Indian" or "Native American," he suggests, homogenize one of the most linguistically and culturally plural areas the world has ever known (1979:147). In recent academic writing, approaches to analysis of oral tradition are converging. With our growing awareness that oral spoken performances are always situated, anthropological attention to cultural categories, cosmologies, and symbols is merging with archaeologists' grasp of the material record and historians' critical evaluation of written documents. Linguists working collaboratively with indigenous storytellers make us aware of the variety of narrative genres grouped under the broad rubric of "Native American literature" (Hymes 1981; Dauenhauer and Dauenhauer 1987; Basso 1996). If there are broad pan–North American similarities in storytelling traditions, they probably have more to do with epistemology than with content. Indigenous people who grow up immersed in oral tradition frequently suggest that their narratives are better understood by absorbing the successive personal messages revealed to listeners in repeated tellings than by trying to analyze and publicly explain their meanings—an approach that contrasts sharply with protocols in many academic disciplines (Morrow 1995:29).

What is too often missing from American Indian studies as a whole, Greg Sarris (1993) suggests, is interruption and risk. Scholars frame the experiences of others with reference to disciplinary norms. Yet unless we put ourselves in interactive situations where we are exposed and vulnerable, where these norms are interrupted and challenged, we can never recognize the limitations of our own descriptions. Academic discourse, Sarris argues, has to be broadly interrogated by other forms of discourse in order to make it clearer what each has to offer the other. He carries on simultaneous conversations with his Pomo aunts—Mabel McKay, Violet Chappell, Frances McDaniel, Anita Silva—and with scholars whose work he admires—Mikhail Bakhtin, Walter Benjamin, Paul

Ricoeur, and Edward Said. His goal is to convey something of that jarring "be-tweenness" of cross-cultural understanding by showing how his aunts' stories cause him to become as sharply critical of his own confident interpretations as of the interpretations of other scholars.

This paper builds on long-term ethnographic work—talking with people about issues and questions grounded in everyday experiences—in a particular region of northwestern Canada. During the 1970s and 1980s, I had the oppor-tunity to work with several elders from the Yukon Territory, speakers of Tagish, Tutchone, and Tlingit and English languages, who were interested in docu-menting memories and having me transcribe their narratives for children, grandchildren, and other family members. Framed as a collaborative project from the outset, this work initially seemed to contribute directly to a larger project of documenting social histories often marginalized in the written record. My search for theoretical guidance grew as I came to see how elders of First Nations ancestry in the Yukon Territory continue to tell stories that make meaningful connections between past and present. Stories, like good theories, make connections that may not at first glance seem straightforward.

In trying to understand issues surrounding transmission of oral narrated histories in northwestern Canada, I have been drawn to questions about narra-tive raised decades ago by scholars working independently in very different parts of the world—Harold Innis, Mikhail Bakhtin, and Walter Benjamin. Each was concerned about the role of oral storytelling in human history, and each deplored the consequences when oral storytelling becomes marginalized by more powerful knowledge systems. Each insisted that narrative is grounded in material circumstances of everyday life and capable of addressing large ques-tions about the consequences of historical events. Such ideas have relevance for ongoing discussions and debates about history that are part of daily conver-sation in Yukon aboriginal communities. Angela Sidney and Kitty Smith, Yukon elders whose work is discussed in this paper, were contemporaries of Innis, Bakhtin, and Benjamin, although they lived much longer and their worlds dif-fered considerably. Their stories certainly do incorporate information about the past, but, more important, the act of storytelling provides ways of making his-torical changes understandable.

Approaches to analysis of oral narrative have become embroiled in broad methodological and theoretical debates in the social sciences that I merely flag here and return to later in the paper. Timeworn arguments about reliability of oral history are familiar enough, but there are deeper issues. To begin with, oral tradition is frequently situated at one pole of centurylong discussions opposing universalist and particularist explanations, now usually framed in terms of local versus global distinctions. My contention is that to relegate them only to the local and the particular is to oversimplify the very real *work* that stories do. Second, oral narrative is frequently positioned on the "mentalist" side of a philosophical divide distinguishing materialist from idealist approaches to understanding power; again, I think this distinction is misplaced. Third, approaches stressing narrative understanding may seem superficially to strand oral tradition on the shores of postmodern relativism when they actually address hierarchies of power in very precise ways. Such troublesome dualisms have a long history, but insights from Bakhtin, Benjamin, and Innis may guide us through this thicket and back to a broader understanding of narrative's role in exploring intersections among knowledge, power, and ideology.

I begin this paper by introducing writings that raised questions about the potential of local oral narratives to engage with global issues long before such issues were taken seriously. I go on to discuss how the shifting power relations described by Innis, Bakhtin, and Benjamin speak to conditions in the Yukon during the late 19th century and early- to-mid-20th century. I draw on work by Angela Sidney and Kitty Smith, briefly summarizing basic understandings about local social organization that each would expect of an intelligent listener, and then illustrate with two stories *about* their stories. I identify where I see convergence among the approaches of these five writers and storytellers. I conclude with a cautionary tale about the late-20th-century reification of oral traditions in legal arenas. My thesis is that local voices from North American indigenous communities provide more than grist for conventional disciplinary paradigms and have the power to contribute to our understanding of historiography.

Late in life, the Canadian economic historian Harold Innis developed an enduring interest in oral tradition. Best known for his economic thesis that mercantile capitalism inevitably produces margins in the process of exploiting them, he attributed Canada's existence to profits it offered imperial Britain, both as a source of unprocessed staples—furs, gold, cod, and timber—and as a market for commodities manufactured in distant industrial centers (Innis 1930, 1940, 1956). Investigating how Empire manages the awkward problem of administering far-flung territories, Innis was drawn to the history of communications. He pointed to the overweening imperial ambition to assert power during periods of territorial expansion by monopolizing and categorizing information and by routinely silencing local traditions that do not fit official categories. A crucial feature of administration in the hinterland is classification and control of activities and authorization of official observations, categories, and statistics in written texts. While this process is conventionally rationalized as both producing knowledge and serving the interests of those administered, it invariably occurs at the expense of existing regional traditions. Innis came to see colonialism as simultaneously economic and intellectual (1950, 1951).

Innis proposed that arctic and subarctic regions provide a visual template for the modernist tendency to conceptualize time as spatially laid out, mechanically segmented, and linear. Colonial projects, he observed, move forward by devising and reinforcing categories—objectivity, subjectivity, space, time—that encourage the annexation of territories and the subjugation of former inhabitants (1956:12–14). Gradually, those at the center monopolize what comes to be considered rational discourse and marginalize those who speak in a different idiom. Innis admired the structural characteristics of oral tradition and saw it as having potential to counterbalance mechanical segmentation of time and space by insisting on the importance of qualitative time in human affairs. Oral tradition, he argued, permits continuous revision of history by actively reinterpreting events and then incorporating such interpretations into the next generation of narrative. Its flexibility allows a gifted storyteller to adapt a given narrative to make sense of a confusing situation (1950:64–100; see also Stamps 1995:48–51).

Innis went on to investigate historical processes by which literacy has displaced the authority of the spoken word, tracing the demise of oral tradition in Egypt, Babylon, Greece, and Rome. He came to view Socrates as the last great exponent of oral tradition and his death at the beginning of the fourth century B.C. as coinciding with a shift from customary law to codified judicial codes (1950:68–69, 81–82; 1951:43–45). Until then, he maintained, oral tradition had given vitality to the written word and had actively prevented concentration of power because a society retaining a central place for orality could not be disciplined to the point of political unity (1951:8–9). Innis was especially intrigued by the ways oral tradition worked in conjunction with writing to provide a kind of dialogue that he saw as a model for social action (Stamps 1995:11). "My bias is with the oral tradition . . . and with the necessity of capturing something of its spirit," he concluded. "The quantitative pressure of modern knowledge has been responsible for the decay of oral dialectic and conversation" (1951:190).

Innis's views about creative potential of oral tradition mirrored those of his contemporary Mikhail Bakhtin, also writing during the 1930s and 1940s, though from more constrained circumstances in Stalinist Russia. They wrote in different languages and neither ever encountered the other's work, but their approaches were similarly eclectic. Bakhtin, like Innis, was drawn to the open-ended possibilities he saw in oral dialogue and the thoroughness with which totalitarian regimes worked to suppress those possibilities. Observing the chilling transformations occurring in 1930s postrevolutionary Russia, Bakhtin concluded that there must be forms of resistance more effective than the violent replacement of one set of leaders by another, and he looked to everyday spoken language for inspiration. He sought out cases where narrative successfully resists such domestication, marginalization, and erasure and was eventually drawn to processes set in motion by conversational forms of oral storytelling. He interpreted what he called its "dialogic," relational possibilities (especially when laced with disruptive humor) as a model inherently opposing authoritarian speech (Bakhtin 1984b).

Bakhtin, with his energetic appreciation of the destabilizing possibilities of folk humor, struggled in 1930s Russia to imagine subversion in totalitarian states. Any adequate reading of contemporary culture, in his view, required an understanding of how ordinary people have used oral communication strategies to resist arbitrary power. In terms applying equally to the capitalist frontier of subarctic Canada and the communist frontier of subarctic Russia, Bakhtin formulated the problem of history as its tendency to foster apparent randomness—for the order of events seemingly to disintegrate. And he saw narrative's role as a constraining, countervailing one of holding things together. The metaphor underlying his model of communication was that of a centrifuge with two countervailing forces: authoritarian speech displacing local ideas to the margins, and irascible, irreverent, brash orality magnetically straining to hold a center (Clark and Holquist 1984:9). His larger point mirrors that made by Innis: narrative challenges hegemonic institutions (Bakhtin 1984a).

A decade later and in another country, Walter Benjamin grappled with similar issues engulfing Europe during the early years of Hitler's ascendancy. He, too, noted the insidious consequences of deteriorating dialogue in modern society, attributing them at least partly to the diminishing role of the storyteller. As communications technology proliferates, he argued, information becomes fragmented and detached from the moral philosophical guidance we think of as knowledge and might once even have called wisdom. Benjamin believed that orally transmitted narratives develop in their hearers a capacity to listen, a deteriorating skill in an age of ever-fragmenting information. He probably would have agreed with Bruno Latour's pithy observation that "information [referring specifically to the Internet] is the enemy of civilized society."[1] The power of narrative storytelling, in his view, lies in its capacity to interweave drama and practical experience with moral content. Storytelling is open-ended rather than didactic, allowing listeners to draw independent conclusions from what they hear. Medieval storytellers recounted events without imposing an interpretation, and their practice had equally important consequences for the arts of telling and the arts of listening. By the very act of telling stories, narrators explore how their meanings work; by listening, audiences can think about how those meanings apply to their own lives. Stories allow listeners to embellish events, to reinterpret them, to mull over what they hear and to learn something new each time, providing raw material for developing philosophy (Benjamin 1969; Stamps 1995:23–40). Once interactive storytelling is replaced by mechanical communication, he alleged, human experience becomes devalued.

What relevance have these ideas to understanding Native North American oral histories from the northwestern part of the continent? Bakhtin's reference point was Russian peasant culture and his target the increasingly authoritarian Soviet state in which he lived, but he drew his examples from how medieval French peasants used ribald, satirical humor to challenge authority through carnivals (1984b). Yet he never, in any of his translated writings, directly discusses everyday storytelling from his own times. Likewise, Innis carried out his economic studies in northern Canada and his historical investigation of classical oral tradition without ever seeming to connect the two. Despite a prodigious appetite for labor-intensive research that took him across northern Canada and an open admiration for the work of his colleague Edward Sapir on indigenous languages, he never seemed to encounter living oral traditions in his own country, reporting, regretfully, that "[W]e have no history of [oral tradition] except as . . . revealed darkly through the written or printed word" (1951:8–9). Had he been aware of the intensity with which indigenous residents were drawing on long-standing oral traditions to interpret the same events he was analyzing near the Klondike gold fields, he might have observed dynamics similar to those that so intrigued him in ancient Greece—the processes set in motion when writing began first to overwhelm narrative traditions and then to actively domesticate or suppress them.

Elsewhere, at greater length, I have illustrated intersections among the ideas of these three scholars and the active storytelling practices that were occurring in northwestern Canada during the decades when each was writing (Cruikshank 1998). Forces bearing down on Yukon communities during the late nineteenth and early twentieth centuries were precisely those discussed by Innis in his account of the Klondike gold rush, by Bakhtin as he observed the mechanics of aggressive state expansion, and by Benjamin whose writings documented the forces mobilizing Nazi Germany. Here, I outline briefly key events experienced by the generation of indigenous men and women born near the upper Yukon River at the end of the 19th century. If we bear in mind that it is not "events" in history we are after but the processes that underlie and shape events, the gold rush in 1896–98 and the construction of the Alaska Highway in 1943 as part of the Second World War effort are worth noting because they incorporate processes that were already contributing to a globalizing world early in this century. Despite their widely differing life experiences, Kitty Smith (b. 1892), Walter Benjamin (b. 1892), Harold Innis (b. 1894), Mikhail Bakhtin (b. 1895), and Angela Sidney (b. 1902) were all contemporaries and each experienced the early years of the 20th century as formative.

The 1890s brought to an end an intensive period of Tlingit-Athapaskan trade that had long shaped human history in northwestern North America. Earliest records of trade between coast and interior are obscured because exchanges largely involved perishables: coastal marine products traded for tanned hides and tailored clothing from the interior. By the time Russian fur traders arrived on the North Pacific coast during the late 18th century, they found Tlingit traders already enmeshed in trading relationships with inland speakers of Athapaskan languages. Following the rapid slaughter of Pacific sea otters, European traders redirected their efforts beyond the mountains to the fur-bearing animals on the upper Yukon River. Coastal Tlingit traders were able to situate themselves as middlemen in this trade and effectively barred whites from the interior even after the sale of Alaska to the United States in 1867. Inevitably, Tlingit held the balance of power in arrangements with inland peoples, using their intermediary position to establish and formalize lifelong trading partnerships, often through marriage (McClellan 1981). As interior groups adopted Tlingit-named clans and concepts of social ranking, prestige came to inhere in Tlingit ancestry and adjacent Athapaskan peoples incorporated Tlingit themes into their storytelling traditions. On a global scale, at the same time, the extreme Northwest was already becoming firmly situated within broader layers of hierarchy centered in international Moscow-, Paris-, and London-based fur markets.

The influx of prospectors from Europe and the United States during the late 1890s dismantled the Tlingit trade monopoly. Coinciding with a world depression in 1896, the gold rush attracted more than 30,000 immigrants to one tributary of the Yukon River within a few years, making Dawson City the largest city north of San Francisco. Much of Harold Innis's work concerns this very topic: the expansion of British interests in North America through the manipulation of commodities like furs, forests, fish, and gold. The British Empire reached its most northwesterly extension in the Yukon where furs and gold coincided, but as Europe spiraled into a depression at the end of the century, furs were replaced by the more lucrative and liquid commodity, gold, as the staple of choice. Local men and women along the Yukon River, speakers of Athapaskan languages, became involved in packing, guiding, and providing food for prospectors and a few years later as deckhands on sternwheelers built to navigate the Yukon River from its headwaters to Dawson City. As well as the disruption of indigenous trade networks, consequences that followed the gold rush included decimation of Tlingit and Athapaskan families by epidemics of smallpox and measles; the expansion of missionaries and the construction of Anglican and Roman Catholic residential schools; and the establishment of a federal and territorial government infrastructure to administer the new territory, the Yukon, as a northern colony of Canada. Following the non-Native exodus after the turn of the century, the population dropped from 27,000 in 1900 to 4,000 in 1921 (Urquhart 1965:14).

What some older people still refer to as the "second rush" advanced during World War II. Hastily constructed in 1942–43, the Alaska Highway was built to deflect an anticipated invasion of North America by Japan. Again, more than 30,000 men, this time U.S. soldiers, arrived to participate in the construction phase, then left as quickly as they had come. Once again, epidemics tore through Yukon communities (Marchand 1943). The new road replaced the Yukon River as the administrative axis of the territory, subjecting indigenous peoples to ever greater bureaucratic surveillance as the "opening of the North" proceeded. The highway acted as a kind of gravel magnet attracting people in search of short-term jobs away from distant settlements (Cruikshank 1984). Its short- and long-term consequences affected both long-standing social institutions associated with kinship and the relationship between indigenous peoples and lands that they had always considered exclusively theirs to use.

From the early 1970s until the mid-1980s, I lived in the Yukon Territory and worked closely with elders engaged in the project of recording their life stories. They and their families wanted to see accounts written in their own words and in the English language describing memories and experiences spanning almost a century. The stories we hear from two of these women, Angela Sidney and Kitty Smith, shift the focus from well-known events to their everyday consequences. Mrs. Sidney's paternal uncles and her aunt were involved in the official discovery of Klondike gold. Four of Mrs. Smith's maternal uncles were charged with murder following an altercation between Tagish people and prospectors and were brought to trial (Cruikshank 1998:71–97). Each woman lost family members in influenza epidemics that accompanied both "rushes." Kitty Smith lost her mother, who returned home in 1898 to comfort her own mother when Kitty's uncles were arrested, and the young mother died of influenza. Angela Sidney watched a son go overseas during World War II and lost a much-loved stepdaughter to influenza. The narratives they tell about those years provide compelling evidence of how ancient narratives provide scaffolding from which to interpret inexplicable events so that families can neverthe-

less carry on. The metaphors central to historical narratives told by Angela Sidney and Kitty Smith are culturally distinctive, highly gendered, and rooted in
mid-19th-century matrilineages. These stories demonstrate how global forces
driving human history are always experienced in locally significant ways. Familiar narratives provide ways to engage with historical events and expand our understanding of the social *work* that stories do.

In telling their life stories, these women make generous assumptions that
listeners or readers have a basic understanding of local concepts surrounding
kinship. Anthropologists use the term *moiety* (from the French "half") to describe a broad organizational principle found in many parts of the world
whereby everyone belongs to one of two "sides." In the Yukon, moieties named
Crow (Kajìt) and Wolf (Ägunda) are transmitted through matrilineal descent so
that everyone inherits his or her mother's affiliation. Moieties are also exoga-
mous, in that well-understood rules prescribe that one must always marry a
member of the opposite moiety. During these women's lifetimes, moiety and
clan relationships were expected to guide behavior at birth, the onset of pu-
berty, marriage, death, and other less formal occasions. This principle pro-
foundly influenced their interpretations of historical changes that have
occurred during this century.

By the time Mrs. Sidney and Mrs. Smith were born, some Athapaskan families were incorporating Tlingit-named clans within moieties, for example,
Deisheetaan (a Crow clan) and Dakl'aweidí (a Wolf clan). The most important
clan property—songs, stories, and ceremonial crests—passed from one generation to the next through the maternal line, and appreciating the significance
of this provides insights into how stories and songs are performed, transmitted, and interpreted by local audiences. Shared assumptions about family and
clan property underscore the broad utility of Pierre Bourdieu's concept of social capital (1991:7–8) and its embeddedness in social institutions. Social capital, Bourdieu argues, accumulates along with practical competence that
eventually reinforces who has the capacity to be listened to, believed, and
obeyed—the entitlement to speak and to be heard.

The life histories these women tell are also grounded in enduring narratives
learned in childhood and told as adults. As we worked, my understanding of
our objectives shifted significantly. Initially, I expected that by recording life
histories we would be documenting events and compiling accounts that could
be stored, like archival documents, for later analysis. I was interested in hearing
these women talk about events chronicled in written documents and tried to
steer our conversations in that direction. I always brought questions to our ses-

sions, but as I began to take increasing direction from the narrators, these questions changed. In the beginning I asked about what might be called secular history—stories they might have heard about the gold rush and about early-20th-century fur trade, their experiences as children and as young adults. I wanted to know about the changes brought by the construction of the Alaska Highway and the subsequent interventions and control over women's lives that followed as government programs expanded north.

Although older women responded patiently to my line of inquiry for a while, they soon quite firmly shifted their emphasis to "more important" accounts they wanted me to record. They would give brief answers to my questions and then suggest that I write down a particular story they wanted to tell me. Usually these were narratives they had learned as youngsters and had heard and told many times, but for an untrained listener they inevitably involved a bewildering series of characters and episodes. At their insistence, I continued on their terms, and it was only later when I saw how they were using these narratives as reference points to talk *about* their life experience that I came to appreciate what they were doing. Narratives about a boy who went to live in the world of salmon, about a girl who married a bear, about men who traveled to the "other world" in search of a lost sister, or about women who went to live with stars provided pivotal philosophical, literary, and social frameworks essential for guiding young and not-so-young people, framing ways of thinking about how to live life appropriately. These narratives erased any distinction between "story" and "history." They were embedded in social life, and in the words of one woman, Angela Sidney, they provided guidance about how to "live life like a story" (Cruikshank et al. 1990). Gradually I came to see the oral tradition less as evidence about the past than as a window on the ways the past is culturally constituted and discussed. In other words, stories were not merely *about* the past, they also provided guidelines for understanding change.

As an anthropologist, I think that theoretical discussions need to be grounded in real cases about everyday life, and so I turn to two instructive ways of history making demonstrated by these women. Each is discussed elsewhere at greater length (Cruikshank 1998:25–44, 98–115). In one series of stories, Angela Sidney shows how a single story can do many different things. In the other, Kitty Smith shows how apparently different stories can convey a unifying message about the importance of matrilineal, matrilocal marital arrangements in preserving continuity in social life. Both women test the boundaries of narrative conventions even within their own culture in ways that would appeal to Bakhtin and Benjamin.

ANGELA SIDNEY'S GIFT

Angela Sidney was born in 1902 in the southern Yukon to a Tlingit mother and a Tagish father. Like their mother, Angela and her siblings were members of the Deisheetaan clan. As the eldest daughter, she had many opportunities to hear about her bicultural Tagish and Tlingit ancestry and her Deisheetaan clan history when, as a young woman, she took on the responsibility of caring for her mother, La.oos Tláa (Maria), who was plagued with ill health. A measles epidemic associated with the gold rush had robbed La.oos Tláa of her four eldest children, who all died before Angela was born. La.oos Tláa never fully recovered herself and eventually lost her eyesight. When Mrs. Sidney and I met in the early 1970s, she was eager to work on the project of recording her life history for family members, and echoing Bourdieu's formulation of social capital she remarked one afternoon, "Well, I have no money to leave to my grandchildren; my stories are my wealth" (Sidney et al. 1977).

I was delighted to have the opportunity to work with Mrs. Sidney on this project. However, after we had collaborated closely for several months and finally produced a 120-page booklet, typed and edited under her supervision, I was somewhat disconcerted by the fact that only 10 to 15 pages had anything to do with what I then would have called life "history." The rest seemed to fall into genres of oral literature that I felt ill equipped to understand involving fabulous characters whose dazzling exploits often eluded my understanding, complex lists of toponyms, songs, and lengthy genealogical sequences interwoven with references to historical events I had usually read about elsewhere. As I continued to listen to and learn from Mrs. Sidney, it became clear to me that she was using these larger narratives as reference points to reflect on her own life experiences, as models both for choices she had made and for explaining those choices to others (Sidney in Cruikshank et al. 1990:37–158). Here I summarize just one story that encapsulates how she earned her reputation as a community historian.

Early on, in 1974, one of the stories she asked me to record was about a heroic ancestor remembered by the name of Kaax'achgóok (Sidney in Cruikshank et al. 1990:139–45).[2] Briefly, Kaax'achgóok was a famous Tlingit ancestor of the Kiks.ádi clan, one of several Tlingit clans. One autumn, he went hunting sea mammals with his nephews but almost immediately received a sign that this was an inauspicious time for hunting and that he should return home. Reluctantly, he destroyed his spears and returned to his winter village, but eventually he could no longer bear the humiliation of having to send his wives to beg for food and hearing about the disrespectful treatment they were receiving. Setting out to sea once again with his nephews, he was blown off course and marooned on a small island. Kaax'achgóok spent the following months devising ways to feed himself and his nephews and perfecting a way to plot the sun's trajectory as it moved north to reach its zenith at the summer solstice. He chose that moment to set sail for home, using the sun as a navigational guide to chart his direction. "I gave up hope, and then I dreamed that I was home," he sang in his account of his travels. Despite his successful return, he faced the difficult business of acknowledging how much life had changed during his absence.

Mrs. Sidney told me this story first in 1974 when we were both primarily interested in transcribing it for publication in a form that she considered accurate. More than a decade later, in 1985, I was visiting her one day when her son, Peter, and his wife arrived. The conversation turned to Peter's experiences as a veteran of the Second World War. He was stationed overseas for a period and Mrs. Sidney began to speak about how she and her husband had bought their first radio "to hear where they're moving the troops so we would know where he is" and her joy when the war ended and they received a telegram announcing his return. The remainder of her story concerned the plans she made to welcome him back when he returned home after the war, hosting a community feast and publicly giving him the most precious gift she could think of: the song sung by Kaax'achgóok on his return, a song she subsequently referred to for the rest of her life as "Pete's song." As a member of his mother's Deisheetaan clan, her son was entitled to receive the song as a gift from her, she pointed out, and she saw it as accurately reflecting the feelings of a man forced to spend an indefinite period away from home and ultimately able to return. Songs constitute some of the most important property of Tlingit-named clans, and she was clearly pleased when her husband complimented her on thinking of such a culturally appropriate gift.

But she then went on to tell a third story about this story—concerning social processes set in motion by her gift. No sooner had she publicly given Peter this gift in 1945 than she was formally challenged by elders from her father's Dakl'aweidí clan who disputed her right to sing it, much less give it to a member of her own clan. They argued that this song was the property of the Kiks.ádi clan and that her Deisheetaan clan had no right to use it. The remainder of her account is the story of how she proceeded with her own ethnographic research to prove that she had acted correctly and had not appropriated another clan's property. She traveled by the same train that had brought her son inland down to the coast to Skagway, Alaska, to interview Tlingit elders about an incident that had occurred many years earlier, sometime during the 19th century. A dispute had broken out between the Kiks.ádi clan and her own Deisheetaan clan and was finally resolved when Kiks.ádi agreed do give this "Kaax'achgóok song" to the Deisheetaan. Her story *about* the story confirmed, to the satisfaction of her elders, that she had acted appropriately. Being able to tell this story 40 years later in the presence of her son (who knew the story well after all and was by now a character in it) and to his non-Tlingit wife and to me reconfirmed her competence in using stories in a socially significant way. By demonstrating the connections between a narrative, a song, and a gift, she was also able to extend her abilities to juxtapose discrete historical events—an ancient clan dispute and a contemporary international war. Missing from this story were the more painful events she told me on other occasions—the loss of an adopted child to influenza in the epidemics accompanying the construction of the Alaska Highway during the war and the loss of another son who died tragically about the same time.

A fourth telling was performed for a very different audience, most of them familiar with Mrs. Sidney and her role as a well-known storyteller but few knowledgeable about this particular story. When a college opened in the Yukon in 1988, Mrs. Sidney was asked to participate in the opening ceremonies. This was an important event for Yukoners because the college allows students to complete part or all of an undergraduate university education without having to leave the North. At the ceremony, Mrs. Sidney decided to tell the story of Kaax'achgóok, explaining in her own words, "The reason I sang that song is because that Yukon College is going to be like the Sun for the students. Instead of going to Vancouver or Victoria they're going to be able to stay here and go to school here. We're not going to lose our kids anymore. It's going to be just like the Sun for them, just like for that Kaax'achgóok" (Sidney 1988).

Very carefully, then, Angela Sidney was able to show how a single story can *do* several different things. She also constructed an important link between a story from long ago and discrete historical events from different periods of time: clan ties that connected coast and interior more formally during the 19th century, a war that caused painful losses ameliorated by the successful return of her own son in the 1940s, the opening of a college in the 1980s, and the continuity provided by the exchange of a gift that weaves these events together. The story also tracks her emerging stature as a person of significance in her community, one who repeatedly demonstrated during her lifetime that a single story, well told, can transform commonsense meanings that "everyone knows" and add significance to everyday life.

KITTY SMITH'S CARVINGS

Kitty Smith was born in approximately 1890, at least 12 years earlier than Mrs. Sidney. She, too, was born into a bicultural family with a Tagish mother and a Tlingit father. Orphaned as a youngster, she was raised by her Tlingit father's mother—an unusual situation in a society where obligations of clan and kinship are traced through one's maternal line. We also began working together in 1974, and, like Mrs. Sidney, Mrs. Smith insisted that I record many stories that initially seemed distant from my understanding of "history." Like Mrs. Sidney she began with detailed genealogical information and only later began talking about critical events in her own life: her mother's disappearance and subsequent death in an influenza epidemic when Kitty was seven or eight years old; her own arranged marriage as a young woman; her decision to leave this marriage some years later (a courageous choice but an unconventional one in the early 1900s); and her eventual reunion with her "mother's people" members of her own Tagish maternal kin group. In describing these events she, too, draws heavily on more foundational narratives she learned as a child to provide explanations for decisions she had made during her own life (Smith in Cruikshank et al. 1990:175–262). In the life story that emerged during our conversations over the years, the reunion with her matrilineage becomes the pivotal event of her life, and narratives about the dangers of distance from matrilineal kin and the loyalty of clan members to one another dominate her account. In trying to learn more about her mother's early death she was led to the tragic story about the circumstances surrounding the arrest, trial, and subsequent execution of her mother's brother, convicted of shooting a prospector in 1898 (Cruikshank 1998:71–97).

During the years we worked together, Mrs. Smith also sometimes referred to carvings that she had made years earlier. Whenever I actually asked her about them, though, she would shrug off my queries about where they might now be—she had sold them or given them away, she said—and would move on to tell the stories that she had carved. Shortly before she passed away in 1989, some carvings in the local McBride Museum were identified as possibly hers. Her granddaughter and another friend made arrangements with the museum's director to bring Mrs. Smith to visit, and when the carvings were brought out, she readily indicated the ones she had made. But nearly a century old by then, she was more amused than surprised by the discovery and not at all inclined to provide an elaborate explication of what they "meant." Instead, she examined her favorite carving, renaming it Azanzhaya/ "it got lost" and enjoying the irony of her own joke.

A few years later, in 1992, I asked her daughter, May Hume Smith, now an elder herself, whether she had ever seen her mother's carvings in the museum. Their continuing existence was a surprise to her, but she recalled childhood memories of her mother carving and was very interested in visiting the museum with me to look at them. With the encouragement of museum staff, we spent two afternoons examining carvings and tape recording May's commentary. She immediately singled out those made by her mother and settled in to talk about them. And then, like her mother, she retold the stories embodied in the carvings. What struck me immediately was that these were the same narratives Mrs. Smith herself had told, several years earlier, to describe critical turning points in her own life.[3]

One carving and story concerns Dukt'ootl', an orphan whose marginal status is vindicated when he is able to perform a task no one else in the community can accomplish, saving both his own life and the lives of other members of the group. The story reflects both the despair and the optimism Mrs. Smith often expressed about her own childhood as an orphan cut off from maternal kin. A second is the story of Naatsilanéi, "the man who made killer whales," one she told me several times as she reflected on the dangers of distance from one's maternal relatives when one is forced to live with affines. In this narrative, a man is abandoned by his opposite moiety brothers-in-law and left to die on an island. He saves himself by the transformative power of carving, fashioning killer whales that carry him back to safety (Smith in Cruikshank 1983:62–65). A third is a carving of the man who abandoned his wife to cohabit with Bear woman, reflecting Mrs. Smith's distress when her first husband announced that he was taking a second wife (Smith in Cruikshank 1983:37–39). Her carving shows the man moving toward his bear wife while the human wife carries away her child, leaving the lovers behind. [4]

NARRATIVE AND HISTORICAL MEMORY

What do these narratives convey about the place and meaning of stories for our understanding of Native American pasts? Sentient bears and whales who encompass personhood and take their place as nonhuman actors in historical dramas are more likely to be classified as "myth" than as historical evidence by listeners raised in a Western tradition. But the issue of how much historical accuracy Homeric poems, Icelandic sagas, Tlingit oratory, or Tagish life stories contain is really beside the point if we understand their contribution as providing social memory, however adequate or inadequate. In the context of Native

American history, the narratives Angela Sidney and Kitty Smith tell make more precise contributions. They directly confront familiar, commonsense categories that take for granted clear distinctions between "nature" and "culture," but they also challenge Euro-American myths that portray official Yukon history as a narrative of frontier individualism.

Ray Fogelson coined the term *epitomizing* to characterize dramatic incidents that condense complex cultural forces and make them easy to grasp in an icon or symbol (Fogelson 1989). The discovery of Klondike gold in August 1896 and the construction of the Alaska Highway in 1943 have both served as key epitomizing events in official Yukon history. Discovery Day, August 17, has long been enshrined as a statutory holiday in the Territory. Both events were commemorated in anniversary celebrations during the 1990s: the 50th anniversary of the highway and the centennial of the gold rush. Individualism remains a cherished self-characterization in Yukon settler society, but as symbols gold rush and Alaska Highway convey quite different messages for indigenous people raised hearing oral narratives from their own elders. The kinds of "freedom" embodied in frontier narratives that portray humans in mortal combat with nature and trying to shed connections in pursuit of individualism must surely appear to Angela Sidney, Kitty Smith, and their contemporaries as the freedom of ghosts—humans approaching the vanishing point (McIntyre 1981:118–119).

Angela Sidney's masterful account of how narrative can maintain human connections across clan, gender, and generation in the face of enormous external pressures demonstrates Benjamin's thesis that a story can do many things and convey many messages. Her gift links events spanning more than a century: the settlement of a conflict between clans through exchange of a narrative; the use of that narrative to welcome a returning son; her public address late in life expressing hopes for the futures of generations of grandchildren. Her story also addresses an international war in the middle of this century that brought a highway and epidemics and took away young men from the Yukon, some of whom did not return. It demonstrates the complex process by which oral history is publicly verified in communities where it is told: her own uncles were prepared to denounce her until she proved to them that she had the right to tell and to give this story, one of the most valued possessions of Tlingit clans. It speaks to late-20th-century attempts to rebuild Tlingit and Athapaskan relationships now severed by an international boundary but critical to bicultural families like Mrs. Sidney's and Mrs. Smith's. If one of her themes is about human connection, another reinforces the point that once things change, nothing is ever quite the same again.

Mrs. Sidney's telling chronicles her expanding reputation in her own community as she persisted in using and reusing one powerful story to make people understand a variety of larger issues. Her work blurs Walter Benjamin's distinction between the historian and the storyteller. "The historian," he suggests, "is bound to explain in one way or another the happenings with which he [sic] deals; under no circumstances can he content himself with displaying them as models of the course of the world. But this is precisely what the chronicler does. . . . Interpreting is not concerned with accurate concatenation of definite events, but with the way these are embedded in the great inscrutable course of the world" (Benjamin 1969:96). To live life "like a story," in Angela Sidney's words, is to confront modernist global narratives with deeply held local ones embedded in a social order in which human and nonhuman persons are deeply interconnected.

Kitty Smith, too, has much to say about the well-lived life. While she knows and tells stories about model lives, where everything proceeds as it should, her own experience taught her that things seldom worked so smoothly. Real life, she might say, is full of contradictions. Narrative gives us ways to think about this. Rather than being clear-cut reflections of ideal life, oral narratives may very well invert social behavior, because one purpose is to resolve symbolically those areas that can't easily be worked out in the sphere of human activity. Orphaned as a child, raised by her father's clan, unhappy in her first marriage, she was drawn to stories that dramatize contradictions and she found them, in Levi-Strauss's terms, "good to think with." Stories of Dukt'ootl', Kaats', and Naatsilanéi began as ancient narratives. They brought their explanatory power to the dilemmas she experienced, and later she began to carve images from those stories in poplar, then sold them or gave them away. Eventually, years later, some reached their current destination as museum artifacts. Mrs. Smith was amused to see them again, but only to a point: in her view, they had already accomplished their work long ago. Yet for young people from her community who continue to see her carvings exhibited in the local museum, they commemorate a life, contribute to social memory, and reinforce a consistent message: ties of kinship must not be torn apart by external pressures.

As noted in the introduction to this paper, oral narratives have become enmeshed in larger cross-disciplinary debates: about the weight that can reasonably be accorded to ideas in the face of material power; about the need to understand local experiences while keeping a sharp eye on the constraints that global forces exert; about the shortcomings of postmodern relativism in the face of modernist neoconservative economics. Yet stories like the ones Mrs. Sidney and Mrs. Smith tell are not simply elaborate mental constructions. They are as grounded in everyday, material conditions as they are in local ideas and practices. Nor are oral traditions in any way natural products. They have social histories, and they acquire meanings in the situations in which they emerge, in situations where they are used, and in interactions between narrators and listeners. The stories Angela Sidney and Kitty Smith tell have their roots in ancient narrative, but their telling emerges at the intersections of power and ideas where larger forces impinge directly on local experience.

In the 1930s, '40s, and '50s, at the same time that Angela Sidney was developing her skills as a teller of clan histories and Kitty Smith was carving her narratives in poplar wood in the Wheaton River valley, the larger potential of oral tradition to destabilize commonsense categories, to promote nonconfrontational ways of reevaluating hegemonic concepts, and to encourage dialogue rather than monologue was being imagined elsewhere. Harold Innis, shaken by his experiences in the trenches of World War I, advanced a thesis about cultural translation that began with economics and moved toward an exploration of how oral tradition challenges imperialist conceptions of time and space. Mikhail Bakhtin, writing from Stalinist Russia, was fascinated by human artistry as communicative behavior and optimistic about the transformative potential of folk culture to destabilize official culture. Walter Benjamin was concerned about deteriorating dialogue under the Third Reich and attributed this in part to loss of oral narrative forms with potential to interweave information, moral content, and philosophical guidance. Each asked thoughtful questions about the relationship between storytelling, cultural translation, and social action. Each was concerned about the role of oral storytelling in human history, yet each based his research on ancient and medieval texts rather than on exposure to practicing storytellers. Their insights and questions provide contemporary opportunities to investigate what this means now, when it is even clearer that control of narrative representation, like transfers of land in contemporary land claims settlements, carries clear material consequences.

In the end, postmodernism presents us with certain challenges by forcing us to confront human life as something that seems always to be falling apart. Yet over and over again, ethnography presents us with ways in which humans construct continuity and integration in the face of disorder. The compelling question, raised by Frederick Barth (1994), among others, is how people enmeshed in this disorderly world create an identity that has continuity especially when there is no script. We do this by working with those strands of tradition we have at our disposal to produce and reproduce the idea that the world is still continuous, and to go on to create those continuities, often by weeding out the really incongruent portions. Culture does not produce itself; rather, images like those of Kaax'achgóok, Kaats', Dukt'ootl', and Naatsilanéi resonate because they become translation devices to explain new experiences that do not seem to have cultural roots. The ways Mrs. Sidney and Mrs. Smith use these images demonstrate their determination to achieve consistency between old values and changing circumstances.

CODA: A CAUTIONARY TALE

In *Envisioning Power*, Eric Wolf directs his attention to situations where culture is, in his phrase, "unmade," where old ideas are rephrased to fit different circumstances, and where new ideas are presented as age-old truths (Wolf 1999:275). Despite growing attention to social processes involved in narrative performance, a textual emphasis in legal and cultural studies still reinforces a century-old tendency to evaluate oral traditions as written words and to sieve for literal meanings that might be compared with competing forms of evidence. A recent Canadian legal case that shifts the legal weight of oral traditions in the direction of such transparency highlights the difficulties. In the late 1980s, the hereditary chiefs of two First Nations in northern British Columbia, the Gitksan and the Wet'suet'en, brought to the British Columbia Supreme Court their petition for a settlement of land claims in a case that has become known as *Delgamuukw v. British Columbia*. They insisted on using long-standing oral traditions as the foundation of their argument and publicly enacted narratives, songs, and dances that had previously been performed only within a restricted ceremonial context. They argued that these ancient traditions demonstrate linkages between people and place, that they are far more than literal history, and that their case should *not* depend on literal accuracy to establish connections between social organization and land tenure. In 1991, the judge hearing the case rejected their arguments and dismissed oral tradition as "beliefs" that he contrasted unfavorably with "facts" best exemplified in archival documents (McEachern 1991:49, 75). Six years later, in 1997, the Supreme Court of Canada reversed this ruling, arguing that because aboriginal rights are constitutionally protected ". . . the laws of evidence must be adapted in order that this kind of evidence can be accommodated and placed on an equal footing with the types of historical evidence that courts are familiar with, which largely consist of historical records" (*Delgamuukw v. British Columbia* [1997] para. 87). By reinforcing archival documents as the standard for evaluation, *both* decisions may once again define oral tradition narrowly and in ways that reduce complex stories to simple messages (Cohen 1989). The implications of this more recent judgment are first being tested in Canadian courts in 1999 (Sieciechowicz 1999).

At a broad level, First Nations in Canada understandably welcome a judgment that seems finally to give their histories legal weight. Nevertheless the power of legal decisions inevitably drives social processes in communities struggling to advance claims that must meet terms laid out by Western courts (Culhane 1998). Again, Eric Wolf is helpful: "Culture is constructed in such encounters, but these are staged, prosecuted, and resolved through the exercise of power" (Wolf 1999:275). A definition that equates oral tradition with archival documents inevitably circumscribes what is heard because it prepares the ground for hearing and assessing "data." Inevitably, certain kinds of oral tradition, especially the disorderly parts that Bakhtin considered so central, slip by—the debates, the silences, the commotion that is often a critical part of oral tradition, as of history. If the court limits its definition to the rules normally followed by academics or lawyers, then official, institutional authority becomes further sedimented. Power inevitably involves deciding who can talk, under what circumstances, in what order, through what discursive procedures and about what topics, and with what credentials (Bourdieu 1991:42, 131,134). A definition that equates oral history with archival documents reinforces the idea that what academics (historians, anthropologists, judges) write is "history" and that local practices are "data" for those official histories. It ignores arguments that equate oral tradition with historiography, the oldest form of historical practice or history making with its own rules and methods of verification. Whether the courts will be willing or able to evaluate oral tradition and oral history on its own terms (rather than as data or sources) remains to be seen.

Growing initiatives to formalize institutional guidelines for recording and conserving oral history will inevitably be fueled by the court decision. In the Yukon, one alternative to this procedure has involved creating structured opportunities, spaces, and places for the public telling and hearing of oral tradition—the creation of social occasions where stories can be told, interpretations debated, and disagreements aired. This occurs, for instance, at the Yukon International Storytelling Festival, which has been held annually since 1988, and at other forums like Elders' Festivals in smaller communities. Occasions like these tacitly acknowledge that history is always located in a social and political universe. They invite different interpretations while enabling public validation. They challenge the authority of institutions like archives or courts without conceding complete relativism. Preservation efforts, following this model, might better be directed toward preserving commemorative *spaces*, where people can tell stories, and significant *objects*, like Kitty Smith's carvings, that act as aids to memory and contribute to the composition and production of history. Social memories associated with such places and objects ensure that "traces of the storyteller cling to the story the way the handprints of the potter cling to the vessel." In such spaces, what is retained of the storyteller's art, even after she is no longer living, is "that slow piling one on top of the other of thin, transparent layers which constitutes the most appropriate picture of the way in which the perfect narrative is revealed through the layers of a variety of retellings" (Benjamin 1968:92, 93).

NOTES

1. Bruno Latour, Vancouver Institute lecture, University of British Columbia, November 8, 1998.

2. This narrative is also recorded by Swanton 1909, nos. 67 and 101, pp. 225 and 321; and in Dauenhauer and Dauenhauer 1987:82–107 and notes 323–333. I have discussed Mrs. Sidney's use of this narrative at greater length in Cruikshank 1998:25–44.

3. Tapes and transcripts of these interviews are filed with the McBride Museum in Whitehorse, Yukon.

4. The story of Dukt'ootl' has been recorded in many versions, including Swanton 1909, No. 93; and Dauenhauer and Dauenhauer 1987:138–151 and notes 348–359. Versions of Naatsilanéi's story can be found in Swanton 1909, nos. 4 and 71; and in Dauenhauer and Dauenhauer 1987:108–137 and notes 334–347. The narrative about Kaats' is inscribed on totem poles from Wrangell to Yakutat and recorded by Swanton 1909, nos. 19 and 69; and in Dauenhauer and Dauenhauer 1987:218–243 and notes 390–406. References to other recorded versions are cited in Cruikshank 1998:98–115 along with photographs of Mrs. Smith's carvings following 128.

REFERENCES

Bakhtin, Mikhail
  1984a The Dialogic Imagination. Austin: University of Texas Press.
  1984b Rabelais and His World. Helene Iswolsky, trans. Bloomington: Indiana University Press.
Barth, Frederick
  1994   Production and Reproduction of Society. Plenary address to Canadian Anthropology Society, Vancouver, British Columbia, May 6.
Basso, Keith
  1996   Wisdom Sits in Places: Landscape and Language among the Western Apache. Albuquerque: University of New Mexico Press.
Benjamin, Walter
  1969   The Storyteller. In Illuminations. Hannah Arendt, ed. Pp. 83–109. New York: Schocken.

Bourdieu, Pierre
    1991   Language and Symbolic Power. John B. Thompson, ed. Cambridge, UK:
            Polity.
Clark, Katerina, and Michael Holquist
    1984   Mikhail Bakhtin. Cambridge, MA: Harvard University Press.
Cohen, David
    1989   The Undefining of Oral Tradition. Ethnohistory 36:9–18.
    1994   The Production of History. In The Combing of History. Chicago: University of
            Chicago Press.
Cronon, William
    1992   A Place for Stories: Nature, History and Narrative. Journal of American His-
            tory 78(4):1347–1376.
Cruikshank, Julie
    1983   The Stolen Woman: Female Journeys in Tagish and Tutchone Narrative. Nat-
            ural Museum of Man Mercury Series, Paper no. 87. Ottawa: National Muse-
            ums of Canada.
    1984   The Gravel Magnet: Some Social Impacts of the Alaska Highway on Yukon
            Indians. In The Alaska Highway: Papers of the Fortieth Anniversary Sympo-
            sium. Kenneth Coates ed., Vancouver: University of British Columbia Press.
    1998   The Social Life of Stories: Narrative and Knowledge in the Yukon Territory.
            Lincoln: University of Nebraska Press; Vancouver: University of British Co-
            lumbia Press.
Cruikshank, Julie, in collaboration with Angela Sidney, Kitty Smith, and Annie Ned
    1990   Life Lived Like a Story: Life Stories of Three Yukon Elders. Lincoln: University
            of Nebraska Press; Vancouver: University of British Columbia Press.
Culhane, Dara
    1998   The Pleasure of the Crown: Anthropology, Law and First Nations. Vancouver:
            Talonbooks.
Dauenhauer, Richard, and Nora Dauenhauer
    1987   Haa Shuká: Our Ancestors: Tlingit Oral Narratives. Seattle: University of
            Washington Press; Juneau: Sealaska Press.
de Certeau, Michel
    1984   The Practice of Everyday Life. Stephen Rendall, trans. Berkeley: University of
            California Press.
Delgamuukw v. British Columbia
    1997   Supreme Court of Canada. Judgment and Reasons for Judgment.
Dorris, Michael
    1979   Native American Literature in an Ethnohistorical Context. College English
            41(2):147–162.
Fogelson, Raymond
    1989   The Ethnohistory of Events and Nonevents. Ethnohistory 36:133–147.
Hinchman, Lewis P., and Sandra K. Hinchman, eds.
    1998   Memory, Identity, Community: The Idea of Narrative in the Human Sciences.
            Albany: State University of New York Press.

Hofmeyer, Isabel

  1993   We Spend Our Years As a Tale That Is Told: Oral Historical Narrative in a South African Chiefdom. Johannesburg: Witwatersund University Press.

Hymes, Del

  1981   In Vain I Tried to Tell You. Philadelphia: University of Pennsylvania Press.

Innis, Harold Adams

  1930   The Fur Trade in Canada. Toronto: University of Toronto Press.

  1940   The Cod Fisheries: The History of an International Economy. Toronto: University of Toronto Press.

  1950   Empire and Communications. Oxford: Clarendon.

  1951   The Bias of Communication. Toronto: University of Toronto Press.

  1956   Essays in Canadian Economic History. Toronto: University of Toronto Press.

Khubova, Daria, Andrei Ivankiev, and Tonia Sharova

  1992   After Glasnost. Oral History in the Soviet Union. *In* Memory and Totalitarianism. Luisa Passerini, ed. Pp. 89–101. Oxford: Oxford University Press.

Leydesdorff, Selma, Luisa Passerini, and Paul Thompson

  1996   Introduction. Gender and Memory. Oxford: Oxford University Press.

Lowie, Robert

  1917   Oral Tradition and History. Journal of American Folklore 30: 161–167.

McClellan, Catharine

  1975   My Old People Say: An Ethnographic Survey of the Southern Yukon Territory. 2 vols. Publications in Ethnology 6 (1–2). Ottawa: National Museums of Canada.

  1981   Intercultural Relations and Cultural Change in the Cordillera. *In* Handbook of North American Indians, vol. 6. Subarctic. Pp. 35–42. June Helm, ed. Washington, DC: Smithsonian Institution.

McEachern, Allan

  1991   Reason for Judgment: Delgamuukw v. B. C. Smithers. British Columbia: Supreme Court of British Columbia.

McIntyre, Alisdair

  1981   After Virtue: A Study in Moral Theory. Notre Dame, IN: University of Notre Dame Press.

Malinowski, Bronislaw

  1926   Myth in Primitive Psychology. New York: Norton.

Marchand, John

  1943   Tribal Epidemics in the Yukon. Journal of the American Medical Association 123:1019–1020.

Morrow, Phyllis

  1995   On Shaky Ground: Folklore, Collaboration, and Problematic Outcomes. *In* When Our Words Return: Writing, Hearing and Remembering Oral Traditions of Alaska and the Yukon. Phyllis Morrow and William Schneider, eds. Pp. 27–51. Logan: Utah State University Press.

Passerini, Louisa

  1987   Fascism and Popular Memory. Cambridge: Cambridge University Press.

  1992   Memory and Totalitarianism. Luisa Passerini, ed. Oxford: Oxford University Press.

Portelli, Alessandro
   1991   The Death of Luigi Trastulli: Memory and Event. *In* The Life and Death of Luigi Trastulli and Other Stories: Form and Meaning in Oral History. Albany: State University of New York Press.
   1997   Trying to Gather a Little Knowledge: Some Thoughts on the Ethics of Oral History. *In* The Battle of Valle Giulia: Oral History and the Art of Dialogue. Pp. 55–71. Madison: University of Wisconsin Press.
Sarris, Greg
   1993   Keeping Slug Woman Alive. Berkeley: University of California Press.
Sidney, Angela
   1988   The Story of Kaax'achgoók. Northern Review 2:9–16.
Sidney, Angela, Kitty Smith, and Rachel Dawson
   1977   My Stories Are My Wealth. Recorded by Julie Cruikshank. Whitehorse, Yukon Territory: Council for Yukon Indians.
Sieciechowicz, Krystyna
   1999   Gossip, Oral History, History and the Role These Play in the Chippewa of Sarnia First Nations 160 Year Old Land Claim. Paper presented at the Canadian Anthropology Society Meetings, Université Laval, Quebec. May 12–16.
Stamps, Judith
   1995   Unthinking Modernity: Innis, McLuhan and the Frankfurt School. Montreal: McGill Queen's University Press.
Swanton, J. R.
   1909   Tlingit Myths and Texts. Bureau of American Ethnology Bulletin, 39. Washington, DC: Smithsonian Institution.
Urquhart, M. C., ed.
   1965   Historical Statistics of Canada. Toronto: Macmillan.
Vansina, Jan
   1985   Oral Tradition as Oral History. Madison: University of Wisconsin Press.
Watson, Rubie, ed.
   1994   Memory, History and Opposition under State Socialism: An Introduction. *In* Memory, History and Opposition under State Socialism. Sante Fe: School of American Research.
White, Hayden
   1987   The Content of the Form: Narrative Discourse and Historical Representation. Baltimore. Johns Hopkins University Press.
Wolf, Eric R.
   1999   Envisioning Power: Ideologies of Dominance and Crisis. Berkeley: University of California Press.

The Story of America: A Tribalography

LeAnne Howe

> It doesn't end.
> In all growing
> from all earths
> to all skies,
> in all touching
> all things
> in all soothing
> the aches of all years,
> it doesn't end."
> —Simon J. Ortiz, *Going for Rain*, 1976

Native stories are power. They create people. They author tribes. America is a tribal creation story, a tribalography.

As numerous as Indian tribes, creation stories gave birth to our people, and it is with absolute certainty that I tell you now: our stories also created the immigrants who landed on our shores. I don't mean that Native people imagined them as their God did, nor "formed man of the dust of the ground, and breathed into his nostrils the breath of life" (Gen. 2:8). But our stories made the immigrants Americans nevertheless.

When the foreigners arrived and attempted to settle in the upper Northeast, they had nothing to eat, nothing to sustain them but their faith in biblical stories. Indigenous people told them new stories of how to live in our world. One example of this is the Native story of the *Three Sisters* (Beauchamp 1897:177). Natives told stories of how to plant their crops, corn, beans, and pumpkins (squash), which sustained the newcomers and taught them how to experiment with their daily diet by adding variety. As a result, Native foods were traded internationally and changed the food cultures of the entire world. According to the National Corn Growers Association's January 2000 statistics, corn is grown in more countries in the world than any other crop, and the United States produces and exports more corn than any other country in the world. Thanksgiving is the holiday in which Americans give thanks to indigenous people for such extraordinary and versatile foods. But the most important story the immigrants would hear from Natives was how to make a united nation by combining people from various tribes. It is this eloquent act of unification that explains how America was created from a story, hence my title: "The Story of America: A Tribalography."

Before I continue with the scholarly account of tribalography, I want to tell you a Choctaw story. My tribe's language has a mysterious prefix that when combined with other words represents a form of creation. It is *nuk* or *nok*, and it has to do with the power of speech, breath, and mind. Things with *nok* or *nuk* attached to them are so powerful they create. For instance, *nukfokechi* brings forth knowledge and inspiration. A teacher is a *nukfoki,* the beginning of action. *Nuklibisha* is to be in a state of passion, and *nukficholi* means to hiccup, or breath that comes out accidentally.

My story begins in September. I was standing on the front porch of my house in Iowa City, Iowa. The sky was bright blue, there was no wind. Rabbits and ghosts of rabbits hopped in the front yard, playing tag with a couple of gray squirrels. After a time I looked at the southern sky and saw what appeared to be black specks of pepper floating in the upper atmosphere. As they glided closer to the earth, I realized they were red-tailed hawks. There were so many I couldn't believe they really were hawks, so I ran into the house and found my binoculars. One, four, seven, twenty-two. Eventually, there were forty-four hawks kettling together, heading for the Iowa River valley. As the first group disappeared, another group of hawks flew into view, their red tail feathers reflecting the midmorning sunlight. For the next 30 minutes, dozens more appeared.

Red-tailed hawks are very special to Choctaw people. They can weigh up to ten pounds, and their body feathers are variegated browns and whites, but their tail feathers are a bright reddish-orange, the color of fire. As I stood in the middle of my yard, their numbers began to dwindle until there were only fours, sevens. Then it happened. One red-tailed hawk flew right over my head and landed in a tree about 30 yards from my porch. He perched on a broken branch and appeared to be looking in my direction. We regarded one another for a while, and it was then that I realized my grandmother was trying to tell me something: the hawks have returned.

Grandmother was a storyteller, and she taught me the power of story. When I was growing up she was the one who told stories late into the night. Sometimes she'd say, "Do you hear what I hear? Listen! *Ygiea-e-e*." Then she would begin a story.

"I don't know if you remember old Lum Jones," she'd say, cocking her head in my direction. "One night, I was looking out my picture window when the Angel of Death walked down the sidewalk in front of my house. He went up on Lum Jones's front porch next door. Before I knew what had happened, he was carrying Lum Jones up through the tree tops," she said. "I'm telling the truth."

From her story, I could see what had happened. A large man-bird first showed himself to her by gliding past her house. Then he slipped soundlessly inside the walls of Lum Jones's house and carried the old man in his beak *up, up, up*, through the loving arms of the gigantic elm in the front yard. Together, the old man and the bird-man, winged their way toward the heavens. Of course, everyone in my family agreed that right after Grandmother saw Lum Jones being carried up through the tree, he was as dead as Andrew Jackson. It was a fact. Grandmother could see life and death, and she told me not to be afraid of either one. That was the first lesson I learned from her.

Then one night while I was in the hospital with rheumatic fever, I overheard someone saying that I was going to die. I had had a lot of heart problems, so in a way I was not surprised, but I was afraid of leaving my family. Later my grandmother appeared to me, first as a huge brown hawk about the size of a person hovering over my bed. I knew it was my grandmother because the bird had a beak shaped like her nose. In the next moment, Grandmother was standing next to me with her hand on my forehead. She had transformed herself from a winged person back into a human person. She said a few words I couldn't understand, then she left. After a long while, I gradually got well. Much later, Grandmother explained that she was the one who visited me as a bird. She said she would always watch over me.

When Grandmother ended a story, she'd squeal in her high-pitched-old-lady-voice: "*Whee-e-e that's enough, I can tell you no more today.*" Then she'd whistle at the canaries and parakeets she kept on her back porch. Then she'd have a smoke.

There were always many varieties of birds around my grandmother's house, and she worried constantly that their numbers were becoming thin. She told me that when she was growing up at the turn of the century dozens of hawks and eagles visited her house. She said that back in the old days it wasn't unusual to see them everywhere, but that wasn't the case in the early 1960s. Hunters had killed a lot of game birds, hawks, and eagles during the first half of the century. Then, farmers had sprayed pesticides that ended up killing all her favorite songbirds.

Right before my grandmother died she said the birds never stopped talking to her, telling her stories. She said that they kept her up all night, making her ears ring, and it was their music that she died listening to, not our voices.

To some who read this story, it may seem like a family memoir. I loved my grandmother and she loved me, and birds. But American and British behavioral scientists have shown that birds have been found to have the same kind of memory that enables people to recall where they left their house keys. A study published in *Nature* (September 17, 1998) marks what researchers say is the *first* demonstration of episodic, or event-based, memory in animals other than humans. Two researchers, Nicola S. Clayton and Anthony Dickinson (1998:272) have shown that birds have memories much the same as humans. "The recollection of past experiences allows us to recall what a particular event was, and where and when it occurred, a form of memory that is thought to be unique to humans. It is known, however, that food-storing birds remember the spatial location and contents of their caches. Furthermore, food-storing animals adapt their caching and recovery strategies to the perish-ability of food stores, which suggest that they are sensitive to temporal factors" (Clayton and Dickinson 1998:272). So birds, like people (who bring their favorite snacks to eat while watching a Saturday afternoon football game on television) can remember not only when and where but what kind of food they've stored for the future.

This is big news to white people, or people educated in mainstream institutions, but not to American Indians who have been telling stories of birds as creators, birds as tricksters, birds as healers, and birds with long memories. At last it seems another group of storytellers, the scientists, have now "proven" that birds demonstrate they too, have episodic, or event-based, memories.

I tell the story about my grandmother because it is a good example of what I am trying to address: the power of Native stories. First, there was the event, the birds, then Grandmother's story and her transformation into a bird, her life and death, and the reappearance of red-tailed hawks. The story I am telling you now is *nukfokechi*. It brings forth knowledge and inspires us to make the eventful leap that one thing leads to another.

Choctaws have many stories about birds. One story says that a long time ago there came to the Choctaws an Unknown Woman. While it is the story about how the Unknown Woman brought corn to the people, it also incorporates birds and their relationship to people. The woman is a stranger who appears in the moonlight atop a great hill. Two hunters see her as if in a vision.

Happening to look behind them in the direction opposite the moon they [two hunters] saw a woman of wonderful beauty standing upon a mound a few rods distant. Like an illuminating shadow, she had suddenly appeared out of the moon-lighted forest. She was loosely clad in a snow-white raiment, and bore in the folds of her drapery a wreath of fragrant flowers. She beckoned them to approach, while she seemed surrounded by a halo of light that gave to her a supernatural appearance. Their imagination now influenced them to believe her to be the Great Spirit of their nation, and that the flowers she bore were representatives of loved ones who had passed from Earth to bloom in the Spirit-Land. [Cushman 1899:277]

The Unknown Woman tells the two men that she's hungry, and they offer her roasted hawk meat. This special meat of the hawk is all they have, so they give it willingly. The woman eats only a small bite, then tells them to return the following midsummer at the same place atop the mound. She promises she'll be there. The next year, at exactly the same time, the two hunters return and find corn growing atop the mound. From the hunters' initial gift of sacred food to the Unknown Woman, Choctaws and other southeastern tribes received the gift of corn. Today we celebrate in midsummer Green Corn Ceremony to mark the coming of the future: corn, our ancient food cache. Another version of this story explains how a black bird brought corn, *tanchi*, to a Choctaw boy.

EVERYTHING IS EVERYTHING

"Everything exists and everything will happen and everything is alive and everything is planned and everything is a mystery, and everything is dangerous, and everything is a mirage, and everything touches everything, and everything is everything, and everything is very, very strange." This quotation is from a painting by the late Roxy Gordon, painted in 1988. An author and artist, Gordon evokes, in a very Choctaw way, the basic principles of Lynn Margulis's scientific theory on symbiogenesis, which says that the merger of previously independent organisms is of great importance to evolutionary change. Margulis is renowned internationally as a biologist for her research on the evolution of eukaryotic cells—cells with a nucleus. As a professor in the department of geosciences at the University of Massachusetts at Amherst she was awarded in March 2000, along with 11 others, the National Medal of Science by President Clinton. She has chaired the National Academy of Science's Space Science Board Committee on Planetary Biology and Chemical Evolution, which aided in the development of research strategies for NASA, and in 1981, she received a

NASA Public Service award. She has written many books on scientific topics, both for children and adults, including *What is Life? Essays in Gaia, Symbiosis, and Evolution* and *Microcosmos: Four Billion Years of Evolution from Our Microbial Ancestors* (coauthored with her science collaborator and son, Dorion Sagan).

> The story of how a human—a being made of nucleated cells—evolves from an ameboid being—a nucleated cell is bizarre. But even this story has a preamble: the evolution of a cell *with* a nucleus. How did such a cell evolve?
>
> The quick answer is by the merging of different kinds of bacteria. Protoctists evolved through symbiosis; twigs and limbs on the tree of life not only branched out but grew together and fused. Symbiosis refers to an ecological and physical relationship between two kinds of organisms that is far more intimate than most organism associations. In Africa, for example, plovers pluck and eat leeches from the open mouths of crocodiles without fear. Bird and beast in this instance are behavioral symbionts; crocodiles enjoy clean teeth in the company of well-fed plovers. Bacteria live in the spaces between our teeth and in our intestines, mites inhabit our eyelashes; all these tiny beings draw nutriment from our cells or our uneaten food, as cells are shed or as they excrete organic excess. Symbiosis, like marriage, means living together for better or worse, but whereas marriage is between two different people, symbiosis is between two or more different types of live beings. [Margulis and Sagan, 1995:96]

In other words, biologists like Margulis have adopted a Choctawan way of looking at the world. "Everything touches everything, and everything is everything," as Gordon phrased it. The theory of symbiosis advanced by Margulis and her colleagues also suggests that evolution is the result of cooperation, not simply competition. "Next the view of evolution as chronic bloody competition among individuals and species, a popular distortion of Darwin's notion of 'survival of the fittest,' dissolves before a new view of continual cooperation, strong interaction, and mutual dependence among life forms. Life did not take over the globe by combat, but by networking. Life forms multiplied and complexified by co-opting others, not just by killing them" (Margulis and Sagan 1986:14). Much like the Choctaw prefix *nuk* that when combined with other words represents a form of creation, Lynn Margulis's scientific theory is also *nukfokechi*.

Consider another storyteller, Pisatuntema, a Choctaw woman who in 1909 told the story of the hunter who became a deer. Her story shows what Margulis says that life does. One thing *combines* with another thing to form "life" the verb, a process that is always in flux:

> One night, a warrior kills a doe and soon afterwards falls asleep near the carcass. The next morning, just at sunrise, the hunter was surprised and startled to see the doe raise her head and to hear her speak, asking him to go with her to her home. At first he was so surprised that he did not know what to reply, so the doe again asked him whether he would go. Then the hunter said that he would go with her, although he had no idea where she would lead him . . . [Ed]. . . . Now all around the cave were piles of deer's feet, antlers and skins. While the hunter was asleep the deer endeavor to fit to his hands and feet deer's feet which they selected for the purpose. After several unsuccessful attempts the fourth set proved to be just the right size and were fastened firmly on the hunter's hands and feet. Then a skin was found that covered him properly, and finally antlers were fitted to his head. And then the hunter became a deer and walked on four feet after the manner of deer. [Bushnell 1909:32]

There are Choctaws, including myself, who consider Pisatuntema's story a biology lesson about creating kin with people and things who are different from ourselves. But there are many possibilities in this story. When all the tribes in the Southeast began to hunt deer to near extinction in the 18th century, a relationship evolved between Indian hunter, deer, and foreigner. This event is what historians have called "the deerskin trade." As the scholar Kathryn E. Holland Braund has noted, "Trade is a mutual affair" (Braund 1993:xiii). This does not mean that all sides are equal, but rather all sides have agency and are networking. "Between 1699 and 1705, Carolina shipped an average of over forty-five thousand deerskins annually to London. And between 1705 and 1715, the trade in deerskins was the most valuable business endeavor in the colony" (Braund 1993:29). She goes on to explain that Indian trading companies forged links to Creek, Chickasaw and Choctaw towns: "About one hundred thousand Weight of Skins were shipped from Augusta in 1741" (Braund 1993: 97). Another event, however, occurs among the Choctaw. In the town of Chickasawhay, a large Choctaw community of the 18th century, hunters forgo the hunting season of 1764. The historian Richard White suggests they did this because deer were becoming scarce. "That the town suffered from a depletion of deer is also suggested by its reputation as a collection of stock thieves and later, more positively, as a center of stock raising in the nation" (White 1983:86). But stories make connections. Choctaws would have been sensitive to being the cause of the scarcity of deer, a source of food. A story of what may happen if the cycle continues seems to hold creative solutions.

Pisatuntema's story explains that the deer are fighting back. Not only does the doe talk, but she lures the hunter into the underground and transforms him. Only through the intervention of the hunter's mother is the hunter's blood returned to the earth and a ceremonial dance held. In the early Choctaw worldview, not being returned to the earth by a bone picking ceremony would be a kind of heresy. I wrote "Danse d'Amour, Danse De Mort" (Howe 1993:447–472) about Choctaw bone picking and what it meant to the people in my story of the 18th century who saw their bodies as food for the animals and earth once they were dead. "Tchatak, the consumer. The animal, the consumed. Tchatak, the consumed. The animal the consumer" (Howe 1993:469). Things are made right when we are returned to the earth as food for the planet. Life continues.

Choctaws have another story to explain a relationship between hunters and deer that also speaks to Margulis's theory of symbiosis. *Kashehotep*, half man, half deer, is a character who will harass hunters if they come too close to his camp where many other animals live. People tell this story to explain what we have learned about the onslaught of ecological disasters caused by the deerskin trade of the 18th and 19th centuries.

For early scholars who studied American Indian stories, and specifically Choctaw stories, the hunter and the doe narrative has been relegated to folklore or myth, a fiction. This troubles many American Indians. The Miwok author Greg Sarris, in an interview for the 1994 film series *The Native Americans*, produced by TBS Productions, explains the prejudice inherent in the belief that Native stories are fictions.

> A team of geologists happened to be working in the creek over here and they unearthed whale fossils from the period of the last Pliocene. And we said, according to the stories that during the time of the flood that there was a whale in that creek. This was told from generation to generation for 10,000 years. They got very interested, these geologists, they said, "these Indians have this myth that there's this whale in the creek and we found the fossils." The Indians also say that during the time of the flood that people went on top of that mountain and went into a cave. Well, they went up to the cave and carbon-dated charcoal on the walls from fire that dated to the same period. If that's a myth, you give me some evidence of Noah's Ark. Do you have any splinters or wood from that? [Sarris 1994]

In the case of the whale story, bones were found to support the Indians' story. Sarris is not arguing about the biblical flood or whether Noah's ark existed; rather he and other Natives in the film point out that no matter what physical evidence Indians have, our stories are thought to be myth.

By this time, you may be asking yourself how my boastful opening remark that America is a tribal creation story relates to Margulis's theory of symbiosis. She suggests that the merger of previously independent organisms, or systems (for the purposes of my article), is of great importance to evolutionary change. I am suggesting that when the European Founding Fathers heard the stories of how the Haudenosaunee unified six individual tribes into an Indian confederacy, they created a document, the U.S. Constitution, that united immigrant Europeans into a symbiotic union called America.

From an Indigenous Story the Europeans and Indians Unite

It is that, therefore,
that in ancient times
it thus came that the hodiyaanehshon,
the Federal Chiefs,
our grandsires,
made a formal rule saying
"Let us unite our affairs; let us formulate regulations."
[Bierhorst 1974:145]

The above is an excerpted translation from Iroquoian of an archaic version of the "Ritual of Condolence," a portion of what is also called the Condolence ceremony. This Iroquois version of the oral drama is spoken by elders and is designed to heal the community and make it a peaceful whole. As John Bierhorst notes in *Four Masterworks*, the ritual drama was the Iroquois attempt to achieve peace between differing tribes and thwart the cult of death and warfare by forming a confederacy (Bierhorst 1974:109–111). The Iroquois Confederacy at the time of contact with the immigrants was scattered over eastern North America and across the contemporary U.S.-Canadian border. They occupied most of New York State and parts of neighboring Pennsylvania, Ontario, and Quebec. When the immigrants settled among them and wanted to create trading networks, the Iroquois told them stories of how their ancestors had learned to live peacefully together: their story would serve as a kind of cultural template for the New World. There are many versions of the story, and what follows is not a direct quote but paraphrased from a variety of sources including the Onondaga elder Oren Lyons's speech at the 1987 conference at Cornell University's American Indian Program, and from his interview in the 1994 six-part film series *The Native Americans*.

A long time ago there was a blood lust among the people. A great war engulfed the land and the people were full of merciless killing and fighting one another for supreme rule. Nations, towns, and families were destroyed and scattered to the four winds. It was proof of the tyranny of which people at that time were capable. Then along came a great visionary leader, Degenawidah, who realized the killing must stop. He began a journey to establish peace, but he knew he had a serious handicap. He stuttered. Since storytelling is an oral art, Degenawidah knew he had to find someone who could speak for him. Along his journey he met the powerful warrior, Ayonwatha, or Hiawatha as his name is pronounced in English. Ayonwatha, an Onondaga by birth and a Mohawk by adoption, was mourning the murder of his wife and children. He had vowed to wipe out his enemies, including the man he saw standing before him. But he knew Degenawidah had combed the snakes out of a powerful wizard's hair, taking away the wizard's anger, so Ayonwatha decided to go with him. Together the two men traveled throughout the land to establish peace. Through Ayonwatha's mighty gift of oratory, Degenawidah proposed that the warring tribes of the upper Northeast form a confederacy.

Degenawidah became known as the Peacemaker. He set up the families into clans, and then he set up the leaders of the clans. He established a confederacy wherein each clan would have a clanmother, and political roles for men and women would be in balance. He made two houses within each nation. One he called the Long House and the other the Mud House. These two houses would work together in ceremony and council establishing the inner source of vitality of their nations. The Peacemaker also made two houses in the Grand Council, one called the Younger Brothers, consisting of the Oneida and the Cayuga Nations, and later (1715) enlarging to include the Tuscarora. The other was the Elder Brothers consisting of the Mohawks, keepers of the Eastern Door; the Onondaga, the Firekeepers; and the Senecas, keepers of the Western Door. Then Degenawidah named the united nations Haudenosaunee: The People of the Long House.

The Haudenosaunee's story remains consistent. The confederacy was founded on the core values the Peacemaker proposed: freedom, respect, tolerance, consensus, and brotherhood. Under the terms and spirit of the *Ne-Gayaneshogowa,* or the Great Law of Peace, all parties pledged themselves to the confederacy's body of laws. United we thrive, divided we fall.

After hearing the Haudenosaunee spokesmen extol the values of unification for over a hundred years, the colonists finally transformed themselves into 13 united states and eventually wrote a document to celebrate the event, the U.S. Constitution. As the historian Robert W. Venables says, "the Haudenosaunee influenced both directly and indirectly the generation of the Founding Fathers and their various efforts to achieve unity" (Venables 1992:68). The power and persistence of a native story convinced the separate peoples of the Old World to merge in their new homeland for their mutual benefit.

Modern scholarly stories place the formation of the Haudenosaunee, the original event, sometime around A.D. 1500 (Ruoff 1990:23). Under these terms a Haudenosaunee governance known as the Council of Fifty was created, and this system gave all Five Nations, later called the Six Nations when the Tuscaroras were included in 1715. Ever since, the Six Nations have gathered to resolve their differences through common consent.

The historian Donald A. Grinde Jr. says that numerous colonial documents exist to support the Iroquois story and its effect on the immigrants. "There is ample scholarly opinion and factual data to conclude that the Founding Fathers respected and used American Indian ideas as the American government evolved" (Grinde 1992:47). Grinde points out that Indian confederacies were so appealing to William Penn that he described the whole of Eastern America as political societies with sachemships inherited through the female side. "Penn was also familiar with the Condolence ceremony of the Iroquois which was crucial for an understanding of their confederacy" (Grinde 1992:49). Again, the ceremony was an oral drama, a story, that the colonists observed. The story was about the unification of the Iroquois, and their aim was to achieve peace and unity.

It is important to remember that the influence the Haudenosaunee had on men like William Penn was derived from Penn's firsthand knowledge of their discourse. In the case of the Haudenosaunee, they made wampum belts to record events but never made written accounts. Rather, their spokesmen were trained to speak and tell stories. The anthropologist Stephen A. Tyler says that "discourse is the maker of the world, not its mirror. . . . The world is what we say it is and what we speak of is the world" (Tyler 1987: 171). Tribal spokesmen used allegory, metaphor, imagination, and inventiveness—all the techniques of storytelling to make their demands come true.

In the case of the Haudenosaunee, their story was about unity. Although the struggle for immigrant dominance was tumultuous, the Haudenosaunee's call for unity in the Northeast remained steady, and it is little wonder why. In the

17th century the Haudenosaunee had to negotiate with seven white colonial governments on the Hudson. "The inter-colonial context was equally stormy. The Haudenosaunee had to deal with New England colonies to their east and the English colonies to the south, which were rivals of the Dutch. After an English government replaced the Dutch in 1664, all the Haudenosaunee white neighbors, except the French in Canada, were now under English rule from London" (Venables 1992:72).

In the summer of 1677, Haudenosaunee spokesmen such as Carachkondie and Connondocgoo joined with English officials from New York, Maryland, and Virginia to speak for a unified colonial policy. The Indians wanted to create a foreign policy with the English in order to cement their trade relationship with them (Venables 1992:72). The Haudenosaunee were major political and economic partners of the English in what is now known as the Covenant Chain. Because the Indians were a counterbalance to French interest in Canada (and key to the English colonists' survival), they often used the councils to retell their origin stories and renew the Covenant Chain. This oratory benefited the Haudenosaunee in two ways. First, it presented a unified Indian image to the colonists. Second, the act of storytelling inculcated what the historian Raymond D. Fogelson (1989:143) calls an epitomizing event for both speaker and listener. Whether the event in question ever happened matters very little to the people who believe it. Therefore, story creates culture and beliefs, the very glue which binds a society together.

In the Western intellectual tradition, the act of writing stories ("documents") has been given hegemony over the act of telling stories. This phenomenon led to a privileged view of text, so much so that written stories of the past became labeled as "history" and their storytellers "historians." Currently, debate persists among anthropologists, ethnohistorians, and literary critics about what distinguishes story from history or ethnography. The anthropologist James Clifford has said in his introduction to *Writing Culture* that much of what is being written about particular cultures is "true fiction."

> Ethnographic writings can properly be called fictions in the sense of "something made or fashioned," the principal burden of the word's Latin foot, *fingere*. But is important to preserve the meaning not merely of making, but also of making up, of inventing things not actually real. (*Fingere*, in some of its uses, implied a degree of falsehood.) Interpretative social scientists have recently come to view good ethnographies as "true fictions," but usually at the cost of weakening the oxymoron, reducing it to the banal claim that all truths are constructed. [Clifford 1986:7]

What Clifford and others are saying is that a particular text within a discipline is not false, but always interpretive, and, most important, the storyteller can never undertake to tell the whole story. The histories of Indian and white relations are replete with documents of how Indians influenced Europeans to unite, but the story remains only partially told. For example, on June 24, 1744, in Lancaster, Pennsylvania, Canasatego, a Haudenosaunee spokesman, gave his first speech on the history of the Covenant Chain and its success in creating symbiotic trade relationships. His manipulation of the image of Indian hegemony in the region was considerable. Canasatego's speech was translated by the interpreter Conrad Weiser. In his concluding remarks given on July 4, 1744, Canasatego repeated the origin story of the Haudenosaunee (Venables 1992:76–81). "Benjamin Franklin printed Canasatego's speech as part of the full record of the 1744 Lancaster negotiations. Franklin sent three hundred copies to London to sell" (Venables 1992:81). Canasatego's story was read by Londoners as well as colonists.

In 1754, Franklin made a proposal called the Albany Plan to unite the colonies. On June 11, 1776, 22 years later, Franklin's revised Albany Plan was given to the committee of the Continental Congress. That group later drafted the Articles of Confederation. James Wilson, a delegate from Pennsylvania and future author of the first draft of the U.S. Constitution, argued vigorously for a confederation that was *similar* to the Haudenosaunee. He declared: "Indians know the striking benefits of confederation . . ." [and we] "have an example of it in the Union of the Six Nations" (Ford 1904–05:1078).

In reading the papers, memoirs, and diaries of influential colonists like the historian Cadwallader Colden, Acting Governor of New York James DeLancey, the Founding Fathers Benjamin Franklin, James Madison, Thomas Jefferson, and James Wilson, as well as the philosopher John Locke, it is clear that they noted the social and political effects the Indians had on them. However, what is most important to the Onondaga elder Oren Lyons is that his community's story remains constant. Haudenosaunee existence predates contact with Europeans. "This is no small achievement," he says. "We have faced off with the white man for three hundred years and right from the beginning he has learned much from us. He just doesn't want to admit it" (Lyons 1994).

I include this long discussion of the Haudenosaunee story, and the early colonial writings, not because I want to enter the debate on whether the U.S. Constitution exactly replicates Haudenosaunee governance. The Constitution, although a kind of nationalist creation story, does not in intent or function imitate Indian governance. Rather, it is my intention to argue that the Haudenosaunee's *story of their union* created an image so powerful in the minds of colonists that they believed if "savages" could unite they ought to be able to do the same thing. That united image remained indelible in the minds of immigrants, so much so that Indians will forever be spoken of as *one group*. Today, it comes as a surprise to college students that there are still over five hundred federally recognized tribes, with distinct cultural practices.

What I suggest is that a native creation story was one of America's authors. If not acknowledged in the "historical credits," American Indians are certainly the ghostwriters for the event, the story of America. So far, I have consciously used *story*, *history*, and *theory* as interchangeable words because the difference in their usage is artificially constructed to privilege writing over speaking. All histories are stories that are written down. The story you get depends on the point of view of the writer. At some point histories are contextualized as *fact*, a theoretically loaded word. Facts change, but stories continually bring us into being.

WHAT IS TRIBALOGRAPHY?

I add my breath to your breath
That our days may be long on the Earth
That the days of our people may be long
That we may be one person
That we may finish our roads together
May our mother bless you with life
May our life Paths be fulfilled [Allen 1986:56]

Now I have come to the place where I must tell you what my term *tribalography* means and how it achieves a new understanding in theorizing on Native studies. This is a tall order for a storyteller, but here goes. Native stories, no matter what form they take (novel, poem, drama, memoir, film, history), seem to pull all the elements together of the storyteller's tribe, meaning the people, the land, and multiple characters and all their manifestations and revelations, and connect these in past, present, and future milieus (present and future milieus mean non-Indians). I have tried to show that tribalography comes from the Native propensity for bringing things together, for making consensus, and for symbiotically connecting one thing to another. It is a cultural bias, if you will.

The Choctaw/Cherokee author Louis Owens writes that the precedent for this wholeness is the oral tradition of American Indians:

Just as significant is the fact that the concept of a single author for any given text, or of an individual who might conceive of herself or himself as the creative center and originating source of a story, or of the individual autobiography, would have made as little sense to pre-Columbian Native Americans as the notion of selling real estate. For the traditional storyteller, each story originates and serves to define the people as a whole, the community. [Owens 1992:9]

The following two books are models of what I am calling tribalography.

From the Glittering World is by the Navajo author Irvin Morris. It is a collection of short stories that connect the Diné with their tribal history and contemporary lives. Throughout his book Morris makes no claims that the stories he tells belong to him alone. The book's subtitle, *A Navajo Story*, shows that the stories he is telling not only have been collected by his people but are about his journey through his people's experience. In essence, he is saying identity is determined by his history and the future.

The stories in the first section are the creation stories of the Diné, which create dichotomies between man and woman, light and dark. Morris tells of a cosmic struggle for survival through flood and drought, as well as tracing the lineages of the original four clans of the Navajo. Following the introduction of Diné cosmology, Morris provides the reader with accounts of his family members. For example, Morris's great-grandmother witnesses the atrocities her people experienced when they were forced off their lands and marched into captivity. Therefore, Morris's stories transcend his own memories, to include those of his relatives and tribal community.

The modern stories in the final section are how Morris connects himself to the shiny and glittering world of the highways of the *bilagaanaa*, or white people. He juxtaposes this against the other world, the traditional *hooghan* life of his grandmother and great-grandmother. Often the telling is dismal. The average annual Diné per capita income for 1980 was only $2,400. Alcoholism takes young men from their homes on weeklong binges. But in the last story, titled "Meat and the Man," Morris offers a comedic version of Navajo life in the 1990s.

An older white man and his dog called "Grabs-the-Meat" come to visit a Navajo family. They are uninvited guests. The *bilagaanaa*, a self-proclaimed tourist, speaks a little Navajo, badly. His car is broken down and he's hungry, so the family feeds him. Eventually he wants to hear stories, so the grandma in the story tells the man about Skinwalkers. The story is so powerful that he actually sees a Skinwalker outside the *hooghan* and faints with fright.

"I told you not to tell those," said Jill, as they watch the man drive away the next morning. "I think you just about scared that man to death. What if he'd had a heart attack?"

"He was awfully nosy," said Grandma.

"But he talked Navajo," Jill's mother said.

"Barely," corrected Grandma.

"I'll bet he never forgets last night," said Jill.

"Yup," said Jim. "He nearly shit his pants. You should have seen him."

"Yaadila," said Jill.

"I thought he was nice—and rather good looking if you ask me," said Grandma. "What did you say his name was again?" [Morris 1997:256–257]

The story ends with Grandma thinking she might take the old white man as a husband. So by the end of Morris's tribalography, another future connection is possible.

What is most significant about Morris's work is that while he is telling specific Navajo tribal history, culture, and his own revelatory stories, he also regards this textual space as a contemplative reflection of identity. What does it mean to be Navajo, but to connect with people who are not? The story continues.

The Yanktonai author Susan Power's novel *The Grass Dancer* is another example of tribalography. Like Morris, Power has written a series of stories that are connected in a novel structure. The story is set in North Dakota on the Standing Rock Sioux Reservation. Power steeps her readers in the connections between Dakota ancestors and the present-day culture. She tells Dakota stories through six central characters. Time travels counterclockwise, and there are multiple narrators giving their versions of events. This creates a multigenerational story that touches all the characters in the book. As each chapter unfolds, the reader is taken backward in time until the final scenes of the book complete the beginning.

One of the central characters, Evie, a Dakota Sioux, believes her father is a Blood Indian from Calgary. Her mother, Margaret Many Wounds, has told the story that she married Sonny Porter and gave birth to twins, Evie, and her sister, Lydia. Evie has believed all her life that she inherited her father's looks, mannerisms, and temperament. Her creation story is that of the Dakota people. What we discover in chapter 4, called "MoonWalk," is that Evie's father is Dr. Sei-ichi Sakuma, a Japanese surgeon from San Francisco. While it is important for Evie to know the identity of her father, she is not destroyed by the fact that he is Japanese because she has been raised with the Dakota, a people with powerful creation stories.

In a lecture at Grinnell College in 1999, Power talked about the stimulus that helped her create *The Grass Dancer* and her second novel, *War Bundles*. She said she believes she is reclaiming American history in her novels of fiction.

As a Native fiction writer I sometimes think of my work as consisting of little more than pointing out the bloody obvious. Ideas that Native peoples have been turning in their minds since the age of five can—once released into the mainstream discourse—find themselves plumped to the status of profundity. For this reason, I don't for a second claim to be covering new ground with my new novel, *War Bundles*, rather following trails familiar to a Native audience which sadly have proven to be revelatory to non-Natives exposed to early versions of the novel.

The message of *War Bundles* is incredibly simple. Native peoples, and their stories and histories are not a social studies unit of an interesting sub-category of American Literature to be haphazardly included in courses such as "Literatures of the Outsider in America," if at all. We are American history, we are American literature. Every track and trace of the American experience runs through our communities, our culture. We have been the transformers so much more than we are ever credited to have been. I am so tired of our image as the transformed—the lost, the dead, always those who are acted upon, always those who have been pushed to the edges, where we can be watched compassionately, nostalgically, seen as little more than a decorative fringe. I don't just want to learn how the writing of Louise Erdrich was influenced by William Faulkner, although that is a fascinating and necessary study, but additionally how so much of the material produced by white Southern writers and African-American writers reflects Native oral traditions. *War Bundles*, then, is not the development of a specifically "Native" history, but a reclamation of moments thought of as exclusively-peculiarly American. We (Natives) have participated in World Fairs and World Wars, witnessed the destruction of cities we also helped to raise; we were gangsters and outlaws, performers and writers. We were there. Always there. Still here. [Power 1999]

While these two books are models of what I am calling a tribalography, there are many others. Currently there are over two million American Indians in the United States, and most of these people, give or take a thousand, are writing stories. The first thing you may think is: LeAnne you maniac, not every Indian in America is writing a book. I know it; some are making movies, or music videos for MTV.

Every Indian I meet is writing a story. A couple of summers ago while I was in Oklahoma conducting research and visiting family, I was invited to lecture at OK Choctaws, a nonpolitical organization in the Oklahoma City area. Many of the elder members of OK Choctaws gathered every day for lunch at the Salvation Army's Native American Center in downtown Oklahoma City to share stories. After lecturing on some of the historical documents I had found concerning Choctaws in the early 18th century, I was asked to come back to help some of the elders who wanted to tell their histories. What I found was that all of the elders were writing stories that had been passed down to them, stories of how their ancestors had survived the 1831 removal from Mississippi to Oklahoma. Our removal began what is known as the Trail of Tears. The Choctaws I met were incorporating the oral stories of their families with the written documents of our removal. They were writing how their ancestors had created new lives in 19th-century Indian Territory, now called Oklahoma.

As we talked about their projects, their World War II experiences, of growing up Choctaw, I realized that they were doing what our ancestors had done for millennia: they were pondering the mysteries of their experiences, telling their stories, and creating a new discourse at the end of the 20th century. Whether they were speaking them into audio tapes, writing them by hand, typing them into computers, or recounting them to future generations of storytellers, Choctaws were doing what the Ojibway author Gerald Vizenor describes as ". . . creat[ing] discourse with imagination" (Vizenor 1993:187). They were integrating oral traditions, histories, and experiences into narratives and expanding our identity. Not only are Choctaws and other American Indians creating a future "literary past" for American Indians, but the textual space, tribalography, creates a literary and literal past for non-Indians as well.

If indeed our world is what we say it is, as Tyler (1987) suggests, then I am saying that a tribalography is a story that links Indians and non-Indians.

In conclusion, I am suggesting that America is a collection of stories. Teaching the stories of Native authors along with stories of historians will be both illuminating and, at times, illusionary. One thing is certain: the landscape of Native stories may remain just beyond the grasp of the reader if the stories are pressed into narrow categories of what is fiction and what is historical truth.

I leave you with what my friend Craig Howe told me when I was a guest lecturer for a program called "Tribal Landscapes" at the Newberry Library in Chicago. I want you to repeat these words after me, because like my ancestors before me, I believe in the power of breath and mind. I am a *nukfoki*, teacher.

"Tribalism will not die, even if all the Indians do."

What I think Craig Howe is alluding to is that our stories are unending connections to past, present, and future. And even if worse comes to worst and our people forget where we left our stories, the birds will remember and bring them back to us.

Whe-ee, that's enough. I can tell you no more today!

REFERENCES

Allen, Paula Gunn
    1986   The Sacred Hoop: Recovering the Feminine in American Indian Tradition. Boston: Beacon.

Barreiro, José, ed.
    1992   Indian Roots of American Democracy. Ithaca, NY: Akwe:Kon Press, Cornell University.

Beauchamp, W. M.
    1897   The New Religion of the Iroquois. The Journal of American Folk-Lore 10, 38 (July–September):175–190.

Bierhorst, John, ed.
    1974   Four Masterworks of American Indian Literature. Tucson: University of Arizona Press.

Bushnell, David I., Jr.
    1909   The Choctaw of Bayou Lacomb St. Tammany Parish Louisiana. Bureau of American Ethnology Bulletin, 48. Washington, DC: Smithsonian Institution.

Clayton, Nicola, and Anthony Dickinson
    1998   Episodic-like Memory during Cache Recovery by Scrub Jays. Nature, 395 (September 17):272–274.

Clifford, James, and George Marcus, eds.
    1986   Writing Culture: The Poetics and Politics of Ethnography. Berkeley: University of California Press.

Cushman, H. B.
    1899   The History of the Choctaws, Chickasaws, and Natchez Indians. Greenville, TX: Headlight Printing House.

Fogelson, Raymond D.
    1989   The Ethnohistory of Events and Non-Events. Ethnohistory 36(2):133–147.

Ford, Paul L., ed.
    1904–   The Works of Thomas Jefferson, vol 6. New York: Putnam.
    1905

Grinde, Donald A., Jr.
    1992   Iroquoian Political Concept and the Genesis of American Government. *In* Indian Roots of American Democracy. José Barreiro, ed. Pp. 47–66. Ithaca, NY: Akwe:Kon Press, Cornell University.

Howe, LeAnne
  1993   Danse D'Amour, Danse De Mort. *In* Earth Sky, Song Spirit. Clifford E. Trafzer, ed. Pp. 447–472. New York: Doubleday.
Lyons, Oren
  1992   Land of the Free, Home of the Brave. *In* Indian Roots of American Democracy. José Barreiro, ed. Pp. 30–35. Ithaca, NY: Akwe:Kon Press, Cornell University.
  1994   Interview. *In* The Native Americans, part 1. The Nations of the Northeast: The Strength and Wisdom of the Confederacies. TBS Productions.
Margulis, Lynn, and Dorion Sagan
  1986   Microcosmos: Four Billion Years of Evolution from Our Microbial Ancestors. New York: Summit Books.
  1995   What Is Life? New York: Simon & Schuster.
Morris, Irvin
  1996   From the Glittering World. Norman: University of Oklahoma Press.
Ortiz, Simon J.
  1976   Going for Rain. New York: Harper.
Owens, Louis
  1992   Other Destinies: Understanding the American Indian Novel. Norman: University of Oklahoma Press.
Power, Susan
  1993   The Grass Dancer. New York: Putnam.
  1999   Formal lecture given at convocation in Grinnell College Chapel, November.
Ruoff, A. LaVonne Brown
  1990   American Indian Literatures: An Introduction, Bibliographic Review, and Selected Bibliography. New York: Modern Language Association of America.
Sarris, Greg
  1994   Interview. *In* The Native Americans, part 2. The Tribal People of the Northwest: Living in Harmony with the Land. TBS Productions.
Tyler, Stephen A.
  1987   The Unspeakable: Discourse, Dialogue, and Rhetoric in the Postmodern World. Madison: The University of Wisconsin Press.
Venables, Robert W.
  1992   Choosing To Be Romans. *In* Indian Roots of American Democracy. Jos Barreiro, ed. Pp. 67–106. Ithaca, NY: Akwe:Kon Press, Cornell University.
Vizenor, Gerald, ed.
  1993   Narrative Chance: Postmodern Discourse on Native American Indian Literatures. Norman: University of Oklahoma Press.

Categories of Analysis

Categories

Nancy Shoemaker

Categories are building blocks in the creation of knowledge and in the application of knowledge to situations. Whether the categories are day and night, self and other, men and women, friends and enemies, or east, west, north, and south, people rely on categories to make a complex world manageable. By paying attention to how people in the past used categories, scholars could better understand historical processes. How do categories come into being and change over time? How do people adapt categories to fit the context? And what kinds of categorizing systems do people in any given society use to comprehend the natural world and to organize the division of labor and the distribution of material goods, rights, obligations, status, honor, respect? I start with two examples from American Indian history that point to the significance of categories in human experience. I then discuss how historians, anthropologists, linguists, and cognitive scientists have dealt with categories as cultural constructions and as universal systems of human thought and how this literature has been used or could be used to provide insights into North American Indian historical studies. I conclude by addressing methodological issues raised by approaching Indian history from this perspective.

TWO CASE STUDIES

In southeastern Indian folklore, there is a story of a ballgame between birds and animals. An eager bat shows up, all ready to play, but wreaks havoc by confounding the categories. The size of a mouse, with teeth, fur, wings, and four feet—what is it? Bird or animal? Whichever side takes the bat (there are different versions), that side wins (Mooney 1992:286–287; Swanton 1929:23). Most obviously, this is a story about taxonomy, about how to apply order to a disorderly world by grouping like things together (Fradkin 1990:425–426). Although the bat plays the role of protagonist in this story, it is as an exception and as such serves to clarify how much easier it is to divide the rest of the natural world into categories based on observable criteria of difference: wings or no wings, four legs or two, fur or feathers.

This story also provides information on southeastern Indian cultural practices because these animals act like humans. They play a ballgame. We know from the documentary record that at least as far back as the 18th century, and probably much earlier, the ballgame publicly displayed the Cherokees' and other southeastern Indians' political organization. Towns played other towns. Often, "red" (war-associated) towns played against "white" (peace-associated) towns. The ballgame thus expressed crucial political divisions (Fogelson 1971; Gearing 1962:27; Hudson 1976:235–237, 408–421). There is another anthropomorphic aspect to this story. No matter how the ballgame unfolds, whether the bat joins the animals or the birds, the bat's odd physical features bring victory to the side of which it is playing. Its ambiguous position between categories was a source of power.

Finally, this story raises the issue of change. Some folklorists have proposed that the ballgame story and other southeastern Indian folktales originated in Africa and were products of African-Indian cultural exchanges in North America. Indeed, there are African stories in which the bat's odd conglomeration of body parts drives the plot, but the stories are not identical. There is no ballgame in the African versions. Either southeastern Indians adapted an African story to their own cultural setting, or maybe the bat is so anomalous in its appearance that Native American, African, European, and Asian taxonomic systems have all had to struggle to account for it (Dundes 1973:123; Lankford 1987:239–242). It is difficult to draw definite conclusions about cultural similarities found through comparative studies. Either changes occurred in southeastern Indian oral traditions or there are common patterns to how people construct categories, or both.

A second example of categories' significance comes from 19th-century Ojibwe (also Chippewa or Anishinaabeg) negotiations with United States treaty commissioners. In 1837, the United States, seeking to acquire the rich pine lands west of the Great Lakes from the Native inhabitants, invited Ojibwe headmen to a treaty. From the perspective of U.S. officials, the Ojibwes then ceded land to the United States, but the Ojibwes for the next 150 years protested this interpretation of their agreement, arguing instead that they had retained rights to use this land and had sold only the pine trees to the United States. The 1983 *Voigt* decision resolved the dispute in favor of Wisconsin's Ojibwe tribes. The judge's decision hinged on transcripts and journal accounts of the negotiations, on Ojibwe elders' testimony about language and culture, and on legal canons delineating that in contract and treaty disputes, courts should lean toward the weaker, non-English-speaking party's understanding of the agreement at the time of entering into the contract (Satz 1991).

The treaty transcripts and later court hearings of evidence abound with references to categories. In his speech to the treaty commissioners, the Ojibwe chief Magegawbaw, also known as La Trappe, divided the world into categories when he said, "We wish to hold on to a tree where we get our living, and to reserve the streams where we drink the waters that give us life." Placing an "oak sprig" on the treaty table, he explained that the tree they wished to reserve for their own use was different from the trees "you wish to get from us" (Satz 1991:18, 142). Magegawbaw's gesture risked being interpreted as a claim to oak trees only, but in the official written transcript of the treaty's proceedings, the secretary scoffed at interpreting this speech literally. Of course, Magegawbaw meant that they wished to continue to hunt, fish, and draw sap from maple trees in the ceded territory. In an 1864 petition, that is how Ojibwe petitioners recalled Magegawbaw's speech, claiming that they had offered to give up the pine timber, but "Again this I hold in my hand the Maple Timber, also the Oak Timber, also this Straw which I hold in my hand. Wild Rice is what we call this. These I do not sell" (Satz 1991:27).

With this speech, Magegawbaw could have been stepping onto the murky "middle ground" of cultural misunderstandings and contrived understandings so eloquently explored by Richard White (1991), but cultural difference is not a prerequisite for mistaken meaning. That categories are contained within categories increases the odds of speakers and hearers coming away with different impressions of what was said, even when speakers and hearers share a common culture and language. An oak sprig could refer to oak trees, to deciduous trees, to trees in general, to all of nature. In this case, at least some Euro-Americans at the treaty grasped the Ojibwe taxonomy of the Great Lakes environment and realized that Magegawbaw, to suit this particular situation, had constructed two new categories from it: pine trees and those useful products of nature's bounty that were not pine trees. In this context, the oak sprig was a metonymical prop that stood for all Ojibwe subsistence needs, which they refused to cede.

Categories presented other problems at this treaty. The need to identify which individuals belonged to which nation undergirded all negotiations in which two polities, represented by authorized individuals, were to meet and come to an agreement. Who had authority to speak for the group labeled "Chippewa" by the United States? By Ojibwe accounts, only the headman of a band could consent to deals regarding resources on that band's territory. However, U.S. treaty commissioners insisted on conducting treaties with the "Chippewa Nation" (Satz 1991:37). Even today, there is no "Chippewa Nation." Instead, many different Ojibwe tribes, some of which still use the word *band* as part of their formal self-identification, joined in bringing to court the lawsuit that ultimately restored, in a fashion, their treaty rights. Since Euro-Americans themselves could be categorized by either cultural heritage or political identity, we have to assume that their refusal to recognize that same distinction operating in Ojibwe society was prejudicial and instrumental. To expedite land acquisition, U.S. treaty commissioners glossed a category based on cultural and linguistic affiliation as a political category.

The treaty negotiations and subsequent dispute reflect some cultural differences in the construction of categories, the subtleties of which passed without comment at the time. In the 1864 petition, the Ojibwes remembered having stated at the treaty council, "I do not make you a present of this, I merely lend it to you" (Satz 1991:27). Although the Ojibwe headmen distinguished between temporary and permanent land transfers, a construction of categories that they may have shared with Euro–Americans, they termed a permanent land cession a "present." Exchanges free from social obligations—"purchases"—may not have existed as a category in Ojibwe thought in the mid-19th century.

Also important at this treaty was the recent emergence of new categories. Magegawbaw or La Trappe, was he Ojibwe or French? Perhaps he was a "mixed blood." U.S.-Indian treaties in the Great Lakes region in the 1830s and 1840s granted or denied "mixed bloods" special payments and are therefore among the earliest official records to group Indians by degree of blood (Kappler 1972:464–465, 543, 568, 573). As Melissa Meyer (1994) has argued for the White Earth Reservation in Minnesota, Ojibwes appear to have based the categories of "mixed blood" and "full blood" on cultural criteria such as dress, language, and economic way of life: "full bloods" engaged in a seasonal round of subsistence activities while "mixed bloods" brought capitalism to the reservation. In the late 19th century, special U.S. agents, hired to figure out which Ojibwes were "mixed bloods," conceived of these categories as biological. To determine who belonged in which category, they looked for differences in hair, skin color, and skull size and charted genealogical descent (Meyer 1994:168–170; Beaulieu 1984). Because some of these 19th-century treaties with Great Lakes Indians treated "mixed bloods" as a distinct group, "mixed" and "full" could be considered nascent political categories. In Canada, "Métis" did become just such a category, a means to distinguish the rights of a body of people within the larger polity. In contrast, in the United States, "mixed blood" and "full blood" survived primarily as cultural referents in many Indian communities. But since most tribes in the United States today use blood quantum minimums, commonly one-fourth, to determine eligibility for tribal membership, it does look as though biological criteria have superseded all others as the basis for tribes' political boundaries (Snipp 1989:361–365).

The stories about the bat and the 1837 "pine tree" treaty and every other story or event in human history depend on intellectual constructs that take the shape of categories. In both these examples, people taxonomized the natural world; organized themselves or other people into groups bounded by cultural, political, or biological criteria; and created new meanings by playing off old categories and inventing additional categories. They also faced the impossibility of ever achieving a culturally constructed system of categories that was fixed, unambiguous, and able to function, without disjuncture or exceptions, in every situation. These processes deserve further study.

THEORIES ABOUT CATEGORIES

Before analyzing other people's categories, we should be aware of our own. Scholars rely on categories, too, but rarely distinguish between categories used by people in the past and their own use of categories as analytical tools. The problem is especially visible in the history of sexuality, where scholars acknowledge the difficulties of defining the boundaries of research projects without recourse to anachronisms such as "gay" and "lesbian" and where the criteria for classifying people by sexuality float uncertainly between sexual acts and sexual identities. American Indian studies faces similar issues. Some ill-suited and confining categories have been exposed and eliminated from academic discourse. "Primitive" and "civilized" have faded in popularity to the point of becoming archaic language. David Rich Lewis (1991) challenged the labels "progressive" and "traditional," which were common in 19th-century parlance and accepted uncritically by 20th-century scholars as legitimate descriptions of reservation populations. But the most unsettling and potentially divisive category is the one that defines the field. Whichever term is used—American Indians, Native Americans, First Nations, or indigenous peoples of the Americas—this category of people does not have transparent, incontestable boundaries. As a contemporary policy issue, the politics of categorizing are particularly pressing. Who determines who is Indian? Tribes? The Bureau of Indian Affairs? Individuals? And what criteria should be used? Blood quantum? Self-identification? Tribal membership? And what does it mean to be Indian? Is it a nationality, an ethnicity, both at once, something else altogether (Thornton 1987:186–224)?

Most of us accept indiscriminately that certain individuals or communities are Indian if our sources identify them as such. If the sources contradict, then the question of categorization becomes explicit. Significantly, however, the most influential scholarship also tends to probe the meaning of categories. James Merrell (1989), for example, in his history of the Catawbas found that "Catawba" as a political identity changed over time and to English users of the term embraced a large group of people who, initially at least, identified themselves differently. In an article on the interpreter Andrew Montour, Merrell (1997) investigated the boundaries of social organization and identities in 18th-century Pennsylvania by demonstrating the difficulty of putting Montour in any one ethnic or national category. Merrell does not take categories for granted but, subtly and implicitly, contextualizes historical figures within their own culturally constructed social and political categories.

Because categories are fictions relevant to particular times, places, and people, it is no wonder that our own categories muddle what we study. One ill-conceived solution to this problem was the antiessentialist fad of the 1990s. Self-conscious about imposing themselves on the past, postmodernists accused other scholars of being essentialists, of identifying people by an essential characteristic, thereby presuming that boundaries between people were self-evident, fixed, and ascertainable. To avoid applying our own cultural constructions to a past world now conceived of as wholly constructed, scholars tried to purge the absoluteness of categories from academic discourse. Consequently, every single word had to be put in quotation marks to show that when we used the word "woman" or "race," we did not want anyone to think that we believed there really was such a thing. However, we are all essentialists to a degree and cannot process complexity or communicate with other people without boiling abstract matter down into manageable categories (Landry and MacLean, 1996:7). The best solution is to be explicit about the origins and nature of categories as building blocks of human thought, to be aware of our own categories as we study the past, and to purposefully seek to discover what categories people in the past have used and why.

One of the few historians to venture in this direction is Joan Scott who, in her landmark essay "Gender: A Useful Category of Historical Analysis" (1988), explained why gender history was surpassing women's history as an area of study. Gender is, of course, not itself a category but what I call a "system of categories." Gender consists, usually, of two categories: male and female. "System of categories" is an apt phrase, for it captures the essence of Scott's thesis that gender analysis, in contrast to women's studies, is relational in its emphasis.

"Women" as a category only exists in juxtaposition to a category of people who are not women—"men." That the term "gender" originated in linguistics and spread to other fields is indicative of larger trends in history, anthropology, sociology, and the newly emergent cultural studies, all of which have looked to linguistics for theoretical insight. Linguists, such as Roman Jakobson, have observed that categories, especially oppositions, work as units. There is no "hot" without "cold," no "day" without "night," no "short" without "tall" (Jakobson 1990:235, 316). Men must be present in women's history; to embrace gender studies only makes this explicit. Similarly, "Indian" is a relational term, a category that is part of a system of categories. Depending on the context, that system might be Indians and non-Indians; Indians, Whites, and Blacks; Indians and Europeans. For "Indians" to exist as a category, there must be people who are not Indian.

Joan Scott and historians in general have most diligently pursued three systems of categories—race, class, and gender—but perhaps too diligently. One should first ask if these were systems of categories in use in the societies under study. For example, among the 18th-century Cherokees, gender, kinship, and age appear to have most influenced daily activities, social relationships, and authority in the community, while towns served as the locus of political identity (Hatley 1993; Gearing 1962; Perdue 1998). Race was just emerging as an idea, and there is no evidence of social classes—of material wealth serving to divide Cherokees into subgroups—until the 19th century (Shoemaker 1997; McLoughlin 1986; Perdue 1979). The single-minded pursuit of race, class, and gender that has preoccupied historians in the past 20 to 30 years was clearly not designed with Indian studies in mind.

Anthropologists, linguists, and cognitive scientists have thought much more about categories than historians, and it is to those disciplines' insights that I now turn. First, I will review anthropological approaches to figuring out why people classify and especially why dualistic oppositions are common classification systems. This discussion will also address liminality, which could be thought of as the gap between categories, and the problems posed by locating structure in worlds that are changing over time. Second, I will discuss ideas about classification originating in linguistics and cognitive science, including theories about the nature of categories, particularly two characteristics: that categories can be marked or unmarked and that categories have centers.

There is no denying that dualistic oppositions, or dichotomies, figure large in the types of categorizing systems humans, including American Indians, have created: red and white towns, mixed bloods and full bloods, men and women, traditional and progressive, primitive and civilized. A major foundational work on this topic is Rodney Needham's *Right and Left: Essays on Dual Symbolic Classification* (1973). Several of the essays in this collection date to the early 20th century when, writing independently, Robert Hertz and Francis La Flesche noted that right and left were commonly used as symbolic opposites in daily custom, ceremonies, and social organization. La Flesche discussed how dualistic divisions—right and left, sky and earth, east and west—structured Osage ceremonies. Hertz more generally summarized that "primitive thought" often associated the right hand with goodness and sacredness, conceived of the left hand as evil or profane, and linked that dualism to other forces of nature: east and west, day and night, hot and cold. Hertz speculated that the shape of the human body, the existence of two hands, might be the basis for binary thought generally and that abstract notions of the right hand's superiority derived from "slight physiological advantages possessed by the right hand" (Hertz 1973:20–21).

Despite these early investigations—Hertz's essay dates to 1909 and La Flesche's to 1916—it was not until several decades later that anthropologists, en masse, were swept away by structural analysis. The big wave came in the 1960s. (Tellingly, Needham reprinted the Hertz and La Flesche essays in 1973.) Anthropologists' curiosity about classification schemes can be traced to the linguist Roman Jacobson, who lectured on the oppositional relationship of sounds, or phonemes, during World War II to a New York audience that included Claude Lévi-Strauss. Lévi-Strauss went on to found a new field of study—structuralism—based on Jakobson's principles but extending his ideas about language to provide a logic for understanding societies and cultures.

Lévi-Strauss's own work is, deservedly, considered incomprehensible, but fortunately he spawned like-minded studies by more comprehensible writers (Lévi-Strauss 1963, 1969; Leach 1989). In North American Indian studies, for example, Fred Gearing (1962) interpreted 18th-century Cherokee society as being in a constant state of tension between "structural poses": young men and old men, red and white towns, peace and war. Raymond Fogelson's (1971:329) analysis of the Cherokee ball game elaborated on Gearing's argument by charting how the practice of the ballgame displayed these and other dualisms central to Cherokee culture:

Peace:	War
Passive:	Active
Old:	Young
Internal:	External

Plants:	Animals
Tame/Cultivated:	Wild
Female:	Male

Structuralism came under a barrage of critiques and, like all theories, collapsed as new ways of seeing rose to take its place. Criticism centered on the seeming rigidity of structure: its incapacity to accommodate exceptions, its resistance to analyses of change over time, and ultimately its incompatibility with postmodernist conceptions of thought and communication as so infinitely varied, relative, and situational that general rules cannot be discerned. Charts summarizing systems of dualistic classification, such as Fogelson's, struck many readers as claims to absolute truths despite their creators' insistence that, of course, there were contexts and exceptions: the right hand was not *always* sacred and the left hand not *always* profane (Needham 1987).

Unfortunately, in the rush to dump structuralism in favor of new theories, some interesting ideas never reached fruition. Fogelson's chart, for instance, does capture some of the underlying categories apparent in 18th-century Cherokee thought, particularly the conceptual associations between white/peace/female/old and red/war/male/young. The town of Chota, which emerged as the capital center of Cherokee politics in the mid-18th century, bore such distinctions as the "ancient town of refuge," "town of peace," and "mother town," and was one of several "*peaceable towns*, which are called 'old-beloved,' 'ancient, holy, or white towns'" (Payne n.d., 2:131; Cheves 1894:332; McDowell 1958–70, 1:258; Williams 1930:166–167). Clearly, concepts such as young and old, red and white—aligned in opposition to each other—were mental devices for organizing political relationships. A structuralist analysis might stop there. However, a more contemporary way to approach these 18th-century references to Chota's status would be to ask who described Chota in these ways and why. By depicting Chota as the head of a lineage of towns and linking it metaphorically to the age, kin, and gender categories associated with peace, certain Cherokees and their English allies may have simply been illuminating Chota's acknowledged role within the larger Cherokee Nation. Or they were using the rhetorical power of "white," "mother," and "old" to create a new image of Chota and elevate its role in diplomacy as a peacemaking authority.

Perhaps the most enduring idea to emerge from anthropological investigations of structuralism was "anti-structure" (Turner 1969), more commonly known as liminality. Victor Turner conceptualized rituals as liminal spaces that marked transformations in social status or transitions in the life course, processes that Arnold van Gennep (1960), writing in 1909, had identified as "rites of passage." Rituals deliberately create an alternative world organized around contrasts to the normal order but in so doing reaffirm existing social and cultural categories. Akin to Turner's work and building on van Gennep's insights, Mary Douglas (1966:96) argued that the threat of disorder generated beliefs about corruption and pollution and that "Danger lies in transitional states, simply because transition is neither one state nor the next, it is undefinable." Ceremonies bring into sharp relief the boundaries between categories, which are liminal spaces, potentially wrought with confusion, mystery, and uncertainty.

As a concept, liminality is useful for explaining the role of ritual in any society and the dislocations caused by people or objects who do not easily fall within a category. In the aforementioned article on the interpreter Andrew Montour, Merrell (1997) did not label Montour "liminal," but Greg Dening suggested as much in his introduction to the collection in which Merrell's essay appeared. Indeed, Dening (1997:2) characterized all of early America as "a place of thresholds, margins, boundaries." A straightforward biography of Montour might accept his contemporaries' account of him as unpredictable and untrustworthy, but the concept of liminality takes us beyond biography and into the realm of social and cultural history, where Montour can serve as a window into 18th-century America precisely because he did not fit the accepted categories. Another liminal figure is the bat in the Cherokee ballgame, which is empowered precisely because it falls in between the categories so easily organized by the physical features of the other animals.

Liminality also offers an explanation for the special status accorded *berdaches*, the men who in some Indian societies adopted women's dress and way of life. The Lakotas called them *winkte*, believed they were *wakan* (endowed with spiritual power), and assigned them special roles in ceremonies as they also did for women who adopted men's ways (DeMallie 1983:244–245). While some scholars have argued for the existence of a "third gender" (Williams 1986; Roscoe 1998), *berdaches* could instead be viewed as liminal. Recognized as exceptions to the norm, their existence in between categories reaffirmed ideas about male and female difference. Liminality also accounts for why men who take on the activities of women or women who take on the activities of men might in some societies be considered polluting or corrupt and in other societies be esteemed for having special access to spiritual power. Across cultures and depending on the context, interpretations might vary as to whether the space between categories is corrupting or transcendent.

Intrinsic to Turner's and van Gennep's treatment of ceremonies as demarcating stages of human experience is the idea that time can be cut up into categories. Societies periodize the life course. Historians periodize epochs.

Significantly, liminality serves as a common narrative device for writing about change over time. For example, Anthony F. C. Wallace's model of revitalization movements, articulated in *The Death and Rebirth of the Seneca* (1969), has a tripartite progression. The first section, "The Heyday of the Iroquois," is an ethnographic description of Iroquois culture not fixed in time but suggesting a precontact, "traditional" Iroquois culture. The book's middle section, "The Decline of the Iroquois," deals with the period following the American Revolution when Seneca reservations, resembling "Slums in the Wilderness," degenerated into a liminal, transitional stage of drinking, violence, depression, and chaos. In the final section, "The Renaissance of the Iroquois," the prophet Handsome Lake emerged with a religious message that was the basis for a new social order. Structure gives way to liminality out of which a new structure emerges.

A more deliberate attempt to accommodate ideas about cultural structure with change over time is Marshall Sahlins's (1981) articulation of "historical structuralism." Using Captain Cook's 1778–79 misadventures in Hawaii as a case study, Sahlins proposed that Hawaiians interpreted Cook's actions in light of their ritual calendar and the expected behavior of certain deities within the annual cycle of ritual events. Cook's arrival in Hawaii, his circling around the island, and his unexpected return led the Hawaiians to treat him as the god Lono and butcher him. At the same time, Sahlins argues, the events surrounding Cook's death changed Hawaiian culture as Cook-lore became incorporated in it. In Sahlins's model, Hawaiian cultural categories shaped their understanding of Cook's actions while the events that unfolded as a consequence simultaneously worked to change the cultural categories.

Of course, change does not really occur so neatly in stages, in discrete categories, but is much messier. As Roman Jakobson (1990:199) wrote in reference to studying historical changes in language, "The static viewpoint is a fiction; it is only a scientific procedure to help us; it is not a particular aspect of the way things are." While we might want to criticize Wallace and Sahlins for simplifying complex changes into two categories divided by a liminal transitional stage (in Wallace's case described as disorder, and in Sahlins's case as a ritual), the pretense that change occurs in stages stems from our own cognitive predilection for turning abstract matter into tangible categories.

Cultural anthropologists wrote the seminal studies on classification, but linguists, cognitive scientists, and cognitive anthropologists have been more active lately at generating new theoretical understandings of classification. Their work opens up entirely new questions for historical research. The linguist George Lakoff's writings have been instrumental in reinvigorating the study of classification and its role in the construction of knowledge. His hefty *Women, Fire, and*

Dangerous Things: What Categories Reveal about the Mind (1987) and a slim volume on metaphors, coauthored with Mark Johnson (1980), argue from the same premise. The experience of the human body is a cognitive framework for creating abstract thought, primarily through metaphor. This idea has ancient roots in Western science. Writing in the 18th century, Giambattista Vico (1968:129) noted that "in all languages the greater part of the expressions relating to inanimate things are formed by metaphor from the human body and its parts and from the human senses and passions." Thus, we use expressions like the head of an organization, a neck of land, the teeth of a comb, and footnotes.

Metaphors are usually classified as figurative language, but Lakoff and Johnson see them operating everywhere. They point to underlying conceptual metaphors that originate in concrete experiences such as the spatial orientation of the human body. Because we experience the body horizontally and vertically, we have the concepts of up and down and often associate the word "up" with activity, the word "down" with inactivity, with sleep or death. Abstract mental states—good moods and bad moods—are metaphorically expressed as feeling up or down. The body as a container is another basic metaphor from which we imagine other objects having boundaries, even such seemingly unbounded objects as, to use Lakoff and Johnson's examples, mountains and street corners. As they say (1980:25), "Human purposes typically require us to impose artificial boundaries that make physical phenomena discrete just as we are: entities bounded by a surface."

The idea that larger concepts underlie everyday speech promises to open up new methods for mining written and spoken texts for insight into cultural values and perspectives. For example, the metaphor I just used—"mining texts"—implies that historical research is an economic enterprise in which raw materials are gathered and processed. It is a revealing choice of metaphor and yet so culturally engrained among academics that it probably slipped by most readers unnoticed. Lakoff and Johnson's awareness of how such metaphors send subtle messages constitutes a useful research methodology. In one of the few applications of Lakoff and Johnson's ideas to a Native American studies topic, linguist Jocelyn C. Ahlers (1997) found that in Hupa, as in English, many commonly used expressions do indeed derive from basic metaphors such as "more is up," "happiness is up," "life is a journey," "time is a landscape," "time is a moving object," and "illness is a fight." Ahlers also noted differences between English and Hupa, primarily in the extent to which certain metaphors appeared. Hupa speakers make much more frequent and varied allusions to illness being like a fight or like an animal that eats or gnaws at its victim. Although Ahlers does not give examples of how Hupa and English cognitive metaphors might differ, I suspect that my analogy equating history with mining would not translate well into Hupa.

Lakoff's work on categories and metaphors offers compelling explanations for why communication across cultures is possible. While Lakoff and Johnson (1980:24) allow for cultural variation, their basic premise goes a long way toward illuminating how Indians and Europeans were able to communicate as easily as they did. Most of the historical literature on 17th- and 18th-century cross-cultural exchanges in North America emphasizes a vast cultural divide. The two works generally characterized as polar opposites in setting up a model for the contact experience—Richard White's *The Middle Ground* (1991) and James Merrell's *The Indians' New World* (1989)—actually agree on this point: both start with the supposition that a great distance separated European and Indian cultures. White and Merrell disagree as to whether this cultural divide was ever overcome and an understanding of the other ever reached. Because most research on early Indian-European relations assumes cultural difference, scholars rarely consider the influence cultural similarities had on Indian-European interactions.

However, they did have similarities. Before they even met, Indians and Europeans shared many ideas stemming from commonalities in their physical worlds and identical cognitive processes for constructing abstract knowledge out of concrete experience. The human body, by analogy, modeled abstract thought. That people the world over tend to count in twos, fives, tens, twenties, or occasionally by fours is no accident but comes from the experience of using the body's appendages as counting tools: two arms and legs, five digits on each hand, ten digits on both hands, twenty digits altogether if the toes are included, and hands with four fingers and one thumb. Which body part served as the original metaphor behind an abstraction is sometimes readily apparent in the language. In English, "digit" and "foot" refer to both a body part and an arithmetical abstraction. Many Indian words for numbers and measurements similarly suggest origins in certain body parts being used as visual demonstrations of size or quantity (Closs 1986; Denny 1986; Kupperman 2000).

Indians and Europeans also had an affinity in their perceptions of geography. Even in their earliest encounters, when Indians and Europeans communicated primarily by signs and with little knowledge of the other's language, Indians easily fulfilled the role of guide to European travelers. In verbal descriptions of a landscape or when drawing maps to show what route to take, Indians and Europeans customarily highlighted the same topographical features travelers would see along the way: mountains, rivers, oddly shaped boulders, and human settlements. For this reason, Indians could, upon request, draw maps that were useful and comprehensible to Europeans, and Indians could read European maps and recognize and correct their errors (McWilliams 1981:48, 60, 71–76; Pownall 1949:30, 126; Henry Bouquet to John Forbes, June 16, 1758, in Stevens et al. 1951–76, 2:95–96; Beauchamp 1916:40; Lewis 1998:60–61; Fossett 1996). Moreover, Indians and Europeans knew firsthand the sensory details of travel. They knew what it was like to move physically through a landscape made up of valleys, mountains, rivers, and boulders and could extend that experience metaphorically to describe other, more abstract situations such as life being like a journey with a beginning and endpoint, obstacles cluttering up the path, and rivers having to be crossed.

More significantly, they all experienced the rising and setting of the sun and consequently conceived of the world as having the same four directions, in English east, west, north, and south (Helms 1988:35). Early English settlers John Lawson (1967:213) and Roger Williams (1973:160) marveled at how Indians had the same eight points or "winds" as they did. The movement of the sun from east to west combined with the shape of the human body—how the body seems to have a front, back, and two sides—constituted raw experiential knowledge from which more elaborate knowledge could be constructed.

Noting commonalities does not refute the simultaneous existence of cultural differences. In the process of exchanging maps, two major differences between Indian and European geographical perceptions became evident. First, Indians measured space in terms of time—the standard measure for long distance travel was one day—an experiential measure that Europeans understood, though they themselves more commonly measured distance in purely spatial terms, such as in miles. Although the Native maps that Europeans solicited solely for the purpose of getting from one place to another marked the same landscape distinctions that European travelers were likely to notice, Indians also drew maps of the human landscape using circles to indicate nations and lines to indicate paths of alliance, cartographic devices which Indian mapmakers had to explain to Europeans (Warhus 1997:2, 104; Waselkov 1989). Because imagination is at the heart of creating knowledge, cultures will develop myriad, varied ideas. However, conceiving of the experience of the human body as a core idea in the construction of knowledge does explain the apparent universality or near universality of certain ideas: the comfort of seeing better in daylight gives rise to fears of darkness, the shape of male and female bodies leads to the idea of two genders, and the symmetry of the human body contributes to the appeal of dualistic classification.

The compulsion to categorize is easily recognized as a basic tool of human cognition, but theorists have probed these processes further to arrive at some common characteristics of categories. One well-known attribute is that some categories are marked relative to other, unmarked categories: in English, "man" is an unmarked category; "woman" bears the mark "wo." Roman Jakobson (1990:134–140) and other Prague School linguists laid the basic groundwork for understanding markedness. Their interest was in grammatical constructs, but they also noted how the hierarchical relationship between marked and unmarked categories often had a broader social significance. For instance, the English language captures a snippet of cultural information in implying that it is women who are different from men, not vice versa. However, markedness patterns vary depending on the context. In the female-dominated nursing profession, "nurse" has an unmarked, gendered connotation and it is the men in that profession who are likely to be marked as "male nurses." Adding the "male" mark to "nurse" informs us that male nurses are the exception to the norm (Battistella 1990:24).

Markedness can thus reveal underlying values. My favorite example is close to home. As I have discussed elsewhere (1996), academia is organized into marked and unmarked categories, consequently reflecting the hierarchy of social groups in American culture. Many universities and colleges have programs in women's studies but not men's studies. The same can be said for American Indian, African American, Latino, and Asian American studies; these programs often exist on college campuses, but there are no departments of white studies. In history, the precedence of the Northeast is readily apparent because only western and southern history exist as subfields with their own conferences and their own journals. These marked areas of study emerged as challenges to the unmarked dominance of men, whites, and the Northeast in research and course offerings, but because they are still marked as different, they retain their marginality. We will know a revolution in American society has occurred when a reversal in markedness transforms relations between categories.

In Native history, reversals in markedness can serve as windows into changes in culture and society. Just as Indian names for newly introduced European items tell us what Indians thought of these items—what categories they put them into—changes in markedness indicate widespread acceptance of that item (Witkowski and Brown 1983). For example, the Cherokees initially named the European-introduced pig after the more familiar *sihgwa* (opossum), but at some later point, as domesticated pigs became central to the Cherokee diet, it was the opossum that came to be the marked animal, garnering the distinction *sihgwa ujetsdi* (grinning opossum/pig) (Fradkin 1990:509). Marked terms are not necessarily inferior to their unmarked opposites. In Cherokee, certain ceremonies call for the use of *tsolagayvli* (ancient tobacco), instead of the more mundane, unmarked *tsola* (Kilpatrick 1997:35). Thus, marked terms represent the exceptions, the nonstandard, infrequent usage.

Another important characteristic of categories is that they have centers, or prototypes, as conceptualized by the cognitive psychologist Eleanor Rosch (1975; 1978; Rosch and Mervis 1975). Rosch studied people's responses in a variety of tests aimed at understanding how people categorize. Her early work expanded on Brent O. Berlin and Paul D. Kay's *Basic Color Terms* (1969), which argued that as societies added new color terms, they did so following a common pattern. Languages with only a two-color scheme conceptualized those two colors as light and dark; languages with three color terms always had red as the third color, and then next came yellow and green, then blue, and eventually brown, purple, pink, orange, and gray. From her experiments, Rosch concluded that while human perception could distinguish between different shades of red, some reds were considered more red than others: color categories had a focal color that seemed to best represent all the colors falling within that named category. Refining these ideas with experiments based on birds as a category, Rosch found that robins and sparrows emerged as prototypical birds, or those birds that best encapsulated the attributes defining the bird category. Instead of having fixed criteria for membership, categories are "fuzzy" and without clear-cut boundaries. Penguins fall on the fuzzy edge of the bird category. In lay terms, when we call up a mental image of a bird, we are more likely to envision a robin than a penguin; however, if asked to put penguins in a category, we would still put them in with the birds (also see Lakoff 1987:39–57; D'Andrade 1995:92–121).

The idea that categories have centers appears in academic discourse even among scholars unaware of Rosch's work. For decades, feminist scholars have debated how to *de-center* women's studies, by which they mean the problem of white, middle-class women often being treated as a prototype. However, like theories of markedness, prototype theory could be employed more explicitly as a window into underlying cultural values. In Indian studies, prototypes may be particularly easy to ascertain if other Indian languages resemble Cherokee. In Cherokee, there is a suffix "-ya" that actually means "true" or "real" (Feeling 1975:310). Interestingly, the Cherokee word for sparrow is *tsisquaya* (true bird), suggesting that Cherokee speakers, similar to Rosch's subjects, view the sparrow as a good representative of the bird category as a whole (Fradkin 1990:183).

Prototype theory also provides a framework for understanding the Cherokee phrase *asgayaya*, which appears in 19th-century documents. In *The Cherokee Phoenix* (January 21, 1829:2), editor Elias Boudinot translated the plural *anis-*

gayaya as "real men" and associated it with "the young and middle aged of the males," whooping, dressing in face paint, and going off "to a ball play, or a meeting of similar nature." *Asgayaya* also could have been translated into English as "much of a man." Trial transcripts from late-19th-century Cherokee Nation court records, which Cherokee clerks maintained in English, are rife with witnesses testifying to some young man having said, "I am much of a man" right before or immediately after having assaulted or killed another man (*Cherokee Nation v. Dunawas Bullfrog* 1884; *Cherokee Nation v. Yartunna Vann and Mitchell Squirrel* 1884; *Cherokee Nation v. John Blair* 1887). In regard to an earlier murder investigation, *The Cherokee Phoenix* (November 20, 1830:2) similarly reported that the young man suspected of murder had bragged that "he was much of a man for he had killed a man," to which a companion of his had responded that "he had also killed a man . . . of course they must all be brave men." In 19th-century Cherokee society, "Are you much of a man?" apparently was a challenge to young men to prove their manhood. The combination of "-ya" and the contexts in which Boudinot and other Cherokees used the expression *asgayaya* point to bravery as behavior considered central to the "young and middle aged" male categories.

While linguists and cognitive scientists have recently been more active than cultural anthropologists at studying how categories work, the two different strains of theory support each other. Robert Hertz's speculations on the prominence of the right hand, in actual lived experience and as a metaphor for social and ritual activities, serves as a good example of Lakoff and Johnson's argument about the body as a model for abstract ideas. And liminal spaces could easily be called "fuzzy."

METHODOLOGICAL ISSUES

By summarizing theoretical approaches to categorization, I hope to suggest possibilities. I am certainly not advocating that structuralism be resurrected or that we embrace the work of linguists and cognitive scientists unquestioningly. When structuralists such as Lévi-Strauss tried to dissect Indian cultural material to expose the operative categories, they looked at myths, rituals, and patterns of social organization without paying much attention to the effects of context or change over time. And when Jakobson, Lakoff, and Rosch speculated on the nature of human thought, they were working narrowly within their own languages and cultures. However, by considering what each of these theorists has proposed, we could arrive at new, possible explanations for the intended meanings and unintended consequences of people's actions in the past. Applying any of these theories to the study of Indian history entails analyzing written texts or spoken language for subtle and perhaps multiple meanings.

While I hope to have offered here a sufficient number of examples to demonstrate the methodological possibilities, I also see two big hindrances to applying theories about categories to American Indian studies. First, few scholars working in North American Indian studies learn Native languages. Since English is the main language used by the majority of Indians living today, fieldwork can proceed and oral histories can be collected, all in English. Moreover, the sparse number of historical documents written in Native languages provides a compelling reason to avoid the painstaking, time-consuming task of learning a new language. And finally, the resources for learning Native languages are scarce and highly dependent on one's location. Universities with an Indian constituency might offer courses in a language from that region, or equipped with audiotapes, grammars, and dictionaries, one could try to pick it up on one's own. Despite these obvious disadvantages to learning Native languages, there is no denying that scholars would enrich their understanding if they would do so.

I suspect that North American studies is about to be transformed in the same way that Latin American ethnohistory has been, where the most creative, innovative research makes use of Native language materials. James Lockhart (1991), for example, traced changes in the Nahuatl language—in the frequency and nature of Spanish loan words—to periodize the impact of Spanish colonization on local institutions in Central Mexico. Similar attention to language as a resource would enrich North American Indian studies as well. Moreover, academic research so often seems divorced from the concerns of Native communities, but making language study a prerequisite for research in Native history could add incentives to building course offerings in Native languages at colleges and universities and help promote language preservation (Valentine 1998). While one can analyze language using materials that have already been translated into English—such as I did with the phrase "much of a man" in the English-language Cherokee court records—translations will not capture every nuance of the original. In addition, familiarity with Native languages could still add insight into historical documents for which the translation from a Native language into French, English, Spanish, or Dutch occurred hundreds of years ago.

A second and larger roadblock to applying theories about categorization to American Indian studies is that all these theories—actually, any theory by definition—implies a universalism that is at odds with the cultural relativism that serves as the basic premise underlying Indian cultural and historical studies.

The very existence of "Indian" as a distinct category posits that there are definable characteristics attributable to Indians that are not attributable to other people. Since the topic of "Who Is Indian" is highly sensitive and the cause of much contention, not many of us want to take a stand on what those characteristics are or should be. Because tribal membership entails certain political rights, tribes are in the awkward position of having to demarcate who is inside and who is outside the category; whenever possible, the rest of us no doubt feel comfortable with "Indian" as a category with fuzzy edges. But even if the attributes of the category "Indian" are left indefinite and open to contextualization, there is one attribute that is certain. "Indian" is part of a system of categories, and so Indian characteristics must differ from those of non-Indians. As with right and left, hot and cold, east and west, we are drawn to oppositions. And if we have this basic assumption that "Indian" has an opposite, we will look for differences in cultures, not for the similarities.

The ideal would be to strike a balance and use theories to open up possibilities but not as straitjackets limiting us to a single stance. Theorists have proposed that categorization adheres to common patterns: people have a penchant for dualistic categorization, uncertainty and mystery shroud the fuzzy boundaries between categories, and the body and other sensory experiences with the physical world can serve as the raw material for building abstract knowledge and communicating meaning to others. Although people around the world may share certain cognitive processes, that does not mean that all cultural knowledge and ideas will be the same.

REFERENCES

Ahlers, Jocelyn C.
  1997   Cognitive Metaphors in Hupa. American Indian Culture and Research Journal 21:63–73.

Battistella, Edwin L.
  1990   Markedness: The Evaluative Superstructure of Language. Albany: State University of New York.

Beauchamp, William M.
  1916   Moravian Journals relating to Central New York, 1745–66. Syracuse: Dehler Press.

Beaulieu, David L.
  1984   Curly Hair and Big Feet: Physical Anthropology and Land Allotment on the White Earth Reservation. American Indian Quarterly 8:281–314.

Berlin, Brent O., and Paul D. Kay
  1969   Basic Color Terms. Berkeley: University of California Press.

Cherokee Nation v. Dunawas Bullfrog.
   1884   Going Snake District Court Records, vol. 125. Reel CHN-40. Oklahoma City: Oklahoma Historical Society.
Cherokee Nation v. John Blair
   1884   Flint District Court Records, vol. 103. Reel CHN-38. Oklahoma City: Oklahoma Historical Society.
Cherokee Nation v. Yartunna Vann and Mitchell Squirrel
   1884   Tahlequah District Court Records, vol. 217. Reel CHN-50. Oklahoma City: Oklahoma Historical Society.
Cherokee Phoenix
   1829– On microfilm.
   1834
Cheves, Langdon, ed.
   1894   A Letter from Carolina in 1715, and Journal of the March of the Carolinians into the Cherokee Mountains, in the Yemassee Indian War, 1715–16. From the Original MS. *In* Year Book 1894, City of Charleston, South Carolina, SC. Pp. 314–354. Charleston: Walker Evans & Cogswell.
Closs, Michael P.
   1986   Native American Number Systems. *In* Native American Mathematics. Michael P. Closs, ed. Pp. 3–43. Austin: University of Texas Press.
D'Andrade, Roy
   1995   The Development of Cognitive Anthropology. New York: Cambridge University Press.
DeMallie, Raymond J.
   1983   Male and Female in Traditional Lakota Culture. *In* The Hidden Half: Studies of Plains Indian Women. Patricia Albers and Beatrice Medicine, eds. Pp. 237–261. Lanham, MD: University Press of America.
Dening, Greg
   1997   Introduction: In Search of a Metaphor. *In* Through a Glass Darkly: Reflections on Personal Identity in Early America. Ronald Hoffman, Mechal Sobel, and Fredrika J. Teute, eds. Pp. 1–6. Chapel Hill: University of North Carolina Press.
Denny, J. Peter
   1986   Cultural Ecology of Mathematics: Ojibway and Inuit Hunters. *In* Native American Mathematics. Michael P. Closs, ed. Pp. 129–180. Austin: University of Texas Press.
Douglas, Mary
   1966   Purity and Danger: An Analysis of Concepts of Pollution and Taboo. New York: Praeger.
Dundes, Alan
   1973   African Tales among the North American Indians. *In* Mother Wit from the Laughing Barrel: Readings in the Interpretation of Afro-American Folklore. Pp. 114–125. Englewood Cliffs, NJ: Prentice Hall.
Feeling, Durbin
   1975   Cherokee-English Dictionary. William Pulte, ed. Tahlequah, OK: Cherokee Nation of Oklahoma.

Fogelson, Raymond
   1971   The Cherokee Ballgame Cycle: An Ethnographer's View. Ethnomusicology
           15:327–338.
Fossett, Renée
   1996   Mapping Inuktut: Inuit Views of the Real World. *In* Reading beyond Words:
           Contexts for Native History. Jennifer S. H. Brown and Elizabeth Vibert, eds.
           Pp. 74–94. Peterborough, Ontario: Broadview Press.
Fradkin, Arlene
   1990   Cherokee Folk Zoology: The Animal World of a Native American People,
           1700–1838. New York: Garland Publishing.
Gearing, Fred
   1962   Priests and Warriors: Social Structures for Cherokee Politics in the 18th Cen-
           tury. American Anthropological Association Memoir, 93. Arlington, VA.
Hatley, M. Thomas
   1993   The Dividing Paths: Cherokees and South Carolinians through the Era of
           Revolution. New York: Oxford University Press.
Helms, Mary W.
   1988   Ulysses' Sail: An Ethnographic Odyssey of Power, Knowledge, and Geograph-
           ical Distance. Princeton, NJ: Princeton University Press.
Hertz, Robert
   1973   The Pre-Eminence of the Right Hand: A Study in Religious Polarity. *In* Right
           and Left: Essays on Dual Symbolic Classification. Rodney Needham, ed. Pp.
           3–31. Chicago: University of Chicago Press.
Hudson, Charles
   1976   The Southeastern Indians. Knoxville: University of Tennessee Press.
Jakobson, Roman
   1990   On Language. Linda R. Waugh and Monique Monville-Burston, eds. Cam-
           bridge: Harvard University Press.
Kappler, Charles, ed.
   1972   Indian Treaties, 1778–1883. Mattituck, NY: Amereon House.
Kilpatrick, Alan
   1997   The Night Has a Naked Soul: Witchcraft and Sorcery among the Western
           Cherokee. Syracuse: Syracuse University Press.
Kupperman, Karen Ordahl
   2000   Indians and English: Facing Off in Early America. Ithaca, NY: Cornell Univer-
           sity Press.
La Flesche, Francis
   1973   Right and Left in Osage Ceremonies. *In* Right and Left: Essays on Dual Sym-
           bolic Classification. Rodney Needham, ed. Pp. 32–42. Chicago: University of
           Chicago Press.
Lakoff, George
   1987   Women, Fire, and Dangerous Things: What Categories Reveal about the
           Mind. Chicago: University of Chicago Press.
Lakoff, George, and Mark Johnson
   1980   Metaphors We Live By. Chicago: University of Chicago Press.

Landry, Donna, and Gerald MacLean, eds.
  1996   Introduction. Selected Works of Gayatri Chakravorty Spivak. New York:
          Routledge.
Lankford, George E., ed.
  1987   Native American Legends: Southeastern Legends: Tales from the Natchez,
          Caddo, Biloxi, Chickasaw, and Other Nations. Little Rock: August House.
Lawson, John
  1967   A New Voyage to Carolina. Hugh Talmage Lefler, ed. Chapel Hill: University
          of North Carolina Press.
Leach, Edmund
  1989   Claude Lévi-Strauss. Chicago: University of Chicago Press.
Lévi-Strauss, Claude
  1963   Structural Anthropology. Claire Jacobson and Brooke Grundfest Schoepf,
          trans. New York: Basic Books.
  1969   The Raw and the Cooked. John Weightman and Doreen Weightman, trans.
          New York: Harper and Row.
Lewis, David Rich
  1991   Reservation Leadership and the Progressive-Traditional Dichotomy: William
          Wash and the Northern Utes, 1865–1928. Ethnohistory 38:124–142.
Lewis, G. Malcolm, ed.
  1998   Cartographic Encounters: Perspectives on Native American Mapmaking and
          Map Use. Chicago: University of Chicago Press.
Lockhart, James
  1991   Nahuas and Spaniards: Postconquest Central Mexican History and Philology.
          Stanford: Stanford University Press.
McDowell, William L., Jr., ed.
  1958–   Documents Relating to Indian Affairs. 2 vols. Columbia: South Carolina
  1970   Archives Department.
McLoughlin, William G.
  1986   Cherokee Renaissance in the New Republic. Princeton: Princeton University
          Press.
McWilliams, Richebourg Gaillard, ed.
  1981   Iberville's Gulf Journals. University, Alabama: University of Alabama Press.
Merrell, James H.
  1989   The Indians' New World: Catawbas and Their Neighbors from European Con-
          tact through the Era of Removal. Chapel Hill: University of North Carolina
          Press.
  1997   "The Cast of His Countenance": Reading Andrew Montour. In Through a
          Glass Darkly: Reflections on Personal Identity in Early America. Ronald Hoff-
          man, Mechal Sobel, and Fredrika J. Teute, eds. Pp. 13–39. Chapel Hill: Uni-
          versity of North Carolina Press.
Meyer, Melissa L.
  1994   The White Earth Tragedy: Ethnicity and Dispossession at a Minnesota An-
          ishinaabe Reservation, 1889–1920. Lincoln: University of Nebraska.
Mooney, James
  1992   Myths of the Cherokees. Asheville, NC: Bright Mountain Books.

Needham, Rodney, ed.
  1973   Right and Left: Essays on Dual Symbolic Classification. Chicago: University
          of Chicago Press.
Needham, Rodney
  1987   Counterpoints. Berkeley: University of California Press.
Payne, John Howard
  N.d.   Papers. Newberry Library, Chicago.
Perdue, Theda
  1979   Slavery and the Evolution of Cherokee Society, 1540–1866. Knoxville: Uni-
          versity of Tennessee Press.
  1998   Cherokee Women: Gender and Culture Change, 1700–1835. Lincoln: Univer-
          sity of Nebraska Press.
Pownall, Thomas
  1949   A Topographical Description of the Dominions of the United States of Amer-
          ica. Lois Mulkearn, ed. Pittsburgh: University of Pittsburgh Press.
Rosch, Eleanor
  1975   Cognitive Representations of Semantic Categories. Journal of Experimental
          Psychology: General 104:192–233.
  1978   Principles of Categorization. In Cognition and Categorization. Eleanor Rosch
          and Barbara B. Lloyd, eds. Pp. 27–48. Hillsdale, NJ: Lawrence Erlbaum Asso-
          ciates.
Rosch, Eleanor, and Carolyn B. Mervis
  1975   Family Resemblances: Studies in the Internal Structure of Categories. Cogni-
          tive Psychology 5:573–605.
Roscoe, Will
  1998   Changing Ones: Third and Fourth Genders in Native North America. New
          York: St. Martin's Press.
Sahlins, Marshall
  1981   Historical Metaphors and Mythical Realities: Structure in the Early History of
          the Sandwich Islands Kingdom. Ann Arbor: University of Michigan Press.
Satz, Ronald N.
  1991   Chippewa Treaty Rights: The Reserved Rights of Wisconsin's Chippewa Indi-
          ans in Historical Perspective. Transactions 79(1). Madison: Wisconsin Acad-
          emy of Sciences, Arts and Letters.
Scott, Joan Wallach
  1988   Gender: A Useful Category of Historical Analysis. Gender and the Politics of
          History. New York: Columbia University Press. Pp. 28–50.
Shoemaker, Nancy
  1996   Regions as Categories of Analysis. AHA Perspectives 34(8): 7–8, 10.
  1997   How Indians Got to Be Red. American Historical Review 102:625–644.
Snipp, C. Matthew
  1989   American Indians: The First of This Land. NY: Russell Sage Foundation.
Stevens, S. K., Donald H. Kent, and Autumn L. Leonard, eds.
  1951–   The Papers of Henry Bouquet. Harrisburg, PA: Pennsylvania Historical and
  1976   Museum Commission.

Swanton, John R.
    1929   Myths and Tales of the Southeastern Indians. Bureau of American Ethnology
            Bulletin, 88. Washington, DC: Smithsonian Institution.
Thornton, Russell
    1987   American Indian Holocaust and Survival: A Population History since 1492.
            Norman: University of Oklahoma Press.
Turner, Victor W.
    1969   The Ritual Process: Structure and Anti-Structure. Chicago: Aldine.
Valentine, J. Randolph
    1998   Linguistics and Languages in Native American Studies. In Studying Native
            America: Problems and Prospects. Russell Thornton, ed. Pp. 152–181. Madi-
            son: University of Wisconsin Press.
Van Gennep, Arnold
    1960   The Rites of Passage. Monika B. Vizedom and Gabrielle L. Caffee, trans.
            Chicago: University of Chicago Press.
Vico, Giambattista
    1968   The New Science of Giambattista Vico: Revised Translation of the Third Edi-
            tion (1744). Thomas Goddard Bergin and Max Harold Fisch, trans. Ithaca,
            NY: Cornell University Press.
Wallace, Anthony F. C.
    1969   The Death and Rebirth of the Seneca. New York: Random House.
Warhus, Mark
    1997   Another America: Native American Maps and the History of Our Land. New
            York: St. Martin's Press.
Waselkov, Gregory A.
    1989   Indian Maps of the Colonial Southeast. In Powhatan's Mantle: Indians in the
            Colonial Southeast. Peter H. Wood, Gregory A. Waselkov, and M. Thomas
            Hatley, eds. Pp. 292–343. Lincoln: University of Nebraska Press.
White, Richard
    1991   The Middle Ground: Indians, Empires, and Republics in the Great Lakes Re-
            gion, 1650–1815. New York: Cambridge University Press.
Williams, Roger
    1973   A Key into the Language of America. John J. Teunissen and Evelyn J. Hinz,
            eds. Detroit: Wayne State University Press.
Williams, Samuel Cole, ed.
    1930   Adair's History of the American Indians. Johnson City, TN: Watauga Press.
Williams, Walter L.
    1986   The Spirit and the Flesh: Sexual Diversity in American Indian Culture.
            Boston: Beacon Press.
Witkowski, Stanley R., and Cecil H. Brown
    1983   Marking-Reversals and Cultural Importance. Language 59:569–582.

"Some Women Are Wiser
than Some Men":
Gender and Native American History

Gunlög Fur

INTRODUCTION

Is gender a useful category of analysis? Joan W. Scott (1988) asked a decade
ago. The question has been answered overwhelmingly in the affirmative
since then, but the use of gender analysis has also been criticized by women of
color, many from the Third World, as being a concept that perpetuates Western ideas of identity and hierarchy, while clouding fundamental aspects of
Western domination and colonization as well as failing to offer valid interpretations of non-Western societies.

It is my firm belief, however, that gender is an extremely useful analytical
tool particularly in historical studies of Native American societies and their interactions with European colonizers. In this article I will draw on examples
from my research on Delaware (Lenape) Indian history to demonstrate how important it is to ask questions about gender, sex, and sexuality. This is not a survey of the now vast number of books and articles dealing with gender in
human societies; rather it is hoped to be a reflective piece providing food for
thought for further considerations. Theories about gender and sex are complicated and therefore the first part of the essay is devoted to an attempt at clarifying some of the issues that gender research brings to the fore. To exemplify,
I use four specific areas where I think gender analysis yields interesting and
significant results. The first of these concerns questions of invisibility in the
historical material and the consequences for our understanding of past events.
The second area, and in this essay the largest, deals with analysis of languages
and texts. Third, I discuss the importance of understanding and respecting the

significance of spirituality and religion within research in gender perceptions and roles. Finally, I focus on sexuality, biological bodies, and ideas of multiple genders as a challenge to binary thinking concerning sex and gender.

Before continuing I want to make a comment on why gender analysis is useful in Indian history. Ideas and practices related to gender and sex have structured and influenced interactions between Indian peoples and Euro-Americans from the first moment of contact, and to me it is obvious that Indian histories simply do not make sense without both men and women. "Indian history" has largely painted images of forests peopled only by men, momentous councils visited only by white and red males, or battles in which warriors performed feats of courage. This is barely more historically justifiable than an older tradition of "Indian history" in which every event had a European or white American originator. We know now that the sources are one-sided and formed in a European patriarchal perspective and that this is a major reason why women are invisible (Perdue 1998:3–4). But it is not sufficient to note that. The theoretical question must be, somewhat flippantly, What did women do when men made history? Women were somewhere and they were decidedly active; they did not exist suspended in a timeless vacuum awaiting the return of the men with the meat and the treaty, or in anticipation of their singular, anomalous appearances in a few sources. A great many studies have shown that women were fully occupied growing maize and other food products, preparing skins, mining lead, healing sicknesses and injuries, leading ceremonies and so on (see Albers and Medicine 1983; Shoemaker 1995; Klein and Ackerman 1995). This knowledge leads to the next theoretical question: What was the significance of men's and women's roles and responsibilities for the whole of the Indian community, for a more holistic understanding of Indian social and individual experiences? How did men's tasks and the changes occurring in them influence women's and vice versa? While some activities may in many societies be coded as either masculine or feminine, the study of gender is not limited to these. It concerns both what people thought about biology and social roles and what they actually did in their lives and how they used gendered metaphors to explain other aspects of social interaction. In all these areas, human beings of different biological sexes, genders, ages, and experiences took part, and to understand the workings of gender in human societies it is as significant to study that which is excluded or unseen as that which is clearly present. Joan Scott reminds us that the knowledge of sexual difference is firmly present in politics or diplomacy (Scott 1988:48–49). Gendered language is and was used to denote the home territory and national identities, as well as to mock or chastise adversaries within and between cultures. It is not the only social category historians must take into consideration, but it is one that cannot be left out if we want a multi-dimensional picture of human societies and interactions of power.

TERMS AND THEORIES:
COMPLICATING WHAT WE ALREADY KNOW?

To many people, maybe most, their sex seems a rather uncomplicated biological given and something that has little to do with culture or ideas. It is a card we have been dealt, and in general not much is or can be done to alter it. That certain expected behaviors and roles are attached to this biology is apparent, but what these are is open for debate and negotiation. In Western research the difference between what appear to be immutable bodies and changeable expectations and performances has led to the adoption of the term *sex* to refer to the body, and *gender* to mean the social practices and thoughts. In the binary model used in feminist research for the past 30 years or so, gender has thus been understood as ideological concepts concerning social categories of maleness and femaleness while sex referred to (likewise) ideological and physical actualities of the body (Moi 1998; Nicholson 1998). This attempt to separate gender and sex first developed in Western feminist writings in the 1960s as a means of escaping the biologism of early-20th-century physiologists who viewed femaleness as an inherent quality of the human female body and argued from these biological assumptions concerning proper behaviors and roles of women. One such female quality was that women by their very nature (that is, biology) were nurturing and peace loving. While feminists in the early part of the 20th century sought to elevate women's status by upgrading the value of these allegedly female qualities, their daughters in the 1960s found that the biological derivation hid the many ways in which society socializes people into behaviors and modes of thinking that are labeled as appropriately male or female (Moi 1998; Scott 1988:29).

Separation of physical sex and social gender has not turned out to be without problems, however, in Western thought and practice. In reality, gender often becomes just the social manifestation of the biological sex, a derivative in other words, and precisely the thing which the 1960s feminists sought to avoid (Nicholson 1998; Roscoe 1998:125; Scott 1988:40). The question then arose: Is this because gender and sex really are ontologically connected and the separation of them just a theoretical exercise seeking to confuse what we all really know—that men and women are two distinct and separate categories? Postmodern arguments, however, deny also the stability of the body, and identities and designations, whether biological or social, are viewed as part of the ruling and nameless discourse outside of which we cannot even conceive coherence (Butler 1993:18). The philosopher Judith Butler has taken another route to criticize the gender/sex pair and the hierarchical relationship between them by suggesting that sex is as much a socially constructed category as gender, and that gender, in fact, is prior to sex (Butler 1990; Butler 1991).[1] This, however, is a difficult pill to swallow for most people. After all, we are constantly reminded in painful or pleasurable ways of our bodies, and it appears incontestable that they are, in most cases, either male or female. At the same time, it is evident that much of our allegedly "natural" assumptions about bodies, sexualities, sex, and gender are open to question, can be changed, and vary in different cultural settings. Attitudes toward female athletes are a case in point, where ideas concerning what women can and cannot do physically have changed dramatically during the past century (Cahn 1994). However, studies from parts of the world other than the West also raise powerful questions about the meaning of categorizations and the foundations upon which they rest (Herdt 1996; Ramet 1996).

Toril Moi speaks of the gender-saturated society of the modern Western world. Everything, she argues, is "drenched" in gender, and perceptions of sex and gender are present in all aspects of social and private life, even when it is not apparent (Moi 1998:74–77). Such a presence of gendered notions is consistent with ideas discussed by the anthropologist Igor Kopytoff as existential versus role-based social identities. Characteristics and behaviors attached to an existential identity are perceived as immanent; that is, individuals do what they do as a consequence of who they are. This means that gender and sexual identities are intrinsically tied to notions of individual identities, as when women are thought to be nurturing, peace loving, and capable of doing several things at once simply because they are female. Role-based social identities, on the other hand, reverse the chain of argument and suggest that people are what they are, in this case "women" or "men," because of their behaviors and actions (Kopytoff 1990:79–80). Kopytoff found, in comparing Western (essentially American) existential gender identities to African (Suku in Zaire), that among the Suku few immanent features were attached to male or female identities. Instead the majority of tasks said to be women's or men's responsibilities were circumstantial, or the outcome of social contracts, rather than "naturally" derived from biological sex (Kopytoff 1990:83–84). He observes: "I could never, however, elicit an identity-personality for either woman or man as such. Characterologically, that is, males and females were not differentiated, the character of a particular person being regarded as a matter of individual variation that cross-cut gender" (Kopytoff 1990:88). By contrast, existential identities of

Western (U.S.) women are associated with a vast number of inherent features: "In America the existential identity is enveloped in a huge mantle of non-negotiable roles" (Kopytoff 1990:93; cf. Amadiume 1987:185–194). As a consequence a woman may take on new tasks, not directly gender-coded (or for which circumstantial gender-coding is changing)—such as becoming an executive for a business—but she cannot easily exchange it for one of the immanent aspects—of nurturing mother or competent homemaker. This may be another way of describing Western culture as gender-saturated.

The past decades have seen an explosion in scholarly studies devoted to various aspects of gender and sex in different societies and times. Viewing the world as divided according to gender and women constantly subordinated to men has been a primary supposition in many of these studies (i.e., Rosaldo and Lamphere 1974).[2] Then come, from non-Western directions, suggestions that the questions concerning gender may be based on the wrong assumptions and that these general principles of gender hierarchies impose Western characteristics on other societies (for Native America, see Strong 1996; Maltz and Archambault 1995). Oyèrónké Oyewùmí writes concerning Yorùbáland, in present-day Nigeria, that none of the social categories used to define people are gender-specific. Instead, they are based on age. Oyewùmí asks: "If the human body is universal, why does the body appear to have an exaggerated presence in the West relative to Yorùbáland? A comparative research framework reveals that one major difference stems from which of the senses is privileged in the apprehension of reality—sight in the West and a multiplicity of sense anchored by hearing in Yorùbáland" (Oyewùmí 1997:14). Following this argument she then challenges researchers that "a preconceived notion of gender as a universal social category is equally problematic. If the investigator assumes gender, then gender categories will be found whether they exist or not" (Oyewùmí 1997:16). Her argument is succinct: "There were no women in Yorùbá society until recently" (Oyewùmí 1997:78). With this she means to say that it would be false to apply a general category of "women" to designate all anatomical females, as "females, like males, have multiple shifting roles from one moment to the next and from one social setting to another" (Oyewùmí 1997:160). The use of gender as a foundational category for human societies imposes Western notions and orders on non-Western cultures, and in fact obscures social and regional categories while proposing to make women visible (Oyewùmí 1997:78, 175–179).

This is indeed a caution that should not go unheeded. Although it would be a mistake, I believe, to throw out the concept altogether, it most certainly needs to be both questioned within specific cultural contexts and historicized in order to become useful for analysis.[3] Let it be a challenge to ethnohistorians

to work out the critique in relation to the material in order to answer fundamental questions about Native societies and processes of colonization. The
questions taken from Oyewùmí would be: Was gender a significant category
within a given society, and, if so, what did it stand for and express? How did
gender function in the cultural encounter, and how and why did perceptions
and practices alter in the process?

An ethnohistorian going to work on the issues of gender and sex in Indian
societies and their interactions with Euro-Americans must look in different directions for inspiration and material. Will Roscoe is concerned with finding a
formula that may include gender, sex, and sexuality. He uses a multidimensional model of gender and sexual difference, defining these as clusters of characteristics, including expected behaviors, ideological concepts, actual
activities, and social responsibilities in specific historical settings. "Although
each society has its own linguistic categories and associated meanings that can
be compared and contrasted, social science research is also concerned with
how people conduct themselves in daily life" (Roscoe 1998:122). The challenge
is to work out both gender ideology—for lack of a better term!—and gender
practices as well as the relationship between thoughts and acts in specific historical situations.

Joan Scott suggests that gender "means knowledge about sexual difference" (Scott 1988:2). Knowledge may be described as the manner in which human beings order and organize concepts concerning human sexual variation.
Scott reminds us that this is not produced freely and at whim according to individual disposition and desire; rather, this knowledge is a matter of constant political contest and serves to establish and maintain relationships of power
(Scott 1988:2). This production of knowledge may be accessed through the
study of language, using methods of text criticism that identify the interplay
between that which is actually stated in the text and that which is not explicit,
but present through negations or repression.[4] Since written sources are central
to the work of most historians, and texts receive a particular emphasis in this
article, Scott's approach is a useful one. At the same time it is important to remember that written sources are not the only kind available and deconstruc-
tion of discourses is only one of several necessary methods in developing an
understanding of the various ways in which societies in the past have lived and
thought out the concepts of sexual difference.

There is always the risk that gender becomes a shorthand for sex. The problem, simply put, is this: What should we do with physiological females or males
who do not conform to expected gender behavior and feelings despite society's overwhelming normative influence from childhood and on? Or vice versa,

people whose gendered behaviors, feelings, and representations do not seem to fit their actual bodies (Nicholson 1998:202–204). If gender is seen as a mirror of sex, then these people are either abnormal or willfully deviant. Both conditions can then be censured or cured to conformity. But if gender and sex are seen as separate, then it is possible to conceive of more than two genders and nonconformity with sex does not necessarily mean aberration. Roscoe cautions: "The challenge, therefore, is to define gender without reducing it to a re-iteration of sex. This can be accomplished by recognizing sex as a category of bodies, and gender as a category of persons" (Roscoe 1998:127). But he is quick to point out that an understanding of the body as constructed does not necessarily lead to "ambiguities of human categories" that "make stable identities and cultural continuity impossible" (Roscoe 1998:5). Rather, evidence from North America suggests that "fluidity leads to the diversification of identities, not their elimination" and that Native gender roles display remarkable historical depth and resilience in spite of centuries of Western domination (Roscoe 1998:5, 209–210). Roscoe's definition leaves the question of numbers open. Bodies and genders need not come in twos, yet the assignation of individuals to these categories may not be an arbitrary exercise dependent on the whim of the moment or political pressures of the day. Instead, these can be identified as continuous categories throughout long periods of time that may be linked to metaphysical explanations and recognized everyday practices.

MAKING SENSE OF INVISIBILITY

Working with absences or lapses is a challenging and valuable approach to the study of gender. Paying attention to gender often means focusing on women as a category, as men are more frequently visible in the historical material. But this focus may be seen as a device, as a means to developing methodologies and theoretical frameworks that allow other groups and individuals to emerge as actors in the past, such as older people, children, those with other gender representations and responsibilities than male or female, refugees, prisoners, mixed bloods, and so on.

We can never enter any research free from assumptions, which will be there whether we acknowledge them or not. In my own research, I have therefore chosen to focus on historical moments that seem to force a clarification of viewpoints and cultural characteristics. The most fruitful approach has been to look at *encounters* between representatives of different cultures, and a method I have found useful is to investigate apparent anomalies. In the instances of meetings between cultures, both sides often find themselves in situations where they need to explain or defend their mode of doing things. At the same time, the unexpected, the inexplicable, or the anomalous occurrences in the sources may be paths into the workings of another culture. It must be remembered, however, that as a historian researching the 17th and 18th centuries, I work with completely one-sided material, most of the words having been spoken by white men and nearly all of them written down by them. Strangely enough, however, I believe this can be an advantage in certain circumstances because it demands a stringent source criticism and thus attention to detail in both that which is present in the texts and that which is noticeable by its absence. The religious historian Wendy Doniger suggests that in a comparative situation knowledge of one of the languages involved can "inspire a proper sense of caution and limited ambitions in the inevitable dealings with translations of texts from other traditions, an understanding of what one can and cannot do with translations" (Doniger 1998:65). The constant reminder of the limits of one's sources, as well as of one's own limited knowledge, can thus serve as a useful and fruitful methodological tool.

My own discovery of the significance of analysis of gender in understanding the history of Indian-white interaction began with an anomaly that intrigued me, and the more I sought an explanation for it, the more I realized that this was an aspect that altered understandings of historical events. A woman, Notike, entered into Swedish and Dutch disagreements over land in the Delaware Valley that both sides argued they had received as donations from Lenape (Delaware) chiefs. Notike, described as the widow of one of these chiefs, supported the Swedish claim to land by stating that the man who had "sold" land to the Dutch did not have the right to do so. The Swedes appeared to have won this round, but what is interesting is how this singular appearance by a woman in the diplomatic record affects the interpretations of the event itself. Notike's assertions were not left unheeded, and it is significant to note that the man she charged as a usurper did not put his mark on the final document drawn up by the Dutch. If Notike's presence is understood as a sign of an internal Lenape political conflict concerning authority over land alienations, an authority with both gender and kin associations, actions on both sides may be explained. But if she is dismissed as a widow who just happened to link two men (a deceased father and a son in his minority), her appearance awakens more questions than it answers. Without attention to gender, some things simply do not make sense, even in the highly male world of diplomacy (Fur 1993:132–135; Fur 1998).

The invisibility of women in Indian history or, indeed, of other categories of members of Indian societies such as old people and children may also be a misconception. The sources from which historians construct their stories must be scrutinized using regular methods of source criticism in order to understand why they are written the way they are, who the intended audience was, what other information they might be dependent on, and so forth. But the theories with which we work, consciously or less so, awaken questions through which we approach, view, or listen to different sources. Attention to various aspects of gender reveals a whole new universe of information contained in well-known sources. And it may lead to the use of other sources. The material left behind by the European side of the encounter is particularly rich in information concerning gendered understandings and metaphors in Native societies (as well as in various European cultures) and signals both pervading Native uses of gendered divisions and profound European discomfort at gender practices that differed from those acceptable to "civilized society."

In 1706 a man named Thomas Chalkley made a visit to the Conestoga town on the Susquehanna River in Pennsylvania. He and his company were treated kindly, and the Indians called a council to discuss religious matters. Chalkley noted how the Indians spoke one after the other "without any Heat or Jarring; (and some of the most Esteemed of their Women do sometimes speak in their Councils)." This observation prompted Chalkley to ask his interpreter "Why they suffered or permitted the Women to speak in their Councils? His Answer was, *That some Women were wiser than some Men*" (Chalkley 1751:50). Much can be made of this brief description, but I will use it here only to point out what I have found to be a central aspect of gender perceptions among the Conestogas and their close allies the Delawares, that performance, capacity, dreams, and age were the important indicators of what position a person would occupy in society, not biological sex, thus suggesting that Oyewùmí's conclusions from Yorùbáland may be of at least theoretical interest also for students of Native American societies (Fur 1998). But the comment does more than that. It demonstrates how *much* biological sex made sense to the English Chalkley as a definer of social responsibilities. This short meeting thus illuminated *both* cultures, reminding the present-day historian, whether she is Indian or white, to keep both eyes open for clues to gender in colonial encounters.

TEXTS AND LANGUAGE

Many of the sources to Native pasts are in the form of texts written down by Euro-Americans as legal documents, council minutes, missionary reports, travel accounts, letters and diaries, and so on. Almost all exist in a European language, but sometimes translations of quotes from Indians are included. Fortunately, it is possible to work with issues regarding texts and languages for both the historian who speaks a Native language and the one who does not. Gendered notions protrude into the language even when it is a translation of Native speech, and both the context of the text and the translation must be questioned. Who is speaking? What terms is the person using? Is it likely to be a reasonable translation? For example, when a woman is called "he" in English, this should raise questions about source criticism and about the purpose of the text (Grumet 1980:52–53; Fur 1998; Oyewùmí 1997:100–107). What is the topic of discussion and what does the nature of the questions reveal about perceptions? As Joan Scott reminds us, there is a risk that the term *language* reduces its meaning to the instrumental activity of the utterances of words. Instead, language "reveals entire systems of meaning and knowledge" that are "the patterns and relationships that constitute understanding or a 'cultural system'"(Scott 1988:59).

Languages differ in their constructions of gender, and there is nothing inherently natural about how different speech systems designate and name male, female, and other categories, although it may seem so to the speaker of any particular language. Grammarians distinguish between languages that have "grammatical" and "natural" gender. In the first case, the linguistic division into gender purportedly has nothing to do with sex, as in German, where *das Mädchen* (the girl) belongs to the *neuter* category, while *die Sonne* (the sun) is *feminine* and *der Welt* (the world) is a *masculine* noun. English, on the other hand, is a language that uses "natural" gender, which means that a noun is categorized according to its actual, biological sex (with a neutered category for nonsexed things). Most Indo-European languages classify nouns according to gender in one of these two ways, although the number of gendered categories may vary.[5] But theoretically, gender is only one of many possible ways of classifying nouns. Other common factors found in human languages are animacy and humanness, dividing things into categories of living versus nonliving or human versus nonhuman (Romaine 1999:66ff.). In Algonkian languages, Lenape (or Delaware) among them, the basic division is between animate and inanimate categories and there are no personal pronouns (Romaine 1999:69; Kehoe 1995:120–124).[6] Many aspects of Delaware customs and ceremonies make a point of establishing reciprocity and balance between women and men, yet when speaking about the world this is not the primary distinguisher. Both men and women are animate, and so from listening to a conversation you would not know whether a man or a woman is discussed unless you knew the context. One consequence of this difference is that the translations of gendered pronouns become difficult. The Lenape sentence *lenape hach nan* can be translated as either "is he a Lenape" or "is she a Lenape." From the grammatical structure of Lenape it is not possible to argue anything regarding the person's biological sex.[7] Conversely, imagine the problem of saying in Lenape, "He met her in the forest"!

This, however, does not mean that Lenape or other Indian languages do not have gendered categories. They do and they are to an Indo-European ear quite elaborate. But whereas in English it is possible to speak about an individual in general by using the pronoun he or she, thus designating the sex of the person, and conversely it is impossible to speak about a person without designating him or her as male or female, in Lenape a person spoken about in general terms would not be sexed, and when speaking about a specific person the words used would designate not only sex but also age, and often the speaker's relationship to the person as well. A recent glossary of Lenape terms for men and women includes the following divisions: "people," "baby" (nonsexed), "child" (nonsexed), "little boy," "boy," "young man," "man," "middle-aged man," "old man," "extremely old and disabled man," "little girl," "girl," "young woman," "woman," "middle-aged woman," "old woman," "extremely old and disabled woman" (Dean 1980:22–23). Among kinship terms Lenape words recognize the difference between uncle (father's brother) and uncle (mother's brother), older brother and older sister, but for younger siblings the same word is used regardless of whether they are male or female (Dean 1980:13).[8]

Such differences between languages beg the question of what the connections are between language and our patterns of thought and perceptions. Studies in this area do not suggest an exact coherence between the gender of words and how we perceive them, but we do seem to associate grammatical gender with our ideas of masculinity and femininity, and there are indications that children form ideas of their own gender earlier if brought up in a language system that employs grammatical gender (Romaine 1999:82–84).

A tantalizing example of how "language" conveys systems of meaning can be found in the impressive document prepared for General Lewis Cass at the American War Department in the 1820s in order to compile a thorough report on all the Indian tribes. Part of it consists of an immense questionnaire filled in from interviews with Delaware and Munsee Indian informants. Many of the questions deal with the respective roles and responsibilities of the sexes, and the questions are oftentimes more interesting and revealing than the answers. Among the questions regarding "government" one was: "At what age are young men entitled to all their rights?" The recorded answer: "No particular age it depends upon the growth and activity of the person" (Weslager 1978:93). The standard against which Delaware and Munsee political life was measured was, as we can see, the American system of democracy with (white) male voters and political actors. Even so, the answer suggests an organization closer to that described by Chalkley's interpreter, a system in which individual capacities and experiences are more important in determining participation than any category such as age or sex. The fact that the response does not reveal the gender of the individual is likely to be a consequence of the Lenape language and which functions without personal pronouns.

In another section dealing with responsibilities in the household the assumptions contained in the questions become quite obvious and one can imagine the bewilderment among the Indian men trying to answer the queries. The question was asked: "Does the manual labor fall upon the wife?"—bringing to mind the image of the squaw drudge. The answer seemingly confirmed this picture: "It does in general." The interrogator continued: "Does all the trouble of moving the camp, etc. devolve upon the women?" and then may have been astonished to hear: "It does not the man and woman share in the fatigue according to their ability." Here again, in answer to questions that clearly aim to distinguish gender differences and household hierarchies, the answers suggest the importance of individual qualities not connected to social gender. The following question contains an expected difference: "Does the woman ever exercise any government over the children?" The answer does not support such a division: "She does equally with the man" (the pronoun, of course, was added in the English translation). The final question under the heading of "Family Government, Social Relations, etc" is loaded with expectations: "Is the woman ever, in fact, at the head of the domestic establishment?" Such an arrangement might suggest to the American interviewer an inverted gender hierarchy and weak husband. Yet the Delawares responding are quite clear: "She is always and the whole care devolves on the woman" (Weslager 1978:105–106). Similar descriptions have also been offered by Delaware Indians in interviews made in the 20th century, and I suggest that it should be understood as a different understanding of gendered responsibilities than that contained in the idea of separate spheres that began to be elaborated during the first half of the 19th century in white America (Fur 1998).[9] The questions may also be understood in the context of early-19th-century insecurities regarding the authority of the patriarchal household (Shammas 1995:133 f.). In Delaware country, as in most Native American societies, women truly controlled the home and her own property in it, as well as the children. What looks similar on the surface— women in the domestic sphere—must be analyzed in its different contexts and then may reveal significant differences.

Let us look at a set of questions whose answers become quite confusing: "Is it common for unmarried women to have children?" The respondents replied: "It is frequently the case." The questionnaire continued: "Is it injurious to the reputation of an unmarried woman to have children?" The answer again must have appeared familiar to the interrogator: "It is very."[10] So far, there seems to be a similarity between white and red American perceptions of women's morals and behavior regarding sex. However, the following exchange suggests that maybe this was an illusion created by the order and shape of questions: "Does it affect her chance of being married?" to which the response was: "Very little" (Weslager 1978:105). The conclusion here is that the whole context must be considered before we analyze a material. In this case, the source is divided into questions and answers, making it obvious how the exchange was planned to develop and that the initiative came from white American men.

Equally significant is to ask oneself in what language(s) the interview was carried out, who translated between the different tongues, and what the consequences may be for the report in front of us. For example, what does it mean that Lenape language does not distinguish only men from women but ages as well? Age is clearly as biological as sex—as undeniable. Moreover, a characteristic of this classification is that it is always changing. A young woman in one account would 20 years later have moved into another definable category altogether. There are suggestions in the material of how responsibilities altered with age, for instance, old women among the Delawares (and others) prepared love medicines eagerly sought after by younger tribespeople (Zeisberger 1910:82–83; Tantaquidgeon 1972:15–16, 45). While for the Cherokees it has been suggested that this skill, by no means insignificant, was clearly linked to women's postmenopausal state (Perdue 1998:36–37), the Moravian missionary John Heckewelder mentions that among the Delawares *both* older women and men had the knowledge to prepare love potions, making it necessary to question assumed links between women's biology and these special abilities (Heckewelder 1819:236). Kinship terms as well as terms designating the age of the individual were often much more prevalent than in English, and this awaits deeper exploration.

Paying close attention to language in its various forms and the formation of texts is thus an important component in the study of gender. Just as ethnohistory is a multidisciplinary approach, gender research necessitates combining the specialties of several fields, but it can also question the foundations on which we base our search for knowledge. My arguments so far have relied heavily on written sources and texts, but colonial texts about *the Other*, in this case, Indians, are at best ambiguous, at worst useless in conveying any kind of information about Native societies.[11] The spoken word as in oral traditions and histories past and present is absolutely vital for an understanding of gender, particularly since women's voices are so often obscured in colonial texts. Here, I believe, are further challenges in which those of us who are non-Native should step aside and listen to the emic perspectives on meanings conveyed in spoken words and stories.

SPIRITUAL RESPONSIBILITIES AND GENDER

A third area in which I think it is of utmost importance to pay attention to gender is within the realm of the *spiritual*. Any analysis of Indian societies must take the spirit world into account. Material culture was not separated from spiritual realities—as indeed it has not been for most people on this earth. What then do myths say about the origins and perpetuation of the world? Do male and female represent differing responsibilities and characteristics? How are they defined? Are there mediating categories between male and female? What can be known about rituals of regeneration and the like? Do Indians use these stories in their attempts to communicate their worldview to Europeans?

Let us look at four accounts of a major Delaware ceremony, taking place at the end of the month of May. Three of the accounts are from the 1760s, the fourth is undated but probably from the 19th century.[12] Two are eyewitness accounts of the same event, one is penning a secondhand observation, and the fourth is apparently written (or recited) by someone with intimate knowledge of the ceremony. From the point of view of gender they are interesting because on a rising scale with the hearsay on one end and the knowledgeable, but anonymous, account on the other, they report on the participation of both women and men and responsibilities connected to gender in the ceremony. James Kenny, Pennsylvania Quaker and Indian trader, reported in 1763 that traders had told him about the yearly ceremony and recounted the importance of the number 12, but in his version it was solely a male event: "They Choose 6 Men head Councilors & 6 Young Men 12 in Numr" and "Hear all of you & take Good Notice that in this manner Your Grandfather's perform'd their Worship" (Kenny 1913:197). The Moravian Christian Frederick Post, who together with John Hays was present at one of these celebrations, noted the participation of women: "Their Priests or Conjurers, with about 10 Women, went first into the Woods to paint themselves according to their different Characters." But his account is otherwise quite unclear and presents a picture of a rather haphazard event without discernible logic (Post 1760). Hays's account of the same event is more sympathetic although similarly vague about the purpose. He supplies more details concerning women's participation throughout the ceremony in ways which indicate that some women, at least, were indeed central to the conduct of the feast in all its parts: "There wase 3 men and Two Wemen and 2 men+2 Wemen and two men and they had rat Bunches of Flours one there heades and was Striped and pinted Be[y]ond Neater Sume Had Grene Rodes in thir hands and Snaks and Birdes + wonder full things Pented on them All colers One mane was Rid + one Womean Black" (Hays 1954).[13]

The fourth account, unfortunately not dated and by an unknown author, shows intimate knowledge of the ceremony and also provides a sense of continuity and reason to the ritual performances. It emphasizes the importance of reciprocity between males and females and between corn and meat:

> Every Morning & Evening during the hunt, one of these aged men, would offer up prayers to the Creator of all things . . . , for the fruits of the Earth the Trees the Springs & Streams of water; for the growing vegitation, for Corn our *Mother*, & for the Thunder or *Grandfather* by which our plants & vegitation are watered. . . . Whilst this hunt is going on, the wife of the chief goes around the village, notifying the women to prepare the *Big House* for the coming festival. [A.A. n.d.]

At the center of the house there stood an upright supporting beam "on one side of it is carved the image of a Man, which they call their Grand Father, and on the reverse side the image of a Woman, this they call their Grand Mother" (A.A. n.d.).

The point of the comparison is not to try to prove certain details but that a source in many ways seeming reliable, such as the Indian trader Kenny's, can be incorrect or ignorant when it comes to women's participation and responsibilities in Indian communities and therefore the whole picture becomes skewed.[14] The fourth source quoted here presents gendered ritual roles as complementary and necessary for the correct procedures of the ceremony. A similar, strictly complementary, description exists from a Munsee-Mahican ceremony focusing on the bear. Throughout the event women and men played strictly defined, complementary parts. When the people gathered in the Big House, the women entered through the eastern door and sat on the east side, while the men entered and sat on the west side. The chief sat on a bench between the north wall and the center post, half of his body on the women's side and the other half on the men's side (Rockwell 1991:165–172).[15]

Yet it is not enough to reveal these seemingly harmonious gendered responsibilities in the spiritual realm. Kenny, in his rendition of the information he had received, noted a generational aspect that returns in the fourth account. Old men, or grandfathers, and young men apparently had different roles to play, and it is quite possible that a differentiation was made between old women, or grandmothers, and younger women as well. This is particularly significant in the light of Oyewùmí's criticism of Western gender notions, as important questions need to be asked about the meaning of vertical relations in age and complementarity between genders. What happens to rituals if some category is denied or suffers extreme losses? That must have been the case when many old people died as a result of infectious diseases or when young men and warriors were exalted as a consequence of contacts with colonial administrations.

Ceremonial obligations tied to gender may suggest that ideas of gender saturate Indian cultures as much as European. But the relationship between individual experiences based on sex and gender and those based on visions and spiritual experiences needs to be clarified. Bruce White concludes an article on Ojibwa women by discussing these connections:

> Scholars must take into account some of the Ojibwa beliefs about women's spiritual power and the accounts of individual women's lives and dreams discussed here. Though the Ojibwa did have a distinct division of labor, one that may have changed at various times in response to interaction with Europeans, women could make a distinct course for themselves through their spiritual power. [White 1999:139]

Among the Delawares both men and women could name children but neither gender nor age determined the distribution of this power (Weslager 1991:71–72). Nora Thompson Dean specifically comments on the paramount importance of spirit encounters when discussing the power of naming: "Age didn't make any difference. Now my father was 90 some years old, and he has often told me regretted he was unable to give names, even in his advanced age because he was sent away to mission school so he did not receive a vision" (Dean 1978). Perhaps the importance of classifications such as gender in Indian societies is mediated, balanced, or stands in contrast to the individual's spiritual guidance. Such a situation would again suggest a similarity with present-day Western notions that must be scrutinized. The individuality of spiritual visions must not be confused with the insistence on individual autonomy in the West today. Although the meaning of spiritual experience and responsibility varied across Native America, it appears to have been (and remains today) firmly lodged in a communal context. In fact, the communities could not survive well without the specific individual gifts, achievements, and experiences. If such assumptions have validity, it would clearly mean that gender could be fundamentally important in dividing, defining, and organizing the world, while at the same time biological sex did not prescribe any individual's life to the extent presumed in the notions of a gender-saturated society.

For many generations of individuals in the Western world, the Bible has stood out as the foundational text regarding the roles and proprieties and expectations of the sexes. It has ruled and influenced interpretations that are decidedly misogynistic, but it has also inspired interpretations that lead up to perceptions of equal values. This does not say, however, that every European colonist thought like ancient Christian philosophers or aristocratic lawmakers. But it does mean that interpretations of the creation texts in the Bible formed the basis for legal statutes regulating and inhibiting females in the European and American societies. It influenced marriage laws, property laws, and certainly laws regulating sexuality. Is there a similar correspondence between Indian creation texts and perceptions and regulations in Indian societies? If so, what do they look like? It is an area of investigation well worth looking into as many recent works demonstrate, even though it promises to be a controversial task (Roscoe 1991:147–169; Kehoe 1995:116–120; Doniger 1998).

SEX, BODIES, AND SEXUALITIES

Anybody studying colonial or imperialist interactions between peoples and cultures cannot avoid noticing that colonists were obsessed with the bodies of others (McClintock 1995; Morgan 1997; also Green 1975). But the simple fact that all humans are bodies does not mean that they are conceived of in the same way nor that they stand in a similar relationship to concepts of gender in different societies and settings (Oyewùmí 1997:1–8, 14–17; Nicholson 1998:202–204). Thus, the body too, how it is understood and used, must be a focus for gender research. As mentioned above, the connection between the body—biology— and its manifestations—gender—has been a vexing problem for Euro-American theorists. Perhaps with a bit of a hope of having found utopia, Western scientists turn to Native multigendered practices such as those first known as "berdaches" or "hermaphrodites." Peeling away all the layers of expectations and fascination and disgust heaped upon the berdaches throughout the centuries, what remains of the idea of multiple genders among American Indians? While some recent works have sought to claim the existence of not just three or four but even up to eight different genders at work in Indian cultures

(Williams 1986; Lang 1998; Roscoe 1998; Jacobs et al. 1997), others have seriously questioned the respect these studies allege adhered to individuals who did not conform to the expectation of one sex, one gender. In fact, these studies claim American Indians were just as opposed to homosexual acts and gender inversion as were the whites who encountered them (Gútiérrez 1989; Trexler 1995; also Sigal 1998). But homosexual practices were not necessarily a trait connected to other gender roles, nor was it limited to them.[16] While the romanticization of "traditional" Indian practices certainly needs to be addressed to make room for significant understandings of Native American experiences in the past, the malleability of human cultural practices is a primary assumption in gender theory and historians must take into account both similarities and differences in seeking to describe cultural approaches to genders, sexes, and sexualities.

The obvious fact of centuries of forceful white indoctrination on Indian communities cannot be disregarded when we approach this issue, but there may be other ways to look at the problem. If—again—the language does not distinguish between two genders, why would two then be the only possible number? The anthropologist Jay Miller discusses three as a basic number in many Native American cultures, with two extremes (such as male and female) mediated by a third entity (Miller 1979; Miller 1982). There exists a large body of evidence from all over Native America regarding gender variation, often recognized in terms of special vocabulary. Sexual practices should not be romanticized, but neither should they be reduced to binary genders or Western concepts of ontological connections between sex, gender, and sexuality, nor should they be ignored because they are difficult to explain or understand. Some Native American perceptions of gender clearly indicate that gender need not be thought of as a mirror image of biological sex and that there are different ways in which human societies deal with the fact that the categories of male and female are not neat and tidy and not all individuals belong to one or the other. Thus, the study of both gender and sexuality leads us to question the binary division of male/female and masculine/feminine. How different societies deal with boundary transgression has much to say about how people perceive both gender and sex.[17]

The Indian body in its shapes, covers (or lack thereof), and practices has been of immense interest to white colonists and administrators from the beginning of contact. Descriptions of physiognomies and physical attributes are common, from early travel accounts, to government officials in the 20th century. Colonists brought along classification systems based on clothing and hairstyles that added an element of both class and gender consciousness to their descriptions of and interactions with Native Americans. To their eyes, Indians displayed a lack of distinctions between social ranks and between men and women, while the category of "hermaphrodite" represented a social and religious abomination (Kupperman 1980; Roscoe 1998:119–123). But Indians, too, placed cultural significance on clothing, and this becomes apparent from numerous exhortations for Indians to return to their traditional garb and cease to use European-manufactured shirts and blankets (Dowd 1992:174).

Concentration on clothing and proper distinctions was not only a concern in early modern contacts, as Tsianina Lomawaima's research on one off-reservation boarding school demonstrates (Lomawaima 1993). Disciplining the Indian body was part of a process in which Indian children were to learn *both* their proper subordinate place in the social hierarchy and the proper roles of the sexes. The latter, it seems, involved a despiritualizing of the body that stood in direct contrast to Native perceptions of the connections between bodies, genders, sexuality, and spirituality. "The body," Jo-Anne Fiske concludes in her article about Carrier women in British Columbia and their experiences in religious schools, "was transformed from the site of inherent mystical powers to the site of sin" (Fiske 1996:674).

It would be hazardous to assume that Native practices and perceptions regarding sexuality were uncomplicated, not least since the tradition of suggesting a liberated Native libido is so prevalent in Western colonial reports from the earliest days up until the present. Human anxieties about the forces of sexuality at work within and between individuals and within communities are ever present, yet these too should be historicized. As I have argued earlier, a comparative cross-cultural approach may yield the most provocative results. Apparent similarities and differences need to be discussed and situated within their historical contexts, and such analyses will point the way to further questions. From the earliest colonial contacts, Europeans took what they saw as a lack of proper marriages as a sign of uncivilized societies (Shammas 1995:109–115; Van der Donck 1841:191). This involved notions of uncontrolled sexual practices. The Dutchman Isaak De Rasieres's comment nicely sums up the judgmental tone and openly sexual gaze of many European accounts: "The women are fine looking, of middle stature, well proportioned, and with finely cut features; with long and black hair, and black eyes set off with fine eyebrows. . . . They smear their bodies and hair with grease, which makes them smell very rankly; they are very much given to promiscuous intercourse" (de Rasieres 1909:106). In sweeping comments, all the differences in practices and moral codes were lumped together in strongly condemnatory phrases. Peter Lindeström wrote in the 1650s about the Lenapes that they "have their mixing together with father and mother, brother and sister like soulless beasts, no one quite knowing, who

is the father of the child" (Lindeström 1962:109). The lack of moral codes regarding sexual behaviors is a standard comment, yet when we turn to sources
that describe actual interaction it becomes obvious that they were not lacking
but often quite different. Such a situation occurred when Moravian missionaries sought to arrange marriages that foundered on much more stringent Indian
rules against incest (Gnadenhütten Diary, May 31, 1755). Women's active roles
in taking sexual initiatives were often described as frightening and contrary to
civilized order, but also tempting. A most frustrated David Zeisberger thun-
dered against the Delaware women who had opposed him:

> The women are much given to lying and gossiping. They carry evil re-
> port from house to house. As long as they are observed they appear
> modest and without guile. All the wrongs of which they are guilty are
> done in secret. That adultery, theft, lying, cheating are terrible vices they
> know, having learned it from their ancestors as well as from the whites.
> Fear of disgrace keeps them from open wrong-doing for they do not
> wish to have a bad name. Secretly, however, they are given to all manner
> of vice. Some are no longer sensitive to shame. There are traces of un-
> natural sins among them, hardly known to any except to those such as
> missionaries who have learned to understand the people well. [Zeis-
> berger 1910:124–125]

It is likely that Zeisberger's experience was colored not only by female opposition but also by encountering a village "where none but unmarried womenfolk
live, who do not want to take any husbands" (Lagundo-Utenünk Diary, May 3,
1770). With reports as well of lascivious female sexual behaviors in the Moravian sources it is not difficult to imagine why Zeisberger considered this town
an unsuitable neighbor for a mission settlement (Shekomeko Diary, May, 1745;
Wellenreuther and Wessel 1995:556–558). But Delawares themselves most
likely viewed it differently. That women could choose to separate themselves
from their villages was neither unheard of nor necessarily indicative of certain
sexual behaviors. The missionary related how Indians critical of his message
told him that they had visited heaven to see what it was like. Among other
things they reported seeing two large towns "in one of which there were only
women, of extraordinary size" (Zeisberger 1912:103). Delawares also told John
Heckewelder of a woman who had chosen to live as a hermit (Heckewelder
1819:200–201). In various ways, then, gendered practices, social organization,
and perceptions of morality and of bodies interlaced to produce generalized
descriptions as well as indigenous defenses.

The emphasis on Native peoples' bodies and sexual practices obviously has much to say about colonists' anxieties and desires, but what does it reveal about Indian perceptions and actions? Cross-cultural studies force us to question all the categories which our various contexts present as "natural," such as the dichotomous division of the world into male and female or the designation of sexualities as synonymous with identities. Yet just as early colonists used choice examples from other societies to question their own, the researcher may be tempted to find in the study of distant lives (in time or space) examples of differences that can bolster contemporary arguments. As always the challenge is to walk the tightrope between attention to actual differences in how people organize their knowledge concerning gender, bodies, and sexualities and the tendency to romanticize and exaggerate these. In many ways, the study of Native recognition of multiple genders brings together the themes that have been the focus of this essay: connections between genders, bodies, and spiritual experiences; the problems of textual representations; the invisibility of all but certain recognized males.

SUMMING UP

In this article I have argued and tried to demonstrate that paying attention to sex, gender, and sexuality is indeed a fruitful approach to Native American history. History, and ethnohistory, is a scholarly practice located ambiguously astride the boundary between theory and empiricism. How we view the past, and time, and change or continuity inspires intense debate, while we seek to relate these theoretical concepts to fragments of lives once lived. It is important, therefore, for all scholars to do their own thinking about the intersections between sources to past lives and perceptions of gender. On one level it is a theoretical issue of defining gender and how awareness or lack thereof operates on different levels of human societies; on another it is an empirical question to investigate what sex difference and similarities mean in specific historical and cultural contexts.

While biological sex may not have been the primary determinant for what an individual could or could not do, I have argued that *gender* as an organizing principle was of paramount significance to most American Indian peoples. Metaphorical and religious language was filled with gendered references that need to be respected and analyzed in order to make sense of historic encounters. We come across these terms in descriptions of kinship and in the metaphors used in diplomatic negotiations. They affect perceptions of power and authority, practices and beliefs surrounding rituals, cosmology and spirituality, as well as production, reproduction, life and death, numbers, and mediations. I have emphasized four aspects as central to an understanding of gender in the colonial encounter and in indigenous communities: paying attention to lacunas or apparent invisibilities, to language and translations, to spiritual responsibilities, and to perceptions of bodies and sexualities. This reveals areas of inquiry that are still insufficiently covered. What does it mean when only certain people are visible in the historical material? Can absences in the material be used to assert that women were excluded from certain situations, or do they primarily raise issues regarding the sources? Can anomalies be used as windows into the workings of another culture and time period, or are they just freak occurrences? Could gender be a significant divider between people *at certain times* but not always, pivotal points in ceremony, for example, but not in everyday life? (Or perhaps the reverse would be more correct.) It is important to look at humans not *only* through lens of gender but also in terms of what constitutes common humanity. The tensions between oppositions need always to be present in the historical analysis: men/women, gendered beings/common humanity, hierarchy/complementarity, and so on. Yet Native American experiences should also caution us against assuming too easily that constructing the world in terms of binaries is the "natural" way to think and act. As in the case with Native practices involving more than two genders, histories of gender relations in Native North America may challenge other dualities as well.

A gendered analysis of Native American history involves a multifaceted approach that takes into account factors of words and translations, individual spiritual experiences and capacities, age-related responsibilities, common legacies of stories, myths, and accounts of creation and ideas concerning proper roles of the sexes and sexuality, as well as actual possibilities and practices— what we may know, in fact, about what human beings actually do.

The significance of studying gender for the understanding of Native history cannot be overstated. It has a direct bearing on issues of cultural continuity. It also sheds valuable light on the interactions and responses to colonization. This is also where Indian history can turn a powerful searchlight on European history. White responses to Indian gendered practices reveal European beliefs and may help explain why Native practices seemed so threatening to civilization projects. The consequences of the traumatic experiences of Indian tribes take on new meanings when viewed through the lenses of gender and age. What did it mean to lose many elder women? What did it mean that Europeans conferred power on younger men? What happened when children were lost? How did such changes alter understandings and relationships to the spirit world? Few attempts have been made so far to assess theoretically the implications of gender for Native American history. It therefore appears to be an urgent venture in which inspiration may be gotten from women's studies and anthropology, while the bulk of the work must be based on Native American lives and experiences.

NOTES

1. Judith Butler writes explicitly that "there are no direct expressive or causal lines between sex, gender, gender presentation, sexual practice, fantasy and sexuality" (Butler 1991:25).

2. The collection of essays in *Woman, Culture and Society* received much attention particularly for the stance that Michelle Rosaldo, Nancy Chodorow, and Sherry Ortner took on the universality of women's subordination to men. It had a major impact on women's studies and history theorizing as well. However, critique came almost immediately from within anthropology, and the most influential were the arguments put forth by Eleanor Leacock (Étienne and Leacock 1980 and Leacock 1981). See also Sherry Ortner's discussions more than 20 years later (Ortner 1996).

3. This is Oyewùmí's conclusion as well. She writes: "gender cannot be theorized in and of itself; it has to be located within cultural systems—local and global—and its history and articulations must be critically charted along with other aspects of social systems" (1997).

4. I use Scott's work and definitions because I find them well argued and her books and articles have become foundational texts for historians working with gender. It is, however, important to recognize her debt to earlier feminist scholars, in particular the French feminists who formulated a critique of the historical canon and discovered the power of discourses before Foucault and Derrida or Lacan began to influence social history. See Canning 1997.

5. Swedish, for example, has two linguistic gender systems, one of which is grammatical, the other semantic and essentially differentiating between animate/inanimate categories (Teleman 1987).

6. Personal communication from Jim Rementer, who has worked closely with Nora Thompson Dean to preserve the Lenape language.

7. Personal communication from Jim Rementer.

8. Also Jim Rementer, personal communication. The Moravian missionary John Heckewelder gives the following words for the concept *woman* in his glossary of Delaware: *ochque*=woman, *wusdóchqueu*=young woman, virgin, *ochquetschitsch*=girl, *quetit*=female infant, *gichtochqueu*=aged woman, *chauchschísis*=very old woman (Heckewelder 1819:363).

9. Oral sources corroborate this from the 20th century as well. Interview with Leonard Thompson, June 6, 1991, *Oklahoma Living Legends*, 91.046, Oklahoma Historical Society, Oklahoma City; Nora Thompson Dean, "Delaware Indian Reminiscences," *Bulletin of the Archaeological Society of New Jersey*, 35, 1978.

10. Moral condemnation may have fallen equally upon a man; see the following exchange: "Is adultery considered criminal in the woman?—It is very much so; Is it so, in the man?—It is equally criminal" (Weslager 1978:104).

11. References to the problem with colonial sources are numerous; important issues for Native American studies are discussed in Martin 1987 and Mihesuah 1998.

12. The source is copied from the Timothy Pickering Papers at the Buffalo and Erie County Historical Society, Buffalo, and contains no information concerning either author, date, or place. A note attached to it informs that John Witthoft judges it to be circa 1820, probably from Grand River Munsees, Ontario. He speculates that the text may have been written down by one of the Moravian missionaries at New Fairfield. The information in it is consistent with a ceremony described from Munsee Delawares, as a springtime annual ceremony (see Harrington 1913:230). But Peter Lindeström refers to springtime ceremonies among the Lenapes (it would have been people later designated as Unami Delawares) already in the 1650s (Lindeström 1962:119, 124).

13. Both Post's and Hays's accounts have recently been published in Grumet 1999:58–61.

14. Those knowledgeable on Delaware and Munsee culture no doubt have more and different questions to pose to these extracts. It is possible that Kenny was referring to a Munsee tradition, while the others had observed an Unami Delaware ceremony. However, this would not alter the basic argument that attention to gender will yield other information and place the sources in a different light.

15. Listen also to oral testimony: "Interview with Anna Anderson Davis, Aug 5, 1968," T-298, *The Doris Duke Collection, American Indian Oral History*, Western History Collection, Norman, Oklahoma; "Interview with Nora Thompson Dean, April 1968," T-296, *The Doris Duke Collection, American Indian Oral History*, "Interview with Bessie Hunter Snake, June 18, 1967," T-88, *The Doris Duke Collection, American Indian Oral History*; "Interview with Mr. Edward Thompson, 13 Feb 1984," *Oklahoma Living Legends* 84.018.

16. Agreement is general concerning this; see, for instance, Lang (1998: 208–212); Trexler (1995:176); Jacobs et al. (1997).

17. An interesting discussion is found in Hopkins (1998). His article looks at how in U.S. culture masculinity is an attribute that is seen as naturally founded in biology and at the same time acquired through proper upbringing and behaviors.

REFERENCES

A.A.
N.d.   A Short History or a Description of the Recitation Festival as Practiced by the Delaware or Munsie Tribe of Indians from Time Immemorial. Timothy Pickering Papers. Buffalo and Erie County Historical Society [BHS], Buffalo.

Albers, Patricia and Beatrice Medicine, eds.
1983   The Hidden Half: Studies of Plains Indian Women. Lanham, MD: University Press of America.

Amadiume, Ifi
1987   Male Daughters, Female Husbands. Gender and Sex in an African Society. London: Zed Books.

Butler, Judith
　1990　Gender Trouble. Feminism and the Subversion of Identity. New York and
　　　　London: Routledge.
　1991　Imitation and Gender Insubordination. In Inside/Out. Lesbian Theories, Gay
　　　　Theories. Diana Fuss, ed. Pp. 13–31. New York: Routledge.
　1993　Critically Queer. GLQ: A Journal of Lesbian and Gay Studies 1:17–32.
Cahn, Susan K.
　1993　Coming on Strong. Gender and Sexuality in Twentieth-Century Women's
　　　　Sport. New York: Free Press.
Canning, Kathleen
　1997　Feminist History after the Linguistic Turn: Historicizing Discourse and Expe-
　　　　rience. In History and Theory. Feminist Research, Debates, Contestations.
　　　　Barbara Laslett, Ruth-Ellen B. Joeres, Mary Jo Maynes, Evelyn Brooks Higgin-
　　　　botham, and Jeanne Barker-Nunn, eds. Pp. 416–452. Chicago: University of
　　　　Chicago Press.
Chalkley, Thomas
　1751　A Journal or, Historical Account of the Life, Travels and Christian Experi-
　　　　ences. . . . London.
Dean, Nora Thompson
　1978　Delaware Indian Reminiscences. Bulletin of the Archaeological Society of
　　　　New Jersey, 35.
　1980　Lenape Language Lessons. (Lessons Three and Four). Dewey, OK: Touching
　　　　Leaves Indian Crafts.
de Rasieres, Isaack
　1909　Letter to Samuel Blommaert, 1628. In Narratives of New Netherland. J.
　　　　Franklin Jameson, ed. New York: Charles Scribner's Sons.
Doniger, Wendy
　1998　The Implied Spider: Politics & Theology in Myth. New York: Columbia Uni-
　　　　versity Press.
Dowd, Gregory E.
　1992　A Spirited Resistance. The North American Indian Struggle for Unity,
　　　　1745–1815. Baltimore: Johns Hopkins University Press.
Étienne, Mona, and Eleanor Leacock, eds.
　1980　Women and Colonization: Anthropological Perspectives. New York: Praeger.
Fiske, Jo-Anne
　1996　Pocahontas's Granddaughters: Spiritual Transition and Tradition of Carrier-
　　　　Women of British Columbia. Ethnohistory 43(4):663–681.
Fur, Gunlög
　1993　Cultural Confrontations on Two Fronts: Swedes Meet Lenapes and Saamis in
　　　　the Seventeenth Century. Ph.D. dissertation, University of Oklahoma.
　1998　Women's Authority and the Anomalies of Vision in Delaware Experiences of
　　　　Colonial Encounters. Working Paper, 98-08. International Seminar on the
　　　　History of the Atlantic World, 1500–1800, Harvard University.
Gnadenhütten Diary
　1755　Gnadenhütten, PA 1754–1755. Box 118, Folder 5. Moravian Archives [MA].
　　　　Bethlehem, PA.

Green, Rayna
    1975   The Pocahontas Perplex: The Image of Indian Women in American Culture.
            Massachusetts Review: 698–714.
Grumet, Robert
    1980   Sunksquaws, Shamans, and Tradeswomen: Middle Atlantic Coastal Al-
            gonkian Women during the Seventeenth and Eighteenth Centuries. *In*
            Women and Colonization: Anthropological Perspectives. Mona Étienne and
            Eleanor Leacock, eds. Pp. 43–62. New York: Praeger.
Grumet, Robert, ed.
    1999   Journey on the Forbidden Path: Chronicles of a Diplomatic Mission to the Al-
            legheny Country, March–September 1760. American Philosophical Society,
            Philadelphia.
Gutiérrez, Ramón
    1989   Must We Deracinate Indians to Find Gay Roots? Out/Look (winter):61–67.
Harrington, M. R.
    1913   A Preliminary Sketch of Lenápe Culture. American Anthropologist, n.s.
            15:208–235.
Hays, John
    1954   John Hays' Diary and Journal of 1760. Pennsylvania Archaeologist
            24(2):63–84.
Heckewelder, John
    1819   An Account of the History, Manners, and Customs of the Indian Nations;
            Who Once Inhabited Pennsylvania and the Neighbouring States. Philadel-
            phia: Abraham Small.
Herdt, Gilbert, ed.
    1996   Third Sex, Third Gender. Beyond Sexual Dimorphism in Culture and History.
            New York: Zone Books.
Hopkins, Patrick D.
    1998   Gender Treachery: Homophobia, Masculinity, and Threatened Identities. *In*
            Race, Class, Gender, and Sexuality: The Big Questions. Naomi Zack, Laurie
            Shrage, Crispin Sartwell, eds. Pp. 168–186. Oxford: Blackwell.
Jacobs, Sue-Ellen, Wesley Thomas, and Sabine Lang, eds.
    1997   Two-Spirit People. Native American Gender Identity, Sexuality, and Spiritual-
            ity. Urbana: University of Illinois Press.
Kehoe, Alice B.
    1995   Blackfoot Persons. *In* Women and Power in Native North America. Laura F.
            Klein and Lillian A. Ackerman, eds. Pp. 113–125. Norman: University of Okla-
            homa Press.
Kenny, James
    1913   Journal of James Kenny, 1761–1763. Pennsylvania Magazine of History and
            Biography 37:1–47, 152–201.
Klein, Laura F., and Lillian A. Ackerman, eds.
    1995   Women and Power in Native North America. Norman: University of Okla-
            homa Press.
Kopytoff, Igor
    1990   Women's Roles and Existential Identities. *In* Beyond the Second Sex. New

Directions in the Anthropology of Gender. Peggy Reeves Sanday and Ruth Gallagher Goodenough, eds. Pp. 77–98. Philadelphia: University of Pennsylvania Press.

Kupperman, Karen O.
1980   Settling with the Indians. Totowa, NJ: Rowman and Littlefield.

Lagundo-Utenünk Diary
1770   Lagundo-Utenünk (Friedenstatt) Diary. Box 137, Folder 1. Moravian Archives [MA]. Bethlehem, PA.

Lang, Sabine
1998   Men as Women, Women as Men. Changing Gender in Native American Cultures. Austin: University of Texas Press.

Leacock, Eleanor
1981   Myths of Male Dominance: Collected Articles on Women Cross-Culturally. New York: Monthly Review Press.

Lindeström, Peter
1962   Resa till Nya Sverige. Alf Åberg, ed. Stockholm: Natur och Kultur. (Also in a reliable English translation by Amandus Johnson. 1925 Geographia America with an Account of the Delaware Indians. Philadelphia: Swedish Colonial Society.)

Lomawaima, K. Tsianina
1993   Domesticity in the Federal Indian Schools: The Power of Authority over Mind and Body. American Ethnologist 20(2):227–240.

Maltz, Daniel, and JoAllyn Archambault
1995   Gender and Power in Native North America: Concluding Remarks. In Women and Power in Native North America. Laura F. Klein and Lillian A. Ackerman, eds. Pp. 230–249. Norman: University of Oklahoma Press.

Martin, Calvin, ed.
1987   The American Indian and the Problem of History. New York:Oxford University Press.

McClintock, Anne
1995   Imperial Leather: Race, Gender and Sexuality in the Colonial Contest. New York: Routledge.

Mihesuah, Devon A., ed.
1998   Natives and Academics. Researching and Writing about American Indians. Lincoln: University of Nebraska Press.

Miller, Jay
1979   A Strucon Model of Delaware Culture and the Positioning of Mediators. American Ethnologist 6:791–802.
1982   People, Berdaches, and Left–Handed Bears: Human Variation in Native America. Journal of Anthropological Research 38(3):274–287.

Moi, Toril
1998   "Vad är en kvinna?" Res Publica 35/36 (1998):71–158. (In English, What Is a Woman and Other Essays.) Oxford: Oxford University Press.

Morgan, Jennifer L.
1997   "Some Could Suckle over Their Shoulder": Male Travelers, Female Bodies,

and the Gendering of Racial Ideology, 1500–1770. William and Mary Quarterly 54(1):167–192.

Nicholson, Linda J.
   1998   Interpreting "Gender." *In* Race, Class, Gender, and Sexuality: The Big Questions. Naomi Zack, Laurie Shrage, Crispin Sartwell, eds. Pp. 187–211. Oxford: Blackwell.

Ortner, Sherry B.
   1996   Making Gender. The Politics and Erotics of Culture. Boston: Beacon Press.

Oyewùmí, Oyèrónké
   1997   The Invention of Women. Making an African Sense of Western Gender Discourses. Minneapolis: University of Minnesota Press.

Perdue, Theda
   1998   Cherokee Women. Gender and Culture Change, 1700–1835. Lincoln: University of Nebraska Press.

Post, Christian Frederick
   1760   Journal of Mr. Christn Fred Post, in Company with Teedyscung, Mr. John Hays, Isaac Still & Moses Tattamy, to the Great Council of the Different Indian Nations, 1760. Microfilm no. 204. (Copied from Mrs. Henry P. Gummere, Upper Darby, PA, in 1942.) American Philosophical Society [APS], Philadelphia.

Ramet, Sabrina Petra, ed.
   1996   Gender Reversals & Gender Cultures. Anthropological and Historical Perspectives. New York: Routledge.

Rockwell, David
   1991   Giving Voice to Bear. Niwot, CO: Robert Rinehart.

Rosaldo, Michelle Z., and Louise Lamphere, eds.
   1974   Woman, Culture and Society. Stanford: Stanford University Press.

Roscoe, Will
   1991   The Zuni Man-Woman. Albuquerque: University of New Mexico Press.
   1998   Changing Ones. Third and Fourth Genders in Native North America. New York: St. Martin's Press.

Saunt, Claudio
   1998   "Domestick . . . Quiet Being broke": Gender Conflict among Creek Indians in the 18th century. *In* Contact Points: American Frontiers from the Mohawk Valley to the Mississippi 1750–1830. Andrew R. L. Cayton and Fredrika J. Teute, eds. Pp. 151–174. Chapel Hill: University of North Carolina Press.

Scott, Joan W.
   1988   Gender and the Politics of History. New York: Columbia University Press.

Shammas, Carole
   1995   Anglo-American Household Government in Comparative Perspective. William and Mary Quarterly 52(1):104–144.

Shekomeko Diary
   1745   Shekomeko, NY, Seidel's visit. Box 112, Folder 11 (2). Moravian Archives [MA]. Bethlehem, PA.

Shoemaker, Nancy, ed.
  1995   Negotiators of Change. Historical Perspectives on Native American Women.
          New York: Routledge.
Sigal, Pete
  1998   Ethnohistory and Homosexual Desire: A Review of Recent Works. Ethnohis-
          tory 45(1):135–141.
Speck, Frank G.
  1931   A Study of the Delaware Indian Big House Ceremony. Publications of the
          Pennsylvania Historical Commission (PHC), vol. 2. Harrisburg: PHC.
Strong, Pauline Turner
  1996   Feminist Theory and the "Invasion of the Heart" in North America. Ethnohis-
          tory 43(4):683–712.
Tantaquidgeon, Gladys
  1972   Folk Medicine of the Delaware and Related Algonkian Indians. Harrisburg:
          Pennsylvania Historical and Museum Commission.
Teleman, Ulf
  1987   Hur många genus finns det i svenskan? In Grammatik på villovägar. Ulf Tele-
          man, ed. (Skrifter utgivna av Svenska språknämnden 73). Stockholm:
          Almqvist & Wiksell Förlag.
Trexler, Richard C.
  1995   Sex and Conquest. Gendered Violence, Political Order, and the European
          Conquest of the Americas. Ithaca, NY: Cornell University Press.
Van der Donck, Adriaen
  1841   Description of the New Netherlands (1653). Jeremiah Johnson, trans. New
          York Historical Society Collections, 2d. ser. I:125–242.
Wellenreuther, Hermann, and Carola Wessel, eds.
  1995   Herrnhuter Indianermission in der Amerikanischen Revolution. Die Tage-
          bücher von David Zeisberger 1772 bis 1781. Berlin: Akademie Verlag.
Weslager, C. A.
  1978   The Delaware Indian Westward Migration. With the Texts of Two Manu-
          scripts (1821–22) Responding to General Lewis Cass's Inquiries about
          Lenape Culture and Language. Wallingford, PA: Middle Atlantic Press.
  1991   The Delaware Indians: A History. New Brunswick, NJ: Rutgers University
  [1972] Press.
White, Bruce M.
  1999   The Woman Who Married a Beaver: Trade Patterns and Gender Roles in
          Ojibwa Fur Trade. Ethnohistory 46(1):109–147.
Williams, Walter L.
  1986   The Spirit and the Flesh: Sexual Diversity in American Indian Culture.
          Boston: Beacon Press.
Zeisberger, David
  1910   History of the Northern American Indians. Archer Butler Hulbert and
          William Nathaniel Schwarze, eds. Ohio State Archaeological Society.
  1912   David Zeisburger [sic] Journal. Ohio Archaeological and Historical Publica-
          tions, 21.

Political Economy

Marxism and Historical Materialism In American Indian History

Patricia C. Albers

Recent deconstructionist, postmodernist, and postcolonialist turns in historical studies, with their emphasis on highly relativistic and culturally constructed readings of American Indian history, appear to have cast aside some of the more generalizing and comparative interpretations of history grounded in material conditions and forces. Indeed, materialism appears passé today whether its theoretical origins are traced to the classical models of laissez-faire markets, the evolutionary paradigms of Darwinian biology, or the labor theory of value in Marxian political economy.

As a mossback scholar with a decidedly materialist and neo-Marxian bent, I am admittingly and unabashedly burdened by a lichenous perspective that, while flourishing in an earlier era, seems to have little place to nest and spread in the scholarly climate of the present. In reflecting upon why some of my own theoretical proclivities are no longer in vogue in today's intellectual circles, I thought it would be instructive to begin at the point of opposition—at the place where the grounds of modern cultural interpretation stand the farthest from some of the materialist places I have sat. By positioning my perspective and historical materialism more generally in the face of its opposition, I hope to be able to critically assess the limits and weaknesses of both. I also hope to articulate their possibilities and strengths, and in the process, suggest how cultural constructionists might meet materialists on common grounds in ways that can enrich each other's work.

LABOR AND HISTORICAL MATERIALISM

One of the many conundrums of modern scholarship in American Indian history is how do we get construction and condition, agency and cause, the subject and its object, to properly dance with each other without overstepping the movement of the other. How do we write histories of American Indian labor, as one example, that simultaneously give expression to the voices and memories of the workers and the forces and events surrounding their work? How do we reveal the historical processes by which the cultural constructs of workers both transform and are transformed by the material conditions under which they work? Can we combine these perspectives, or in the end are we obliged to write different sorts of histories?

Approaches to cultural constructions and material conditions typically meet history on different grounds. On one side of the ledger are scholars who interpret historical phenomena as constructed from human thought and imagination. Railing against empirical positivism and naive forms of realism, they deny the ontological existence of an object world outside a universe of culturally mediated signs and symbols. Human agency is heavily weighted by the cultural memories that people bring to their action. It is relative and particularized. It is grounded, contingent on the historically specific context of its creation, and interpreted at the sites of its making. Essentialism in all of its forms is opposed because agency is presumed to have no generic dimensions or eternal truths. On the other side are scholars who interpret history as an epiphenomenon of the material universe. Standing opposed to cultural idealism and conventionalism, they reduce all symbols and their meanings to a physical object base and deny them a separate ontological status. Human agency is largely ephemeral, impacted and conditioned by forces that reside in the recurring properties of the material world. Generalized patterns and causal processes can be discovered and explained for these properties through neutral and comparative methods of analysis that, idealistically at least, stand outside the historically situated appearance of the phenomena under study and the vagaries of human subjectivity. Of course, most historical scholars do not follow either extreme: they sit somewhere in between and muddle (or should I say fudge?) their way through the subjectivist/objectivist quagmire. What differentiates them is not whether they displace a thing by its thought, or vice versa, but the prevailing direction from which they enter and leave their historical studies. And this is certainly true for most historical and ethnographic studies of American Indian labor, including those which begin and end their work at the doorstep of materialism.

In its most generic sense, materialism identifies any of a variety of approaches that take it as axiomatic that the physical world and its myriad corporeal properties have an existence independent of the way we deal with them. A book, a table, or a spoon has an object constancy. Except for alteration and deterioration, their appearances remain stable over time and space. For materialists, the fixed conditions of these objects have a bearing on how they get confronted, interpreted, and used, even in different culturally mediated settings, and as such, these must be considered (although not necessarily privileged) in the process of analysis.

How historical scholars travel a materialist path is quite varied, however. But of all the different materialist road maps, the one that has had the most profound and lasting influence on studies in American Indian history draws on the insights and work of Karl Marx (1947, 1963, 1967, 1970, 1973) and his associate, Friedrich Engels (1947). Both men were much influenced by the earlier writings of Lewis Henry Morgan (1851, 1871, 1877) who was known not only for his ethnographic research among the Iroquois but for his ethnological theories on kinship and evolution as well. Theoretical approaches that trace their intellectual roots to Marx and Engels generally fall under the rubric of historical materialism whose dialectical methodology differentiates it from the more ahistoric and empiricist materialisms that have long dominated thinking in the American social sciences.

Historical materialism entered studies of American Indian history in the 1940s, but due to the anticommunist and antisocialist sentiment of the times, its Marxian intellectual origins went largely unacknowledged (Klein 1980; Moore 1980, 1993; Leacock 1982). It was most evident in a body of studies, including works by Oscar Lewis (1942), Esther Goldfrank (1945), and Joseph Jablow (1951), that focused on various tribal nations in the Plains. In this and later periods, writings on the Pueblo (Wittfogel and Goldfrank 1957), the Tlingit (Oberg 1973), Innu (Leacock 1954), Dene (Aberle 1967), and Anishinabe (Hickerson 1960, 1967, 1971, 1973) extended the application of historical materialist theory to other regions of North America. And in 1971, Eleanor Leacock and Nancy Lurie coedited a popular textbook that contained historical materialist approaches to reconstructing tribal histories.

By the end of the 1970s, historical materialism began to take root in other areas of American Indian historical study, and it did so largely in three different but related bodies of scholarship. It held a significant position in the literatures on the European trade where it was especially evident in the work of scholars such as Rolf Knight (1978), Bruce Cox (1984), John Moore (1974), Alan Klein (1977), and Adrian Tanner (1979). Eleanor Leacock (1978, 1981) was also instrumental in introducing Marxian theory to the newly developing field of feminist studies, and many of the writings (Nowack 1976; Perry 1979; Rothenberg 1980; Conte 1982; Albers 1985) about American Indian women from this and later times reveal the influence of a historical materialist perspective. The writings of Joseph Jorgenson (1971, 1972, 1978) opened the door to historical materialism and dependency theory in studies of economic development and the making of government policy in Indian country. Louise Lamphere (1976), Richard Clemmer (1977), Gary Anders (1979), Lorraine Ruffing (1979), Cardell Jacobson (1984), Thomas Biolsi (1992, 1993), Matthew Snipp (1986a, 1986b), and Lawrence Weiss (1984) are among the long line of scholars whose work is tied in one degree or another to this branch of historical materialism.

Whether scholars connect their work to Marx or not, it is clear that his ideas have permeated a significant segment of the scholarly writings in American Indian history, especially those which touch on various facets of political economy. What much of this writing shares in common is an interest in understanding the transformative power of material forces at the sites where they intersect with society and ideology. The introduction of the horse, for example, brought considerable change to tribal nations in the 18th- and 19th-century Plains. The conditions of its material presence, including access to grazing grounds, certainly affected how the animal became incorporated into the life of the region as the determinists (Osborn 1983) claim, but they did so through the engagement of human labor shaped by complex social relationships and ideologies preexisting within the region's various modes of production (Albers and James 1985, 1991). It is the socially and ideologically mediated articulations of material forces at particular sites of production that draw the interest of historical materialists. Over the years, it has been common for critics (Churchill 1983) to equate historical materialist approaches with economic determinism. And while there is no question that some of the scholarship linked to Marx represents a crass, simplistic, and overly reductionist form of materialism, historical materialist methodology is not unidirectional but dialectical (Hobsbawn 1980).

Human labor is the starting point for studies that draw on the theories and methods of historical materialism (Hobsbawn 1980:12–13; Wolf 1982:73–75). Indeed for Marx, labor was a definitive and essential condition of the human species. It consists of the actions, both mental and manual, by which humans transform nature into products for their own use and exchange. Not only does it include the various transactions, techniques, and knowledges by which nature is transformed, but it also covers the communicative relationships through which the transformations are enacted. As such, labor is implicitly a sociocultural phenomenon, and for Marx (1970:31–32), it was at all times and places a particularized phenomenon. Labor is the point at which the material (or natural) world is appropriated and mediated through human action and thought, the point at which social relatedness is created and challenged in the making of human existence. Historical materialism certainly favors the material world in its analyses, but it does not equate or reduce human existence to that world.

As Eric Hobsbawn (1980) writes in his introduction to Marx's *Pre-Capitalist Economic Formations*, historical materialism is a multidimensional theory in which the economic, social, and ideological dimensions of history are inseparable and enfolded in certain elementary assumptions about human labor. Insofar as historical materialist theory posits certain axioms about a universal dimension to human labor, it carries with it the burdens of many essentializing theories that "naturalize" a particular construction of humanness. But insofar as it also entertains the idea that labor unfolds dynamically in the simultaneous and dialectical engagement of the relations of production and forces of production, it is not reductionist or deterministic. The social order is not a consequence of the material order, or vice versa; the two have coevolved historically and changed in tandem with the contradictions their relationship inevitably provokes. How the two get connected, however, is historically specific. There was no universal history for Marx, but there were broader configurations, or modes of production, that represented generalized constructs of the possible ways labor gets realized in the engagement of particular social formations and material forces at different points in history (Wolf 1982:21).

CULTURAL CONSTRUCTS

One of the most positive outcomes of the deconstructionist turn in modern scholarship is that it has forced those of us interested in materialist histories of American Indians to revisit and rethink some of the ways we have come to understand and represent this subject. One of the central weaknesses of historical materialist theory has been its reliance on European-derived analytical categories, and its failure to fully describe and understand the cultural constructions that have defined work and exchange for particular tribal nations at specific times in history. It still surprises me how we know so much about the material conditions and outcomes of various acts of labor but understand so little about the experience of performing labor and even less about the languages and cultural constructs within which its agency gets expressed.

In the area of American Indian ethnography, there is an enormous literature that focuses on the techniques, tools, and products of labor. There are in-depth descriptions of subsistence work from salmon fishing to the preparation of acorn meal and from buffalo hunting to the cultivation of corn. There are detailed accountings of the methods behind the making of baskets, canoes, bows, and cradles, and even more comprehensive representations of the form and design of the finished products. In historical research, analyses of traders' ledgers yield solid data on the volume and types of furs, hides, and provisions traded to Europeans, the identities of the producers, and the timing and location of their production. By and large, the semantic and cultural frameworks within which particular labors and their products are conceptualized and applied remain largely uncharted. This is true for all types of labor whether it is a form of waged employment, petty commodity production, household labor, or subsistence work. And it stands in marked contrast to the "thick descriptions" of systems of naming and meaning associated with medicine, religion, ethnoscience, and kinship. Although cultural constructionists have applied a great deal of effort to unraveling the language and logic behind these areas of knowledge and experience, most have not been as eager to examine them in the flow of ordinary life events associated with work and day-to-day provisioning.

With limited exception, the communicative context of labor and laboring in American Indian history is unexplored. One of the exceptions is found in the literature on the fur trade where attempts (Tanner 1979; Brightman 1993) have been made to identify and interpret the cultural perspectives that surround hunting. The word *respect*, as one example, frequently appears in this literature to gloss a particular cultural attitude that involves a special kinship and spiritual reverence toward the taking of beaver, buffalo, white tail deer, and other animals whose products entered the European trade. Its interpretation provides a way to make sense of the motivations and choices behind certain hunting practices and behaviors. And this has been especially useful in understanding how the ideological and material worlds of American Indians interfaced in complex and sometimes even contradictory ways to resist, challenge, and accommodate the intrusion of European modes of production.

The idea of respect certainly carries spiritual values, but it also embodies other dimensions. Among the Dakota, as one example, it has a much broader usage. The word *ohoda* (to honor or to respect), is a synergistic concept that blends and weaves a single idea across many different areas of experience. When speaking in English of their labors in quilt making, Dakota women use the word "respect" to reveal a regard for the materials, skills, knowledge, and inspiration required in making quilts of high quality and striking design. It also expresses a reverence for the spiritual figures who enable the labor and an admiration for the people who will be honored and gifted by its completion. The word has many different but related applications that reveal not only a multifaceted relationship to quilt making but also an intrinsic sense of connectedness between the quilter and her social, material, and spiritual worlds (Albers and Medicine 1983; MacDowell and Dewhurst 1997). As such, it provides a critical point of entry for following the threads of meaning, desire, and motivation that enrich a woman's labor and the cultural universe within which she works.

Understanding what words mean and how they get used can be a daunting task because it requires a full-dress review of a language and the ability to hear words at work, no pun intended, in the situations in which they are most likely to be uttered. What does Dene sheep raising "talk" sound like, what about the language of Yurok salmon fishing, the factory speech of Anishinabe assembly line workers, or the Micmac conversations that surround potato picking. And what about the various vernaculars of "reservation" English, French, or Spanish in which a rich body of idiomatic expression surrounds economic activity that is not easily equated with customary usage among other European language speakers. Some may groan over what might be considered an excessively relativistic turn here. Yet it is safe to say that we cannot reliably discuss acts of historic, much less modern, American Indian labor unless we can be sure we are talking about the same thing from a Hopi, Haida, or Hochunk language perspective. Without prior linguistic and cultural knowledge, it is easy to essentialize indigenous perspectives in terms of the categories and assumptions that dominate mainstream economics.

Many may argue that while in-depth reconstructions of the semantic meanings behind labor and their application in concrete work situations are an ideal we ought to strive toward, at least in theory, they are hard to put it into practice especially when most of the documentary sources historians rely upon for reconstructing the social economies of the past do not permit this. My response is that if we have detailed knowledge of language practice, which can be derived for a number of languages including Ojibwe, Cree, Dakota, Lakota, Cheyenne, Cherokee, Navajo, Apache, and Shoshone, we can engage a practice that Frederic Gleach (1996) has called "controlled speculation." In the face of alternative interpretations, we can identify those which seem to make the best fit or the most sense in relation to native language practice. Of course, language usage today is not what it was two hundred years ago, but it's better than nothing at all and certainly superior to using words such as "sharing," "gifting," "making," "hunting," "trading," and "hiring" without any appreciation for subtle meanings and uses in Native languages much less Native vernaculars of English, French, or Spanish.

Knowing what concepts are used for labor and its associated work activities and understanding how these are applied contextually are more than an intellectual exercise. They can have concrete bearing on the outcome of legal cases where courts are required to interpret how American Indians understood the language of treaties to which they were signatories. In an important fishing rights case involving the state of Idaho and the Shoshone-Bannock Tribes, the widely respected linguist Sven Lljeblad argued that the language that preserved hunting rights in the Fort Bridger Treaty of 1858 would have been understood by Shoshone- and Bannock-speakers to include activities customarily labeled fishing and gathering in English. In these Numic languages, the word glossed as "hunting" is identified with a specific style of procural that can be applied equally well to the pursuit of fish, plants, or game. As Lljeblad argued in the trial proceedings (*State of Idaho v. Gerald Cleo Tinno* 1970), the Shoshone and Bannock who signed the treaty would have understood a more general reading of "hunt" than is typically the case in English. By the way, the court ruled in favor of the Shoshone-Bannock litigant (*State of Idaho v. Gerald Cleo Tinno* 1972).

As we know little of the particular cultural constructions or semantic expressions surrounding labor in a concrete or abstract sense, we also have a long way to go in understanding the specific agencies, motivations, desires, and needs that have drawn American Indian people to specific labors at different times and places. Life histories and autobiographies represent a starting point for these understandings, and there are some, including *Guests Never Leave Hungry* (1969), which contain very compelling narratives about people's involvement in work and the cultural reasoning behind particular kinds of labor. There are also encouraging signs in some of the recent writings (Hosmer 1991, 1997, 1999; Littlefield and Knack 1996; Iverson 1997) on wage labor and entrepreneurship that give voice to the workers and their experiences. Yet, overall, a comprehensive knowledge of the cultural principles and sensibilities surrounding work, either in a specific or general sense, is still lacking. What we need to know is how do indigenous cultural perspectives shape the ways people experience labor at particular work sites, and how do these perspectives change and/or persist in the context of this work?

Above all, studies need to go beyond generalized lists (Vinje 1985; Trosper 1999) of value orientation, many of which fail to show how a cultural principle or sensibility gets expressed in concrete worlds of discourse and experience. For example, if the labor surrounding the acquisition and disbursement of wealth is interpreted differently in American Indian cultures than it is in the mainstream cultures of Euro-Americans, what does this mean in specific tribal settings? Does it carry the same meanings for the Pequot as it does for the Yakama? What implications does it have for tribal groups entering the world of casinos and high stakes gambling? How do these new forms of wealth creation get inscribed, experienced, and even contested on the casino floors where tribal members work and play, in the offices of the tribal governments and management companies that run high-stake gaming, and in the flow of tribal life outside the bingo hall? What kinds of tensions and contradictions emerge when different expectations about the acquisition and disbursement of wealth collide? For cultural constructs to be something more than vacuous abstractions, they need to be studied in concrete contexts. In the fashion of Loretta Fowler's work (1987) on the contested meaning of symbols among the Atsina, we not only need to know the cultural constructs tribal communities actually share around the acquisition and disbursement of wealth, but we also need to understand how these are expressed, negotiated, and challenged in the places where people actually produce and distribute their wealth.

Scholars who study labor in American Indian history have much to gain from understanding the cultural constructs that express and give agency to a people's economic activity, but there are dangers, too. One of these is the tendency toward an exoticism that either overdetermines the cultural uniqueness of what people are doing or misinterprets the cultural cues that govern certain labor efforts and their associated exchanges. Above all, we need to ask whether certain cultural representations really reveal any concrete tribal perspective or are simply another European-based construction dressed in exoticized cultural clothing. Attempts to interpret the cultural markers of work and trade sometimes imply, if not downright deny, the possibility that any sort of pragmatic logic stands behind individual and group choices. All kinds of forces, from the aesthetic to the spiritual, become driving influences in interpreting the motivations of American Indians without due weight given to material considerations. But to say that practical knowledge and choice exist is not to say that these follow the same lines of rationality present in mainstream economic thought, because they clearly do not. There is reason to be leery of certain constructionist efforts to read the cultural content of economic activity, not because meaning is unimportant but because we need to respect the difficulties involved in representing things correctly. Not being able to do this, it is sometimes better to acknowledge the inherent biases of using outside analytical categories rather than pursuing reconstructions of Native discourse that end up being something other than what the authors purport them to be.

Myopism is also a danger in cultural constructionist approaches. The inquiry gets so centered on the details that the larger conditions under which labor unfolds and the structures within which it operates elude the researcher or get discounted because they do not flow within the discourse of the inquiry itself. Although it has become fashionable of late to dismiss the "reality" of social arrangements outside and beyond the agency of individual actors, this denies the possibility of history and the social weight that prior generations bring to bear on the outcome of their successors' lives and future. Like many of today's postmodernists, I once dismissed the existence of superordinate structures, in cultural constructs, social formations, or modes of production, seeing the general as simply the totality of all its individual representations and transactions. Over the past three decades, I have come to recognize that the cacophony of individual agency, action, and expression is realized within the existence of a series of shared constructs, albeit not always consensual, that make up not only the languages and worldviews in which we think and voice our ideas but also the social formations and material orders in which we realize and engage our actions.

Language and ideologies do have their own structures and movements that are dependent on the people who engage them but are independent of them as well. Insofar as language, ideas, and symbols transcend individual lives and lifetimes, they exist as abstractions and carry qualities that are not determined by the agency of single actors. These larger orders involve frames of reference that differ, both logically and logistically, from those that focus on the discourse and actions of individuals.

Historically, there were abstract and conventionalized expectations for assigning labor along gender lines in American Indian societies. These expectations were embedded in a series of complex cultural constructs about personhood, age, kinship, and rank. They were also shaped by cultural ideas about the conduct of work under particular circumstances and in relation to specific tools and resources. Importantly, cultural constructs about the division of labor are not always tightly wedded to the way things actually get enacted. They do not follow immovable, formulaic paths. Nevertheless, they still exist as a body of ideas that people share and engage when they conduct their work. These constructs form a map: they are points of reference when negotiating various domains of work experience. They are not, however, the territory where the work actually unfolds.

The territory encompasses the social and material worlds that labor engages. It involves the people who collaborate in the act of production, the resources that are transformed in the process, and the tools that enable the transformation. The territory often contains features not easily read or even registered by a preexisting and culturally constituted map, and, indeed, the two may even stand in contradiction to each other. When the historical settings under which American Indian women and men worked were changed by colonization, tribal nations not only confronted new material conditions and social relationships for carrying on their labor but also new ideas and maps for engaging their work. One of the most bitterly contested sites of colonial domination stood and still stands on the back of gender and its relation to work (Leacock 1980; Shoemaker 1995; Perdue 1998). Colonization created grounds for innovation and change but also resistance and continuity in the way American Indian people labored. Unless we see the maps and their territories as distinct, at least heuristically, it is impossible to understand how the two intersected.

When theorists use cultural constructs to absorb the layers of social relationship and praxis in which labor is actually enacted, they enter what Margaret Archer (1990) describes as the pitfall of conflationism. Lacking an independent analytical status, action simply becomes a mirror of thought without its own agency. Of course, action and thought are related and labor is both a mental and manual process, but in order to understand how these pairings relate to one another, they need to be disentangled in the course of analysis and interpretation. Otherwise, the results are endless tautologies. Or else, they become spurious distinctions where subsistence is identified as an economic act under capitalism but a social one in indigenous economic settings. In both situations, these acts engage labor that is socially constituted, and in both, nature is transformed into products, goods, and commodities. The difference does not lie in the relative sociality of the acts but in the particular social agencies from which and to which production is directed. That economic activity appears to lack a social or cultural referent under capitalism is only an illusion that hides the relations of power in this particular mode of production.

Historic and ethnographic studies (Brightman 1993; DeMallie 1993; Kan 1993; Basso 1996; Schwartz 1998) with constructionist leanings have advanced our understanding of the many-sided ways cultural knowledge and sensibilities permeate and permutate local discourse and praxis. But the question that still must be addressed is whether cultural interpretations are sufficient for representing the complex set of stories that make up American Indian history. The answer depends, of course, on what kinds of knowledge are being pursued through a particular inquiry. If the point of study is to determine how meaning and agency interface, or how people invest their work with meaning, then hermeneutic forms of interpretation are the most appropriate path to follow. But when questions seek materialist forms of explanation, the lines of inquiry travel different routes. Let me illustrate.

One of the most contested subjects in American Indian studies is the origin of potlatching among the tribal nations of the Northwest Coast. In the 1960s, several anthropologists (Suttles 1960; Vayda 1961; Piddocke 1965) explained the potlatch, its associated labor and exchange, as a mechanism for redistributing resources in the face of environmental variation. Without question, the constraints and opportunities for prestige giving were influenced by their material contexts, including the character of local environments, population demographics, and the wider economies of the fur trade and industrial capitalism. It is problematic, however, to argue that any of these conditions necessitated, much less created, the complex cultural constructions that "caused" potlatching in the first place (Drucker and Heizer 1967). Importantly, what motivates people to potlatch is different from what enables them to do so, and the answer to one does not explain the other. Sergei Kan's masterful constructionist approach (1993) to the Tlingit potlatch reveals how this institution is embedded in a complex series of symbols and beliefs that address the immortality of individuals and the social groups to which they belong. In order to understand why Tlingit hold these ceremonies and invest considerable labor in their performance, historical interpretation requires a constructionist course. That potlatches may have other intended and unintended outcomes, including the redistribution of wealth, is beside the point because intentions and consequences are not the same thing. On the other hand, a constructionist interpretation begs the question of why the Tlingit have the capacity to perform the potlatch in the particular ways they have done so in historic times or, to put it another way, what conditions in the Tlingit's material and social universe allow the potlatch and the cultural symbolism associated with it to reveal themselves.

MATERIAL CONDITIONS

Karl Marx's famous and oft-quoted dictum (1963:15) that "men make their own history, but they do not make it just as they please" is relevant here. For while the thick representations of language and cultural agency enlighten and bring rich texture to our understanding of people's experience, they are still inadequate to the task of accounting for many of the conditions under which people live and make their choices (Dirlik 1999). How labor is performed, what products it produces, and how these get exchanged are constituted in and constituted by universes of social relationship that include, but at the same time exist beyond, the actors and the cultural meanings they bring to their experience. To presume otherwise is to engage in a naive form of solipsism.

The universes of plants, animals, and minerals that humans transform for use and exchange exist under conditions independent of any perceptions we may have of them, and although we have a selective awareness of them and even appropriate them through the legacy of our own cultural knowledge, their presence in our lives is not totally determined by ours. Humans enter other natural (material) worlds in mutually determined and dialectical ways. Some studies (Bishop 1972; Feit 1988) clearly show this, and one of the ways they have been able to do so is through materially based considerations of plant and animal ecologies. Even some of the most scientifically positivist approaches (Hayden 1992) are useful here. By providing insights into the conditions within which various species survive, flourish, and decline, we are in a better position to see how a particular resource's existence enters into a tribal nation's ideas and acts of production, and also to understand the variable ways in which American Indian people were (and still are) able to engage these resources to their own ends and purposes. Unquestionably, the fundamental conditions of species survival have been altered by a human presence, including, as some scholars (Cronon 1983; White 1984; White and Cronon 1988; Krech 1999) argue, by the approaches American Indians took to their environment. The uses to which nature is put and the conditions of its appropriation clearly shape the way it exists both within and outside a world of human discourse and praxis. But again to understand how the two affect and are affected by each other's presence, each needs to have a separate analytical status.

It is not the conditions of the material world alone that participate in the making of labor, because humans work within discursive spaces where their efforts are also interwoven into far-reaching networks of social relationship. The path of our individualized labors radiates out and is connected to others in local, regional, and global landscapes. In the process, the patterns of these wider landscapes return and exert an influence on both the position and course of our individualized efforts. Making this claim in no way presupposes, or even demands, any essentialist theory or canon. It dismisses neither the strength of individual agency nor the press of particular meanings and desires; it only argues that these do not emerge in isolation divorced from other worlds of agency and meaning.

More than any other place in American Indian historical studies, research on the fur trade clearly reveals the press of wider forces on local lives and agency, and it has done so in many different ways. Research on the fur and hide trades (Knight 1968; Bishop 1974; Ray 1974, 1988, 1990; Klein 1977, 1993; Kay 1979; Ray and Freeman 1978; Cox 1984, 1993; Krech 1984; Swagerty 1988) has given evidence of how participation in European markets altered the technologies of work, the prioritization of tasks, the sites and timing of production, and the relationships that organized particular labor activities as well as managed access to land and resources. It has also shown how involvement in the trade influenced the locations and movements of tribes as well as the hostilities and alliances between them (Wishart 1979; Swagerty 1988; Albers 1993, 1996). Studies (Knight 1978; Cox 1984, 1993; Foster 1988; Klein 1977; Moore 1996) that follow a historical materialist approach have also attempted to document patterns of dependency and to show how peoples' livelihoods were affected by the forces and movements of markets beyond their borders and outside their direct control. For historical materialists, American Indian labor and its associated modes of production were altered in fundamental ways under colonization, not only through the arrival of new tools and other commodities but also through the introduction of foreign institutions and relationships that made access to these things possible.

In recent years, there has been a great deal of discussion and debate surrounding the extent to which American Indians were able to press their own cultural agendas and express their own agency in the face of economic institutions with global power and reach (R. White 1983; Krech 1999). There is no question that tribal nations exercised agency in negotiating their positions in the European trade. They certainly shaped the social and cultural fields in which the trade was conducted in their own communities, they demonstrated discriminating taste in selecting what was offered at the trader's counter, and they made decisions about the level and character of their participation in particular trades (B. White 1982, 1994; Anderson 1984; Merrell 1989). It is clear that individual and collective tribal agencies played a role in directing the course of fur trade history. And in some instances, these agencies might be construed as "causal" or determinative of the directions that particular trade formations took (Usner 1992). One would be hard-pressed, however, to deny the fact that at a wider level most tribal nations, particularly in the eastern regions of North America, had become dependent in some degree on market forces and formations governed by mercantile capitalism, and that their dependency unfolded as a result of conditions and terms of engagement outside their direct or even indirect control. Recognizing its historical and regional peculiarities, European mercantilism established conditions, structures, and processes that had to be reproduced in order for its markets to survive and expand (Hickerson 1973; Wolf 1982). Unquestionably, these had an influence on the social arenas within which tribal nations and trading companies were able to reveal their respective agencies.

If attention to the structure of forces and formations beyond local agency is required of scholarship for the fur trade era, it goes without saying that it is indispensable for research in 20th-century history. It is hard to make sense of the constraints and opportunities under which American Indian people exert their cultural agencies in modern-day economies unless we understand how these are also shaped by wider national and international conditions. Many of the forces that impacted 20th-century American Indian agrarian enterprises demand approaches that consider how property, capital, and class intersect within and outside local reservation economies (Trosper 1978; Knack 1986, 1987; McLaughlin

1988; Carter 1990; Iverson 1997; Lewis 1997; Sattler 1998). Without question, many of the choices American Indian people made in their farming and ranching endeavors were motivated by their respective cultural agencies. Yet, at the same time, these agencies generally unfolded under political economic conditions that linked local affairs to national and even global interests.

Also, the conditions that push today's American Indians into particular labor markets and force them out of others require a knowledge of broader economic structures and processes, including patterns of labor force segmentation and the workings of public versus private sector labor markets. Again, knowing the character of wider market forces and their role in influencing labor force participation does not deny the press of local cultural agencies. The ways in which American Indian people negotiate employment opportunities is clearly influenced by cultural attitudes about work, but the fact also remains that the character of the markets in which this agency is exercised is also conditioned by forces and formations outside their direct control (Knight 1978; Fairman-Silva 1993; Littlefield and Knack 1996). The fact that the labor markets American Indians enter are dominated by private sector work in Oklahoma while those in North Dakota are predominately public sector helps us understand not only the different ways women and men participate in these labor markets but also some of the relative disparities in their incomes (Albers and Breen 1996). Acknowledging the press of regional, national, and international market forces requires perspectives radically different from those that focus their lens on single events, eras, or tribal histories. It demands approaches that take a bird's-eye view of their subject, that paint the broad strokes of history, that seek answers through comparative analyses, and that draw on theories that make the embeddedness of tribal nations in today's transnational modes of production intelligible (Hall 1988; Moore 1989; Champagne 1992; Wilkins 1993; Jorgenson 1998).

One of the problems with approaches that focus on determinative conditions, structures, and forces is their steamroller effect. They tend to level everything in their path to fit the agency and raison d'être of an institution without due consideration of the resistance, conflict, and contradictions it faces. American Indian labor history in California, for example, is not a one-sided story of Spanish military power conquering Native peoples and forcing them into labor servitude. It is also a story of the active resistance and rebellion of American Indian populations indentured to the Spanish (Swagerty 1984; Hurtado 1988). The point to be made is that forces and formations that carry a "causal" weight in particular situations do not do so in an unobstructed way. There are always countervailing pressures, evoked and shaped by other conditions and structures and the agencies of the people who are affected by them. Recognizing this does not demand, however, that we throw the proverbial baby out with the bathwater.

If conflationism is a problem in constructionist approaches, then reductionism is a flaw of many materialist forms of explanation. Labor becomes little more than a rote response to some condition or structure. It lacks not only autonomy and agency but also a language, logic, and moral compass whose origins may be related to, yet independent of, the material universe in which it is located. Today, the harvesting of wild rice for family use and market trade is an important arena of production among the Anishinabe of Minnesota and Wisconsin. In the 20th century, its commercial viability was increasingly challenged by competition from agribusiness producers of cultivated "wild" rice (Vennum 1988). As a result, Anishinabe earnings from wild rice production declined; and just in the last decade, the price of hand-processed wild rice plummeted from $10 to $5 per pound. There is no question that various corporate market forces are impacting the grounds and terms on which the Anishinabe are able to sustain their own production for subsistence, ceremonial, and commercial purposes, nor is there any doubt that some of these forces operate in circles difficult for the Anishinabe to penetrate and transform. Nevertheless, alarmed by the inroads of the cultivated varieties on their own production, and now by corporately financed research on the wild rice genome, Anishinabe throughout the upper Midwest are mobilizing to protect their control over and interests in the integrity of the region's remaining stands of naturally occurring wild rice. And they are launching their political and legal efforts through arguments and actions that cannot be exclusively or even easily reduced to material terms. As Thomas Vennum's history (1988) on the subject documents, wild rice is more than a material means to make a living. It is a food heavily laden with social and spiritual meanings, ends, and desires. Its historic and contemporary position in Anishinabe life cannot be adequately understood without reference to its cultural anchorings, and certainly the Anishinabe's labor investments in wild rice production are motivated by cultural issues that may include but certainly transcend the material value of wild rice either as subsistence or as a commercial commodity. Understanding these issues clearly demands a perspective with constructionist leanings. Yet, at the same time, knowledge about how and why Anishinabe interests in wild rice are continually threatened in the modern world requires a historical materialist approach that can make sense of the political and economic machinations of American agribusiness.

Again, the construction of labor and the condition of labor, though related, are not the same thing. Understanding the cultural constructions behind peoples' intentions produces a knowledge that lends itself to forms of interpretation different from those that seek to account for the material base on which people stand. Not only do the methodological and theoretical strategies differ, but the way the questions are formulated differs. By extension, they lead to dissimilar sorts of understandings neither of which needs to subvert or displace the other. What happens in one arena of inquiry informs the other, but from an analytical perspective neither can be reduced to the other (see Archer 1990). These approaches are not irreconcilably antagonistic, as some scholars would lead us to believe, but dialectically related positionings whose very presence is revealed through the process of their mutual articulation.

HISTORICAL MATERIALISM REVISITED

In the past, tribal nations in North America represented what Eric Wolf describes as a "kin-ordered mode of production," which he defines as "a way of committing social labor to the transformation of nature through appeals to filiation and marriage, and to consanguinity and affinity" (1982:91). In other words, kinship identifies and organizes the relationships upon which people make claims to their material and social universes and through which they labor in the making of their own existence.

In the 20th century, kinship remained central to the language of social relations that organized labor in many tribal communities and it also became a critical force in tribal survivance and autonomy (Lamphere 1977; Knack 1980; Albers 1982; Hedley 1993). When I did fieldwork among the Dakota of the Mniwakan Oyate (Spirit Lake People) Reservation in North Dakota 40 years ago, which I believe now qualifies as history, I wrestled with issues of construct and condition especially as these related to understanding how kinship persisted as a viable social formation for sustaining and reproducing the tribe's material survival within a capitalist economy where most socially productive labor becomes alienated from kin-based relations.

Before I arrived at Spirit Lake in 1968, I knew the importance of various cultural values that supported the importance of kinship, sharing, and generosity among the Dakota from reading available ethnographies, oral histories, and linguistic texts. Over the four years I lived there, I heard these values expressed, and I saw them enacted in the flow of everyday life and over a wide range of public events. People talked about their responsibilities to their kin; they spoke about their own acts of sharing and generosity as a way to underscore their identity as Dakota. Giving and sharing among kin were commonplace topics in the conversations that Dakota held when they visited each other. I heard them speak of their desire "to take care of their relations," "to help each other out," and to "be of use to people." I listened to stories about individuals whose actions illustrated generosity and also those whose behavior revealed its antithesis in "stinginess." I watched parents admonish their children, "Don't be stingy" or "Share that with brother." Indeed, ideas about kinship, sharing, giving, and generosity entered discourse in such constant, seamless, and pervasive ways that one could hardly doubt that these were at the heart of the Mniwakan Oyate's scheme of values.

Not only did I hear these values expressed in countless conversations, but I saw them enacted in a wide range of contexts. The sharing of food and cash were routine among kin. Women often gifted each other with clothing, yard goods, blankets, dishes, and a host of other domestic goods in the absence of a special occasion. They gave up a nice shawl because a friend admired it, or they gave a warm coat to someone who did not own one. Help in gardening, food preparation, child care, wood cutting, automobile repair, and housework were commonplace as well. Beyond the everyday acts of giving, generosity was revealed in a host of public "doings" where people gave their time, money, and goods to support a dance or a prayer meeting and where families came together to honor their own through elaborate feasts and giveaways.

Yet I also heard people express their reluctance to give, and I saw many situations where people did not share because they were unable to do so. I also witnessed occasions when people were capable of meeting a request but failed to honor it. I was witness to countless occasions where values were not upheld, where fractures in social relationships even among close kin mitigated against sharing, or where requests to give had become too burdensome to meet. People did make choices, often hard ones, about giving and sharing that sometimes conflicted with and contradicted their own espoused values. But this did not surprise me because I did not expect that an "ideal" universe of values would always be realized in a "real" world of lived experience.

What perplexed me more was the persistence of a larger pattern of kinship and sharing. Why had it continued, albeit in an altered form, after the Dakota were incorporated into a political economic formation governed by capitalism? It would have been easy for me to appeal to a constructionist argument, in which ideas are privileged in defining how people engage their worlds, how they shape and resist outside influences, and ultimately how they persist without destroying the integrity of their own cultural universes. There was no question in my mind that the cultural constructs surrounding the Dakota's notions of kinship and sharing had endured over time and changing circumstance. Nor did I have any doubt that the Spirit Lake Dakota's ideas held considerable force in interpreting how they explained their actions and agency in everyday life. I could have left my interpretation at that, but I did not do so because it begged the question of why the ideas about kinship, sharing, and generosity still exercised such a powerful presence in people's lives.

If I had made the assumption, as many scholars do, that kinship and sharing are determined by the press of ideology, their persistence could have been explained as a form of cultural lag (the passive answer) or cultural resistance (the active response). Here cultural constructs are conservative, that is, traditional, elements that continue from one generation to the next largely through processes of socialization and identity maintenance. The problem as I saw it (and still see it) is that persistence gets enclosed in an ideological vacuum, severed from the social connections and existential conditions that give it life.

Instead, I took the position that kinship and the moral responsibilities it inspires remain vital because they have work to perform in the present (Albers 1982:253–254). More specifically, I argued that the particular manner in which Dakota reservations were linked to the political economic formations of capitalism fostered the persistence of an attenuated arena of domestic provisioning where a historically developed pattern of kinship continued to exist as the dominant relations of production. The purpose of my analysis was to show not only how this pattern of kinship dialectically engaged the material forces and conditions that defined the Dakota's universe of work and provisioning three decades ago, but also how it created a sense of cultural autonomy in a situation where people had become dependent on transfer payments and transient wage labor for their survival. In the end, I explained how this particular pattern of kinship and sharing offered a workable solution for surviving the depths of poverty that the wider economy and its federal policies had imposed on the Dakota.

For Native North America, an important historical question is when and under what conditions have kinship and its associated moral obligations been diminished rather than redeployed as was in the case for the Dakota at Spirit Lake. One answer is offered by Max Hedley (1993) in his study of the Walpole Island Reserve in Canada. His work shows that kinship cooperation and support were effective until World War II. After the war, when mass movements into wage labor took place, customary patterns of collaboration among kin were disrupted. Even though many kinship values continued to be upheld, at least as ideals, the social relations through which these were realized in day-to-day provisioning eroded as other agencies and interests laid claim to people's labor and resources. But wage labor is not always erosive of kinship and its values. Kurt Peters's work (1996) on Acoma and Laguna railway workers transported to California suggests that they recreated many aspects of their kinship and domestic social formations in their new home as is the case with Mohawk steelworkers in Brooklyn (Voget 1953; Hill 1987; Katzer 1988). That wage labor does not always undermine kinship as a basis for organizing relations of provisioning and support in American Indian communities does not mean, however, that it should be ignored in understanding the persistence of kinship in its various forms. It only implies that the articulations between wage labor and kinship are variable and need to be tracked and understood in relation to the historically specific situations in which they are engaged.

Although many writings that draw on historical materialism as a theory and methodology contain narrow, unidirectional, and even doctrinaire interpretations of what happens when kin-ordered social formations and modes of production meet capitalism, these are not the inevitable and only result of this approach. Quite the contrary, and notwithstanding some of Marx's own misguided reconstructions of the place of kinship in various stages of history (which most scholars now recognize were limited by the information available to him in the 19th century), historical materialism is a perspective that can offer much insight for understanding how labor is enveloped in the totality of relationships connecting conditions, relations, and ideas and in the process shaping the way history unfolds at particular places and moments in time.

CONCLUSION

Reading American Indian history with a heavy culturally relativistic hand often creates an overly conventionalized view of human labor that conflates cultural constructions with lived experience. It can lead to spurious and overly exoticized separations between the experiences of American Indian people and those of European American, African American, and Asian American origins. On the other hand, reading with a materialistic grip that is too tight often ignores the culturally distinct and conventionalized ideas that mold and shape the ways people confront their historical circumstances. It can create monolithic, unidirectional models overdetermined by the weight of material conditions and forces in history.

Historical materialism offers one methodology for bridging the divide between cultural constructs and material conditions, even though it is often misunderstood and read in reductionist terms as a form of economic determinism. Insofar as it understands material conditions as having a profound press on the human condition, it does give priority to the concrete corporeal world. But it is not restricted to this. Good historical materialist work engages dialectically and dynamically the conditions under which labor is engaged with the constructions that shape its outcome—just as the poetics and politics of good cultural theory dialectically and dynamically engage the constructions fashioning labor against the conditions that serve as limits and possibilities to its final unfolding.

REFERENCES

Aberle, David
    1967   The Peyote Religion among the Navajo. Chicago: Aldine Press.

Albers, Patricia
    1982   Sioux Kinship in a Colonial Setting. Dialectical Anthropology 7:253–269.
    1985   Autonomy and Dependency in the Lives of Dakota Women: A Study in Historical Change. Review of Radical Political Economics 17(3):109–134.
    1993   Symbiosis, Merger, and War: Contrasting Forms of Intertribal Relationship among Historic Plains Indians. In The Political Economy of North American Indians. J. Moore, ed. Pp. 94–132. Norman: University of Oklahoma Press.
    1996   Changing Configurations of Ethnicity in the Northeastern Plains. In Culture, Power, and History: Ethnogenesis in the Americas, 1492–1992. J. Hill, ed. Pp. 90–118. Iowa City: University of Iowa Press.

Albers, Patricia, and Nancy Breen
    1996   Reaching Gender Parity: The Case of American Indians on or near Tribal Reservations and Historic Areas. Race, Class and Gender 3:75–95.

Albers, Patricia, and William James
    1985   Historical Materialism vs. Evolutionary Ecology: A Methodological Note on Horse Distribution and American Plains Indians. Critique of Anthropology 6(1):87–100.
    1991   Horses without People: A Critique of Neoclassical Ecology. In Explorations in Political Economy: Essays in Criticism. R. K. Kanth and E. K. Hunt, eds. Pp. 5–31. Savage, MD: Rowman and Littlefield.

Albers, Patricia, and Beatrice Medicine
    1983   The Role of Sioux Women in the Production of Ceremonial Objects: The Case of the Star Quilt. In The Hidden Half: Studies of Plains Indian Women. P. Albers and B. Medicine, eds. Pp.123–142. Washington, DC: University Press of America.

Anders, Gary
    1979   The Internal Colonization of Cherokee Native Americans. Development and Change 10(1):41–55.

Anderson, Gary
    1984   Kinsmen of Another Kind: Dakota-White Relations in the Upper Mississippi Valley, 1650–1862. Lincoln: University of Nebraska Press.

Archer, Barbara
    1990   Culture and Agency: The Place of Culture in Social Theory. New York: Cambridge University Press.

Basso, Keith
    1996   Wisdom Sits in Places. Albuquerque: University of New Mexico Press.

Biolsi, Thomas
    1992   Organizing the Lakota: The Political Economy of the New Deal on the Pine Ridge and Rosebud Reservations. Tucson: University of Arizona Press.
    1993   The Political Economy of Lakota Consciousness. *In* The Political Economy of North American Indians. J. Moore, ed. Pp. 20–42. Norman: University of Oklahoma Press.

Bishop, Charles A.
    1972   Demography, Ecology, and Trade among the Northern Ojibwa and Swampy Cree. Special issues: The Fur Trade in Canada. Western Canadian Journal of Anthropology 3(1):58–71.
    1974   The Northern Ojibwa and the Fur Trade: A Historical and Ecological Study. Toronto: Holt, Rinehart and Winston of Canada.

Braund, Kathryn E. Holland
    1993   Deerskins & Duffels: The Creek Indian Trade and Anglo-America. Lincoln: University of Nebraska Press.

Brightman, Robert
    1993   Grateful Prey: Rock Cree Human-Animal Relationships. Berkeley: University of California Press.

Carter, Sarah
    1990   Lost Harvest: Prairie Indians and Reserve Farming. Montreal: McGill-Queen's University Press.

Champagne, Duane
    1992   Economic Culture, Institutional Order, and Sustained Market Enterprise: Comparisons of Historical and Contemporary American Indian Cases. *In* Property Rights and Indian Economies. T. Anderson, ed. Pp. 195–213. Lanham, MD: Rowman and Littlefield.

Churchill, Ward, ed.
    1983   Marxism and Native Americans. Boston: South End Press.

Clemmer, Richard
    1977   Hopi Political Economy: Industrialization and Alienation. Southwest Economy and Society 2(2):4–33.

Conte, Christine
    1982   Ladies, Livestock and Lucre: Women's Networks and Social Status on the Western Navajo Reservation. American Indian Quarterly 6(1–2):105–124.

Cox, Bruce
    1984   Indian "Middemen" and the Early Fur Trade: Reconsidering the Position of the Hudson's Bay Company's "Trading Indians." *In* Rendezvous: Selected Papers of the Fourth North American Fur Trade Conference, 1981. T. C. Buckley, ed. St. Paul.
    1993   Natives and the Development of Mercantile Capitalism: A New Look at "Opposition" in the Eighteenth-Century Fur Trade. *In* The Political Economy of

North American Indians. J. H. Moore, ed. Pp. 87–93. Norman: University of Oklahoma Press.

Cronon, William
1983   Changes in the Land: Indians, Colonist, and the Ecology of New England. New York: Hill and Wang.

DeMallie, Raymond
1993   "These Have No Ears": Narrative and the Ethnohistorical Method. Ethnohistory 40(4):515–538.

Dirlik, Arif
1999   The Past as Legacy and Project: Postcolonial Criticism in the Perspective of Indigenous Historicism. In Contemporary Native American Political Issues, T. R. Johnson, ed. Pp. 73–98. Walnut Creek, CA: AltaMira Press.

Drucker, Philip, and Robert F. Heizer
1967   To Make My Name Good: A Reexamination of the Southern Kwakiutl Potlatch. Berkeley: University of California Press.

Engels, Friedrich
1948   The Origin of the Family, Private Property, and the State. Moscow: Progressive.

Fairman-Silva, Sandra
1993   Multinational Corporate Development in the American Hinterland: The Case of the Oklahoma Choctaws. In The Political Economy of North American Indians. J. H. Moore, ed. Pp. 214–239. Norman: University of Oklahoma Press.

Feit, Harvey
1988   Waswanipi Cree Management of Land and Wildlife: Cree Ethno-Ecology Revisited. In Native Peoples, Native Lands. B. Cox, ed. Pp. 75–91. Ottawa: Carlton University Press.

Forbes, Jack D.
1991   Envelopment, Proletarianization and Interiorization: Aspects of Colonialism's Impact upon Native Americans and Other People of Color in Eastern North America. Journal of Ethnic Studies 18(4):95–122.

Foster, J. E.
1988   The Home Guard Cree and the Hudson's Bay Company: The First Hundred Years. In Native Peoples, Native Lands. B. Cox, ed. Pp. 107–119. Ottawa: Carlton University Press.

Fowler, Loretta
1987   Shared Symbols, Contested Meanings: Gros Ventres Culture and History, 1778–1984. Ithaca, NY: Cornell University Press.

Gleach, Frederic
1996   Controlled Speculation: Interpreting the Saga of Pocahontas and Captain John Smith. In Reading beyond Words: Contexts for Native History. J. Brown and E. Vibert, eds. Pp. 21–42. Toronto: Broadview Press.

Goldfrank, Esther
1945   Changing Configurations in the Social Organization of the Blackfoot Tribe in the Reserve Period. American Ethnological Society Monograph, 8. Seattle: University of Washington Press.

Hall, Thomas D.

1988   The Patterns of Native American Incorporation. *In* Public Policy Impacts on American Indian Economic Development. C. M. Snipp, ed. Pp. 23–38. Albuquerque: Native American Studies. Institute for Native American Development. University of New Mexico Development Series, 4.

1989   Social Change in the Southwest, 1350–1880. Lawrence: University Press of Kansas.

Hayden, Brian, ed.

1992   A Complex Culture of the British Columbia Plateau: Traditional Stl'átl'imix Resource Use. Vancouver: University of British Columbia Press.

Hedley, Max

1993   Autonomy and Constraint: The Household Economy on a Southern Ontario Reserve. *In* The Political Economy of North American Indians. J. Moore, ed. Pp. 184–213.

Hickerson, Harold

1960   The Feast of the Dead among Seventeenth Century Algonkian of the Upper Great Lakes. American Anthropologist 62:81–107.

1967   Some Implications of the Theory of Atomism. Current Anthropology 8:313–345.

1971   The Chippewa and Their Neighbors: A Study in Ethnohistory. New York: Holt, Rinehart, and Winston.

1973   Fur Trade Colonialism and the North American Indians. Journal of Ethnic Studies 1:15–44.

Hill, Richard

1987   Skywalkers: A History of Indian Ironworkers. Brantford, Ontario: Woodland Indian Cultural Educational Center.

Hobsbawn, Eric

1980   Introduction to Karl Marx's Pre-Capitalist Economic Formations. New York: New World Paperbacks.

Hosmer, Brian

1991   Creating Indian Entrepreneurs: Menominees, Neopit Mills, and Timber Exploitation, 1890–1915. American Indian Culture and Research Journal 15(1):1–28.

1997   Reflections on Indian Cultural "Brokers": Reginald Oshkosh, Mitchell Oshkenaniew, and the Politics of Menominee Lumbering. Ethnohistory 44(3):493–510.

1999   American Indians in the Marketplace: Persistence and Innovation among the Menominees and Metlakatlans, 1870–1920. Lawrence: University Press of Kansas.

Hurtado, Albert

1988   Indian Survival on the California Frontier. New Haven: Yale University Press.

Iverson, Peter

1997   When Indians Became Cowboys: Native Peoples and Cattle Ranching in the American West. Norman: University of Oklahoma Press.

Jablow, Joseph

1951   The Cheyenne in Plains Indian Trade Relations, 1795–1840. Monographs of the American Ethnological Society, 19. Seattle: University of Washington Press.

Jacobson, Cardell K.

1984   Internal Colonialism and Native Americans: Indian Labor in the United States from 1871 to World War II. Social Science Quarterly 65(1):158–171.

Jorgenson, Joseph

1971   Indians and the Metropolis. In The American Indian in Urban Society. J. O. Waddell and O. M. Watson, eds. Pp. 67–113. Boston: Little Brown.

1972   The Sundance Religion: Power for the Powerless. Chicago: University of Chicago Press.

1978   A Century of Political Economic Effects on American Indian Society, 1880–1890. Journal of Ethnic Studies 6(3):1–82.

1998   Gaming and Recent American Indian Economic Development. American Indian Culture and Research Journal 22(3):157–172.

Kan , Sergei

1993   Symbolic Immortality: The Tlingit Potlatch of the Nineteenth Century. Washington, DC: Smithsonian Institution Press.

Katzer, Bruce

1988   The Caughnawaga Mohawk: The Other Side of Ironwork. Journal of Ethnic Studies 15:39–55.

Kay, Jeanne

1979   Wisconsin Indian Hunting Patterns, 1634–1836. Annals of the Association of American Geographers 69:402–418.

Klein, Alan

1977   Adaptive Strategies and Process on the Plains: The 19th Century Cultural Sink. Ph.D. dissertation, State University of New York at Buffalo.

1980   Plains Economic Analysis: The Marxist Complement. In R. Wood and M. Liberty, eds. Anthropology on the Great Plains. Lincoln: University of Nebraska Press.

1993   Political Economy of the Buffalo Hide Trade: Race and Class on the Plains. In The Political Economy of North American Indians. J. H. Moore, ed. Pp. 133–160. Norman: University of Oklahoma Press.

Knack, Martha

1980   Life Is with People: Household Organization of the Contemporary Southern Paiute Indians. Socorro, NM: Ballena Press Anthropological Papers, 19.

1986   Indian Economies, 1950–1980. In Handbook of North American Indians, vol. 11. Great Basin. W. L. d'Azevado, ed. Pp. 573–591. Washington, DC: Smithsonian Institution Press.

1987   The Role of Credit in Native American Adaptation to the Great Basin Ranching Economy. American Indian Culture and Research Journal 11:43–65.

Knight, Rolf

1968   Ecological Factors in Changing Economy and Social Organization among the Rupert House Cree. National Museum of Canada Anthropology Paper, 15. Ottawa.

1978   Indians at Work: An Informal History of Native American Labour in British Columbia, 1858–1930. Vancouver: New Star Books.

Krech, Shepard, III
    1984   The Subarctic Fur Trade: Native and Social Adaptations. Vancouver: University of British Columbia Press.
    1999   The Ecological Indian: Myth and History. New York: W. W. Norton.
Lamphere, Louise
    1976   The Internal Colonization of the Navajo People. Southwest Economy and Society 1:6–13.
    1977   To Run After Them. Tucson: University of Arizona Press.
Leacock, Eleanor
    1954   The Montagnais "Hunting Territory" and the Fur Trade. Memoirs of the American Anthropological Association, 78. Menasha, WI.
    1978   Women's Status in Egalitarian Society: Implications of Social Evolution. Current Anthropology 19:247–276.
    1980   Montagnais Women and the Jesuit Program for Colonization. In Women and Colonization. M. Etienne and E. Leacock, eds. Pp. 25–42. New York: Praeger.
    1981   Myths of Male Dominance. New York: Monthly Review Press.
    1982   Marxism and Anthropology. In The Left Academy. B. Ollman and E. Vernoff, eds. New York: McGraw-Hill.
Leacock, Eleanor, and Nancy Lurie, eds.
    1971   North American Indians in Historical Perspective. New York: Random House.
Lewis, David Rich
    1997   Neither Wolf Nor Dog: American Indians, Environment, and Agrarian Change. New York: Oxford University Press.
Lewis, Oscar
    1942   The Effects of White Contact upon Blackfoot Culture. Monographs of the American Ethnological Society, 6. Seattle: University of Washington Press.
Littlefield, Alice, and Martha Knack, eds.
    1996   Native Americans and Wage Labor: Ethnohistorical Perspectives. Norman: University of Oklahoma Press.
MacDowell, Marsha L., and C. Kurt Dewhurst
    1997   To Honor and Comfort: Native Quilting Traditions. Santa Fe: Museum of New Mexico Press in association with Michigan State University Press.
Marx, Karl
    1963   The Eighteenth Brumaire of Louis Bonaparte. New York: International.
    1967   Capital, vol. 1. New York: International.
    1970   A Contribution to the Critique of Political Economy. New York: International.
    1973   Grundrisse. New York: Vintage Books.
Marx, Karl, and Friederich Engels
    1947   The German Ideology. New York: International.
McLaughlin, Castle
    1988   Nation, Tribe, and Class: The Dynamics of Agrarian Transformation on the Fort Berthold Reservation. American Indian Culture and Research Journal 22(3):101–138.
Merrell, James H.
    1989   The Indians' New World: Catawbas and Their Neighbors from European Con-

tact through the Era of Removal. Chapel Hill: University of North Carolina
Press.

Moore, John

1974   Cheyenne Political History, 1829–1894. Ethnohistory 2:329–359.

1989   The Myth of the Lazy Indian: Native American Contributions to the U.S.
Economy. Nature, Society, and Thought 2(2):195–215.

1993   Political Economy in Anthropology. In The Political Economy of North American Indians. J. H. Moore, ed. Pp. 3–19. Norman: University of Oklahoma
Press.

1996   The History of Cheyenne Work in the History of U.S. Capitalism. In Native
Americans and Wage Labor: Ethnohistorical Perspectives. A. Littlefield and
M. C. Knack, eds. Pp. 122–143. Norman: University of Oklahoma Press.

Morgan, Lewis Henry

1851   League of the Ho-dé-no-sau-nee or Iroquois. Rochester, NY: Sage Books.

1871   Systems of Consanguinity and Affinity of the Human Family. Smithsonian
Contributions to Knowledge, 17.

1877   Ancient Society. New York: Henry Holt.

Nowack, Barbara

1976   Women's Roles and Status in a Changing Iroquois Society. In Sex Roles in
Changing Cultures. A. McElroy and C. Matthiasson, eds. Pp. 95–111. Occa-
sional Papers in Anthropology, 1. Buffalo: Department of Anthropology,
State University of New York.

Oberg, Kalervo

1973   The Tlingit Social Economy. Seattle: University of Washington Press.

Osborn, Alan

1983   Ecological Aspects of Equestrian Adaptations in Aboriginal North America.
American Anthropologist 85:563–591.

Perdue, Theda

1998   Cherokee Women. Lincoln: University of Nebraska Press.

Perry, Richard

1979   The Fur Trade and the Status of Women in the Western Subarctic. Ethnohistory 26:363–376.

Peters, Kurt

1996   Watering the Flower: Laguna Pueblo and the Santa Fe Railroad, 1880–1943.
In Native Americans and Wage Labor: Ethnohistorical Perspectives. A. Little-
field and M. C. Knack, eds. Pp. 177–197. Norman: University of Oklahoma
Press.

Piddocke, Stuart

1965   The Potlatch System of the Southern Kwakiutl: A New Perspective. Southwestern Journal of Anthropology 21(33):244–264.

Ray, Arthur

1974   Indians in the Fur Trade: Their Role as Trappers, Hunters, and Middlemen in
the Lands Southwest of Hudson's Bay, 1660–1780. Toronto: University of
Toronto Press.

1988   The Hudson's Bay Company and Native People. In Handbook of American

Indians, vol. 4. History of Indian-White Relations. W. Washburn, ed. Pp. 335–350. Washington, DC: Smithsonian Institution.

1990   The Canadian Fur Trade in the Industrial Age. Toronto: University of Toronto Press.

Ray, Arthur, and Donald Freeman
1978   Give Us Good Measure: An Economic Analysis of Relations between Indians and the Hudson's Bay Company before 1763. Toronto: University of Toronto Press.

Rothenberg, Diane
1980   The Mothers of the Nation: Seneca Resistance to Quaker Intervention. *In* Women and Colonization. M. Etienne and E. Leacock. Pp. 63–87. New York: Praeger.

Ruffing, Lorraine
1979   The Navajo Nation: A History of Dependence and Underdevelopment. Review of Radical Political Economics 2:25–37.

Sattler, Richard A.
1998   Cowboys and Indians: Creek and Seminole Stock Raising, 1700–1900. American Indian Culture and Research Journal 22(3):79–100.

Schwartz, Maureen
1998   Molded in the Image of Changing Woman. Tucson: University of Arizona Press.

Shoemaker, Nancy, ed.
1995   Negotiators of Change: Historical Perspectives on Native American Women. New York: Routledge.

Snipp, C. Matthew
1986a   American Indians and Resource Development. American Journal of Economics and Sociology 45:145–157.
1986b   The Changing Political and Economic Status of American Indians: From Captive Nations to Internal Colonies. American Journal of Economics and Sociology 45:457–474.

Spradley, James P., ed.
1969   Guests Never Leave Hungry: The Autobiography of James Sewid, a Kwakiutl Indian. New Haven: Yale University Press.

State of Idaho
1970   State of Idaho v. Gerald Cleo Tinno, District Court of the Seventh Judicial District of the State of Idaho in and for the County of Custer, State of Idaho (April 1), 04-759. Court Transcript of Testimony.
1972   State of Idaho v. Gerald Cleo Tinno, District Court of the Seventh Judicial District of the State of Idaho in and for the County of Custer, State of Idaho (June 8), 04-759. Court Transcript of Supreme Court Decision.

Suttles, Wayne
1960   Affinal Ties, Subsistence, and Prestige Among the Coast Salish. American Anthropologist 62(2):296–305.

Swagerty, William R.
1984   Spanish-Indian Relations, 1513–1821. *In* Scholars and the Indian Experience: Critical Reviews of Recent Writing in the Social Sciences. W. R. Swagerty, ed.

Pp. 36–78 Bloomington: Indian University Press for D'Arcy McNickle Center for American Indian History, Newberry Library, Chicago.

1988   Indian Trade in the Trans-Mississippi West to 1870. *In* Handbook of American Indians, vol. 4: History of Indian-White Relations. W. Washburn, ed. Pp. 351–374. Washington, DC: Smithsonian Institution Press.

Tanner, Adrian

1979   Bringing Home Animals: Religious Ideology and Mode of Production of the Mistasini Cree Hunters. St. John's Institute of Social and Economic Research, Memorial University of New Foundland.

Trosper, Ronald

1978   American Indian Relative Ranching Efficiency. American Economic Review 68(4):503–516.

1999   Traditional American Indian Economic Policy. *In* Contemporary Native American Political Issues. T. R. Johnson, ed. Pp. 139–162. Walnut Creek, CA: AltaMira Press.

Usner, Daniel H., Jr.

1992   Indians, Settlers, & Slaves in a Frontier Exchange Economy: The Lower Mississippi Valley before 1783. Chapel Hill: University of North Carolina Press.

Vayda, Andrew

1961   A Re-examination of Northwest Coast Economic Systems. Transactions of the New York Academy of Sciences, ser. 2, vol. 23:618–624.

Vennum, Thomas, Jr.

1988   Wild Rice and the Ojibway People. St. Paul: Minnesota Historical Society Press.

Vinje, David

1985   Cultural Values and Economic Development. *In* American Indian Policy in the 20th Century. V. Deloria, ed. Pp. 155–175. Norman: University of Oklahoma Press.

Voget, Fred

1953   Kinship Changes at Caughnawaga. American Anthropologist 55:385–395.

Weiss, Lawrence

1984   The Development of Capitalism in the Navajo Nation: A Political-Economic History. Minneapolis: Marxist Educational Press.

White, Bruce

1982   "Give Us a Little Milk": The Social and Cultural Meanings of Gift Giving in the Lake Superior Fur Trade. Minnesota History 48:2–12.

1994   Encounters with Spirits: Ojibwa and Dakota Theories about the French and Their Merchandise. Ethnohistory 41(3):369–406.

White, Richard

1983   The Roots of Dependency: Subsistence, Environment and Social Change among the Choctaws, Pawnees, and Navajos. Lincoln: University of Nebraska Press.

1984   Native Americans and the Environment. *In* Scholars and the Indian Experience: Critical Reviews of Recent Writing in the Social Sciences. W. R. Swagerty, ed. Pp. 179–204. Bloomington: Indiana University Press for D'Arcy McNickle Center for American Indian History, Newberry Library, Chicago.

White, Richard, and William Cronon

    1988   Ecological Change and Indian-White Relations. *In* Handbook of American Indians, vol. 4: History of Indian-White Relations. W. Washburn, ed. Pp. 417–429. Washington, DC: Smithsonian Institution Press.

Wilkins, David E.

    1993   Modernization, Colonialism, Dependency: How Appropriate Are These Models for Providing an Explanation of North American Indian "Underdevelopment"? Ethnic and Racial Studies 16(3):390–419.

Wishart, David J.

    1979   The Fur Trade of the American West: 1807–1840: A Geographical Synthesis. Lincoln: University of Nebraska Press.

Wittfogel, Karl, and Esther Goldfrank

    1957   Some Aspects of Pueblo Mythology and Society. Journal of American Folklore 56:17–30.

Wolf, Eric. R.

    1982   Europe and the People without History. Berkeley: University of California Press.

Primary Sources: Indian Goods and the History of American Colonialism and the 19th-Century Reservation

Jacki Thompson Rand

"Culture" is never separate from, and cannot be understood apart from, politics and economy.
—Micaela di Leonardo, *Exotics at Home*, 1998

Throughout the last half of the 19th century, American Indian tribes throughout the Great Plains signed treaties and moved onto reservations carved out of traditional Native homelands. Through their scholarship, historians and anthropologists alike have made reservation boundaries synonymous with a now standard break in the periodization of American Indian studies.[1] For historians, the time before reservation boundaries involved a great struggle between westward expansion and tribal retention of political autonomy and homelands.[2] Anthropologists write of the time before reservations as one of cultures untainted by the radical changes imposed on tribes during the reservation period. Following reservation treaties Native history becomes one of economic, political, and cultural decline in the wake of individual tribal struggles and failures to stop the American advance across the Plains (Mooney 1979:ix–x, 218).

Through more recent reservation literature runs a common thread that indirectly challenges the reservation boundary as a fixed and impermeable temporal marker, as well as a social, cultural, and political barrier (Asher 1999; Hoxie 1995). Was the reservation boundary impermeable? Did it function in the ways treaty documents described? What place did the reservation boundary have in daily life? The quick answer is that reservation boundaries affected

Native American lives in different ways. In some, the significance of the boundary is not whether it kept people in or out but how daily life required them to transcend it. For others, the reservation boundary imposed a segregation from mainstream American society that only reinforced tribal cultures and identities.

This essay participates in the inquiry that revisits the reservation period in American Indian history. Taking material objects and the pathways they follow as a point of exploration, it complicates the history of a more or less purposeful and progressive "rational plan" of American hegemony over Native tribes, the outcomes for Native peoples, and the idea of the reservation as a final chapter. Following Nicholas Thomas's work on colonial culture, Arjun Appadurai's study of the social life of things, and other theoretical sources, this essay is taken from a larger project focused on the Kiowa tribe of the southern plains that challenges the presumed inevitability of conquest. The question "What endures?" frames the ironic consequences of peoples' daily lives, the social lives of things that contribute to and interact with human practice, and the histories of peoples joined to the objects with which their lives were intertwined.

Colonialism, Thomas argues in *Colonialism's Culture: Anthropology, Travel and Government* (1994), has been misunderstood as a static, transhistorical condition, the product of imposed hegemonic control by a metropolitan society over peoples who are organized along tribal principles. This model is characterized by primarily unequal economic and political relationships based in a Western ideology of racial hierarchy and European quest for empire. Control over indigenous peoples was a key function of colonial governments, according to this interpretation of colonialism, which they carried out through the deployment of effective, consistent, and unified policies and goals. The structure and purpose of colonialism were rational, progressive, and replicated from one locale to another.

Thomas challenges the conventional concept of colonialism as an artifact of the 19th century and its binary opposite of a postcolonial world. Rather, he offers a model of an ongoing cultural process that creates and is created by economic, social, and political relationships between the colonized and colonizers. In addition to relegating colonialism to the distant past, scholars, Thomas argues, have exaggerated historic colonial power and granted it a consistency and uniformity of purpose and action that is assumed rather than an accurate reflection of local conditions. As a consequence scholars discount indigenous noncompliance (ranging from rebellion to covert retention of cultural practices), diplomatic ingenuity, and other various strategies as temporary obstacles to an inevitable conclusion. Colonizers were exploitive and destructive, but they also exhibited anxieties, limitations, and inadequacies that interfered with the rational plan. It was not necessarily the best and brightest who peopled the front lines of expansion, carried out colonial administration, fought tribes, and implemented policies. Colonizers could be dependent on the peoples they aspired to overcome, and even, at times, at their complete mercy. Except in cases of total genocide, brute force was an option that frequently failed as a means to establishing long-term total control. Rather, indigenous agency, colonial compromise of its own mission, local conditions, and collaboration based frequently on antithetical motives tell other complicated histories that lie beneath the narratives of official colonial administrations and national histories.

The Kiowa reservation period, the subject of this essay, is a history of war (Nye 1968), but it is also a history of conspiracy between the environment and politics that brought starvation to the Kiowas' feet. In the face of American expansion, food and other goods continued to circulate, now across reservation boundary lines. This activity provides a glimpse of the early reservation economy and Kiowa society, particularly involving relations between young men and on- and off-reservation leaders. Young Kiowa men, archetypes of warrior culture and youthful audacity, maintained Kiowa social conventions and values that shaped them, and challenged a weakening resolve among band leaders to reject the reservation.

Negotiators of the 1867 Treaty of Medicine Lodge Creek, which defined the Kiowa reservation, had verbally promised rations for the Indians if the leaders signed the agreement (Kappler 1972:977–984). Rations were crucial to a transition from Plains to reservation as envisioned by the United States government for the Kiowa people. The government proposed, however, to supplement, not replace, the Indians' traditional diet with rations as they embarked on the hoped-for transition to agriculture. The ill-conceived plan reflected the government's failure to recognize the implications of the Kiowas' dwindling traditional sources of nutrition. A decreasing buffalo population in the southern Plains reduced an important food source, requiring more time and labor to sustain subsistence levels. Meanwhile, the reservation plan would divert the Indians' hunting and trading time and labor to agricultural start-ups. The combined diversion of Indian labor to farming and delimited hunting territories reduced the Indians' subsistence sources drastically.

The offering of food and annuities was consistent with the prereservation history of diplomacy on the southern Plains. Gifts had long played an important role between the tribes and earlier colonial occupiers.[3] Kiowa and Comanche leaders first grew accustomed to receiving annuities and rations in the form of gifts during the Spanish and Mexican colonial occupation of the Southwest and Texas. After the 1820 Mexican revolution, levels of gift giving in New Mexico and Texas became uneven and sporadic, but shortly thereafter the American presence on the southern Plains introduced another source of gifts, while the Texas Republic also used gifts in its political relations with the southern Plains tribes (Anderson 1999).

The 1853 Treaty of Fort Atkinson between the United States and the southern Plains tribes provided an $18,000 annuity as payment for the tribes' cooperation, and "for the better support and the improvement of the social condition of the said tribes" for a period of ten years (Kappler 1972:600–602). The government used the annuity payment for its purposes, the acculturation of Native tribes, rather than turn the funds over to the Kiowas for their own use. Thereafter, the Kiowas, Comanches, and Apaches gathered on the Arkansas River for the annual distribution of goods paid for with their compensatory funds. The tribes' experience with the Americans insinuated a suggestion of dependency in their relationship, which the Kiowas routinely rejected by "audacious and insolent" behaviors during the distribution of goods (Cumming 1856:72; Manypenny 1856:11).

Kiowa aggression was evident the following year, when annuity goods arrived at Fort Atkinson on July 8 from Westport, Missouri. Again, the Kiowas confidently displayed their usual contempt for the agent, Robert C. Miller, and disregard for the authority he tried to exert. When he attempted to delay the distribution until all the bands had arrived, the Kiowas left in great displeasure only to return with armed young men who threatened to take the goods by force. The Comanche contingent's intervention prevented violence, but the Kiowas claimed the upper hand, the agent reported: "They said they knew their Great Father sent them presents because he feared them; that he was no brave, or he would not talk so much, but would act; would send the soldiers. . . ." Agent Miller could only lament what he perceived as a practice of rewarding the Kiowas with "presents as if they had done no wrong, and this regularly every year" (Miller 1857:143). The wrong Agent Miller alluded to was Kiowa aggressions against American travelers and settler homesteads in violation of their agreements with the government.

The initial reports to the Commissioner of Indian Affairs from the Indian agent of the Upper Arkansas attested to the changing face of southern Plains diplomacy and economy as a result of the American presence. Dohausen, the highly respected headman who was probably the last to command recognition of his leadership from all Kiowa bands, described it himself as quoted in the agent's report for 1857.

The white chief is a fool; he is a coward; his heart is small—not larger than a pebble stone; his men are not strong—too few to contend against my warriors; they are women. There are three chiefs—the white chief, the Spanish chief, and myself. The Spanish and myself are men; we do bad towards each other sometimes, stealing horses and taking scalps, but we do not get mad and act the fool. The white chief is a child, and like a child gets mad quick. When my young men, to keep their women and children from starving, take from the white man passing through our country, killing and driving away our buffalo, a cup of sugar or coffee, the "white chief" is angry and threatens to send his soldiers. I have looked for them a long time, but they have not come; he is a coward; his heart is a woman's. I have spoken. Tell the "great chief" what I have said. [Miller 1858:99]

Dohausen rightly recognized that the Americans did not conform to the spirit of the old southern Plains economy. The establishment of the Santa Fe Trail in the 1820s, the annexation of Texas in 1846, and a growing number of military posts brought American settlers into the region. Demands to protect these fledgling commercial links from hostile tribes guaranteed a growing federal presence on the southern Plains. In 1857, as the Kiowas observed, the military presence on the southern plains was indeed small and ineffective, a situation favorable to the Kiowas, who found isolated American settlers inviting sources of stock and captives for trade.

Ten years later, the Kiowas, Comanches, and Apaches signed the 1867 Treaty of Medicine Lodge Creek. From the outset, irregularities in the delivery of rations strained relations between the reservation agent, Jesse Leavenworth, and the Kiowa leaders. One account described a confrontation between Stumbling Bear and other Kiowa leaders and Agent Leavenworth. They charged the agent with requiring Kiowa horses, mules, and cattle in exchange for the promised rations. Stumbling Bear, speaking for the other leaders, said, "It is a better thing to trade [Indian goods] then [sic] take them by force" explaining the Kiowas' willingness to exchange their animals for food (Stanton 1867).

Stumbling Bear's indictment of the agent's activities calls attention to the distinction between *Indian goods* and *trade goods*. The term *Indian goods*, commonly found in primary government documents, is a polyvalent category and object of exchange, that is, one defined by a process of circulation that designates the receivers and the givers as Indians. Indian goods might refer to trade goods such as horses (stolen or traded), blankets, buffalo robes, hides of various game animals, and other masculine objects of exchange. It might also

signify goods, including cloth, beads, German silver, and rations presented by
the authorities to Indian negotiators during treaty talks. Indian goods, therefore, can be synonymous with other terms that appear in government documents. Trinkets or goo-gaws and curios may refer to items produced mainly by
Indian women, such as beaded moccasins, beaded bags, and jewelry, using Indian goods or manufactured goods such as Czech beads, metal studs, silver
buttons, and the findings required for the production of trinkets.

Indian goods, in treaty parlance, signified rations and annuity goods; *trade
goods* referred to horses, mules, and cattle, as well as manufactured goods that
circulated among tribes and traders. Stumbling Bear's admonition to the agent
made clear the Indians' awareness of the distinction. They were not interchangeable. Indian goods were a payment for ceded lands and cooperation.
They were not a gift, nor charity, but rather the government's obligation to the
Kiowa people for their signatures to the treaty of Medicine Lodge Creek. But
Stumbling Bear, and apparently other Kiowa headmen, were willing to provide
their trade goods for the Indian goods although they were not bound to do so
by treaty. According to Stumbling Bear, it was a "better way to trade for our
own goods, then take them by force," suggesting that the Kiowas had trade
goods and the means of force available to them, but chose the path of exchange over confrontation with the authorities.

The objects and the pathways they followed help to recover the histories of
people who are not so apparent in conventional sources. As Arjun Appadurai
reminds us:

> Even if our own approach to things is conditioned necessarily by the
> view that things have no meanings apart from those that human transac-
> tions, attributions and motivations endow them with, the anthropologi-
> cal problem is that this formal truth does not illuminate the concrete,
> historical circulation of things . . . even though from a *theoretical* point
> of view human actors encode things with significance, from a *method-
> ological* point of view it is the things-in-motion that illuminate their hu-
> man and social context. [Appadurai 1986:5]

Subjects may endow objects with significance, but we locate it along the pathways objects follow from production through exchange(s) to destinations far
from their production points. When objects divert from conventional pathways, that, too, is significant (Appadurai 1986:26).

Objects of indigenous trade or of trade between colonized and colonizers
are entangled in ideas about the nature of indigenous economies. Prereserva-

tion "subsistence" economies have been viewed as something outside and inferior to Western market forces. In this paradigm, trade becomes a means by
which Western forces impose external economic pressures and thereby sub-
sume Native peoples into dominant markets. Those market forces have power
to degrade, overwhelm, and destroy Native economic systems. Tribal exchange
patterns (barter, gift, and so on) are presumed to escape rational calculation,
while Western trade is driven by calculation (and devoid of "culture"). Appadurai sees calculation and "culture" in both (1986:11). To recognize calculation in
indigenous systems we need to observe the exchange of goods over a longer
period to accommodate reciprocity. Scholars have categorized reciprocity in
precapitalist exchange as a cultural convention, significant to social rather than
economic relations.

Further, Appadurai argues that the context in which exchange takes place
determines the value of goods exchanged. Colonial exchange contexts were
characterized by unequal power relations among trading peoples in which a
higher value was attached to the goods of colonizers than the goods of the colonized. The most famous example is the "sale" of Manhattan by the Indians to
the Europeans for manufactured beads. Presumably at the time of the exchange
of land for beads (if that indeed is what occurred), each party came into the
transaction with its respective ideas as to the value of the land and beads. Concerned with wanting to complete the exchange, each side was unconcerned
with trying to understand the other side's rules of the game, in which exchange
is carried out with varying degrees of common agreement, producing alternative values in exchange. This allows us to consider the cultural dimension and
distinctive calculations and strategies of exchange. Suspending the determining themes of hierarchy and power allows exchange to become an economic
and cultural meeting ground where desire and sacrifice can come together regardless of whether the traders involved possess a shared value of goods or not
(Appadurai 1986:15).

On its face, the transactions that propelled Kiowa horses and other stock
along this new pathway amounted to a simple story of white corruption and
exploitation of Indians. The agent acted in violation of promises made at Medicine Lodge Creek. Stumbling Bear, speaking on behalf of the other half dozen
leaders, told Leavenworth as much when he said "Indian goods" and "trade
goods" were different. But, he went on, "The only way we can get our goods
[government rations] is to give him our ponies, our robes, and our furs. He kept
them [rations] from us. The great Father sent them to us. He thinks his time will
be short and he wants to make a good bargain." And, indeed, Leavenworth did
make a good bargain from the sale of government rations. He and business

partner William Matheson sold the Kiowa livestock to Arkansas City, Kansas, traders and pocketed the profit (McCusker 1868).

Stumbling Bear and the others traded with Leavenworth not out of fear of him but out of a desire to avoid force, and because they had the means, horses and mules, to do it. "But it is a better way [for us] to trade for our own goods, then [sic] take them by force. The braves [young men] that bring him most horses get most goods, more than one third of our tribe gets none [rations] at all for they have not any [horses] to give" (Stanton 1867). But the statement also raises the possibility of constricting resources. Perhaps the off-reservation bands were unable to sustain themselves and reservation bands from the buffalo hunt, and therefore improvised to gain access to rations.

This exchange context reflected antithetical systems, motivations, bases of calculation, and outcomes all resulting from the exchange of goods dispersed by and received by Indians. The agent's demands for further payments for rations represented exploitive colonial calculation expressed as rational exchange with a view to individual profit. But it also reinforced conventional Kiowa practices in the acquisition of trade goods and social relations within Kiowa bands. The theft of horses, mules, and cattle, the distribution of government rations, and the sale of stolen stock—activities involving off- and on-reservation Indians and government authorities—constituted a new arena of exchange that transcended the reservation boundary and rendered it irrelevant to the containment of Indians.

At the center of this new irregular trade network were off-reservation young men, vilified with their band leaders as outlaws (Nye 1968:204). For the most part, the young men were anonymous, known to us only in specific circumstances, such as the occasion of the death of the son of Lone Wolf, a principal headman. The primary sources represent them as a criminal element outside a normalized reservation system that, over time, became increasingly aberrant (Sheridan 1872; Beede 1873). Although their junior status and anonymity went hand in hand, young men held significant roles in Kiowa society. Organized into autonomous residence groups or bands led by more senior men, a gendered division of labor characterized Kiowa life. Women accompanied their husbands on expeditions and provided camp-based support, principally focused on childbirth and childrearing, food and hide production, clothing and shelter production, and preservation of craft traditions, such as beadwork. Men's energies were organized into group activities such as hunting, raiding, trading, and carrying out revenge against enemies.

In this context, young men were a significant source of labor. By participating in raids and hunting parties, they trained to be accomplished senior men, potential leaders, and full members of the realm of adult males. Until such time, young men occupied a cusp that reflected the multiple demands of a successful transition to manhood (Mishkin 1992:41, 45–47). Young Kiowa men were most commonly known to have great capacities for risk-taking and audacity, which earned them recognition for bravery and martial skills such as riding and shooting. Too much audacity earned them reputations for being arrogant and foolish, reflecting a kind of vanity that could imperil themselves and others. Their training included an emphasis on generosity and concern for band members. Young men needed both kinds of skills—individualistic daring and courage, as well as a spirit of communal responsibility—to earn the esteem of family and band leaders. Their training, then, continued traditions of social interdependence by providing both material support, including food production, and signs of respect to community members. Thus, we may understand an elderly woman's comment that young men were then required to be "kind-hearted, thoughtful, willing, helpful, dependable to be respected," because they guaranteed the tribe's future.[4]

The work of food production was divided between men and women in the prereservation period. Kiowa bands of extended kin bore responsibility for the band's collective well-being, including feeding its members. For much of their history Kiowas had relied on the buffalo herds of the Plains to feed and clothe themselves and to provide housing. Men and women made up hunting parties, whose leaders determined the timing and location of the collective hunt. Male members organized the effort to bring the animals down. The tribes' adoption of the Spanish horse had improved their proficiency in hunting, and old methods of corralling and driving buffalo off cliffs fell away. Women controlled butchering the animals and dressing valuable hides. Both men and women participated in the distribution of fresh meat. Back in the individual camps, however, women assumed complete control over the food, including preparation, storage, and distribution. Women's control of camps pertained whether on fixed sites or on the move with raiding, trading, and hunting parties. Food acquisition and production, therefore, were the shared work of male hunters and female processors from the hunting of the animal to the distribution of prepared food to relatives attached to individual camps. Young men and women constituted a significant portion of a band's labor force, and both must have felt acutely the pressures of disappearing resources and reduced hunting territory.

Military societies offered young Kiowas the company and example of adults whom they would emulate in their growth to maturity. There, too, young people were inculcated with values identified with community obligations, including feeding the people, an aspect of their history that scholarly preoccupation with the war complex has overshadowed. There have been eight Kiowa military societies since the late 18th or early 19th century, the most recent of which, the Ohomo, being introduced in the late 19th century. From a very early age, Kiowa children have held a place in the military society membership, beginning with the Polahyup, or Rabbits (Meadows 1999:40–41). As children mature into young adulthood and beyond, other societies are available for those who demonstrate skill, character, and accomplishment along the way. The military societies reinforced the ranked nature of Kiowa social organization based on kinship, achievement, and status.

Military societies by their very name connote the war complex with which the Kiowa people are so strongly associated in the historical literature (Kracht 1989; Meadows 1999). While achieving respected warrior status was probably paramount, young men were immersed in Kiowa knowledge, which included cultivating life values integral to individual good character and the well-being of the community. Underlying all activities that a young man might excel at, even warfare, was an ethic of community service (Mishkin 1992:42, 48). The training began not only with young Rabbits but within the circle of all adult military societies as well (Meadows 1999:40–41). Each society included young male assistants to the *aljoqi. Aujoqi* (those who keep things handy) and *ijeqi* (distributors or rationers, in reference to serving during feasts) were usually *audetalyi* (favored boys). These young members were adopted into the society and granted kin status to every other member. The boys and the regular society members used reciprocal kin terms for each other's relatives. The boys' labor, which included maintaining the fire, serving food, heating the dance drum, running messages, and providing general assistance, thus became an obligation to relatives and things to be done well to avoid bringing shame on his family (Meadows 1999:51). Labor, obligation, and service to a broader network of relatives beyond immediate family were interwoven.

The duty to feed relatives was powerful enough to cause a man to disregard band law regarding policed hunts, a punishable offense. Wolf Appeared and two of his male relatives tried to obtain fresh meat for his sick sister, wife to Kicking Bird (the reservation leader). Their actions violated the no-hunting rules then in effect, requiring the Jaifegau military society to mete out a punishment. While the two relatives ran away to escape sure punishment, Wolf Appeared remained. The punishers struck him with bows, killed his horse, and broke his bows and arrows (Meadows 1999:86). Even a Ten Medicine Keeper such as Wolf Appeared could not circumvent the laws with impunity, but neither could he ignore the obligation to feed his relative. He chose to break the no-hunting rule to obtain food for his sister, and to accept the Jaifegau's sanctions. Wolf Appeared did have the last word, however. Subsequently, in his role as war party leader he gained a reputation for abusing Jaifegau members whose fear of his powers as a Ten Medicine Keeper kept them from retaliating (Meadows 1999:86).

Despite a prickly disposition that he exhibited frequently, Wolf Appeared's actions illustrate the values inculcated in young Kiowa men. Properly socialized young men, and later as older men, balanced a fierce individualism that underlay their quest for war honors such as counting coup with responsibility to the larger network of relatives, whether on the battlefield or hunt. Through war honors young men gradually built up their credibility as warriors, the demands of which were arduous and risk-filled. But it was only by building up credibility as warriors that a young man earned others' trust with their well-being, indeed with their lives. The competing claims of intense individualism and broader social commitments were reconciled in the Kiowa value system (Mishkin 1992:39).

The unique dual roles of young Kiowa men were pointedly memorialized in the case of one fallen young warrior. Set-angya (Sitting Bear) set out with a few followers in the spring of 1870 with the intention of raiding settlements in Texas. He was shot and killed during one of the attacks on a house and his fellow raiders hid his body in Texas. Later, after the last Kiowa Sun Dance, the young man's father by the same name went with some friends to recover his son's body from Texas. Set-angya the father returned with the bones wrapped in a bundle atop a led horse. Back in his band's camp he built a tipi with a raised platform inside. He hosted a feast in his son's honor and invited all his friends, "telling them, 'My son calls you to eat.'" Thereafter he left food and water for the son he claimed to be only sleeping, not dead. The son's remains atop a led horse accompanied Set-angya the father whenever he went out on marches. In these ways—the tipi, the feast, the march—the father memorialized Set-angya the young man until his own death at Fort Sill in 1871. Friends of Set-angya the father interred the remains, but the son, his death, and his father's memorial to him are preserved in Kiowa history through the winter count of 1870–71 (Mooney 1979:325).

Set-angya the father was leader of Qoichegau (Sentinel Horse) at the time of his death. Qoichegau was one of six Kiowa military societies at the time and was distinguished by rigorous battle obligations (Meadows 1999:40–43). Composed of ten sash wearers, ten assistants, retired members, and young "colts," Qoichegau members were known for being the first society into battle and the last to retreat. The society formally obligated members to stake themselves down (by an arrow through the sash) while the other warriors were in retreat and to continue fighting until they themselves were slain. Only *ode*, or those born of the highest rank, whose status was reinforced with many war honors, could gain membership to Qoichegau. Sons did not inherit the father's position in Qoichegau, but they were taken in as colt members and were expected to rise through the ranks by war honors. The highest war deed, even higher than counting coup, was performed by the warrior who fell back to divert the enemy or take more enemies as his comrades retreated, thereby protecting the escaping party members. In a march, be it a revenge or raiding party, the brave warrior who was not Qoichegau but undertook such a role did so voluntarily (Mishkin 1992:39), but the Qoichegau were obligated to do so (Mooney 1979:285). When Set-angya died in 1871, he was a prisoner of the United States government. The United States Army was transporting him to a federal penitentiary in Texas when he sang his death song, leaped from the wagon, and was shot down by soldiers (Mooney 1979:329).

The year before he died, Qoichegau friends and followers would likely have attended the father's feast for his son. A family's honoring of a son's achievements in battle was expected in Kiowa ranked society. Typically, an account was spread throughout the camp to create public awareness of the young warrior's deed, enhance a growing reputation, and increase the young man's status (Mishkin 1992:41). A more elaborate honoring might involve the giving away of a horse and other gifts in the name of the young warrior. In this case, female relatives of the two Set-angya's probably prepared the meal, which in 1870 might not have resembled feasts of earlier days when meat was plentiful. Nevertheless, the meal was the focal point of the honoring. There are no references to a public giveaway. Set-angya the father spoke the son's invitation to eat, to come and be with him and share a common meal. In his death the young man's dual responsibilities as "rationer," or provider of food, and warrior were recognized simultaneously. Set-angya the father fulfilled his responsibilities to his son in multiple ways. Following his retrieval of the bones, he took revenge for his son's death by killing a white settler and honored his son with the feast. But the meals of meat and water left for the son by the father went further, acknowledging and memorializing the obligations between warriors and the people as well as providing for the life that follows death.

Between 1867 and 1870 food acquisition, storage, and distribution practices were undermined by environmental changes, unfulfilled promises of insufficient rations, and a federal policy of buffalo extermination. The developments combined with a military strategy of targeting Kiowa winter camps, destroying food, and keeping the Kiowas on the move affected both reservation and off-reservation bands and their leaders. Kiowas responded in multiple ways with varying results. Headman diplomacy carried on for the most part by Kicking Bird and other reservation leaders consisted mainly of ineffective promises to rein in the off-reservation bands. Those bands moved in and out of the reservation and continued to raid, primarily against Texas settlers, Indian tribes of eastern Indian Territory, their old enemies the Navajos and Utes, and travelers on the Santa Fe Trail. Food acquisitions came from rations distributions, continued off-reservation hunting, and the old practices of raiding and trading.

The Kiowas' subsistence in this period required utilization of all sources. Both on- and off-reservation bands had access to resources that the other needed. Kicking Bird's people by their presence ensured the continued distribution of rations, no matter how irregularly or inconsistent in quality. The off-reservation bands continued to acquire cattle, horses, mules, and trade goods through raiding. While the government and military made efforts to herd all Indians onto the reservation, the boundaries were indeed porous and ineffective. Off-reservation bands came and went at will, effecting an exchange of goods acquired in ways consistent with the old southwestern economy for rations and annuity goods. A succession of Indian agents and military authorities expressed exasperation with the off-reservation bands' access to rations. They either showed up for distributions or relied upon relatives to divide their rations with them (Tatum 1870).

Relations between young men and older leaders showed signs of strain from the effort to exploit the reservation and the old, now outlawed, Plains system. In July of 1870, as Set-anya retrieved the bones of his young son from his hidden grave in Texas, the young men challenged the reservation leader Kicking Bird to join them in a raiding party. Kicking Bird, stung by their accusation that he had become soft and "like a woman" and perhaps mindful of the grieving Set-anya, helped lead a party of 100 raiders into Texas in July following the Sun Dance. Later, leaders employed harsh rhetoric to denounce the young men's activities. For example, Lone Wolf promised to punish the young men for their raids by humiliating them, taking their horses and making them walk home (Horse Back 1870; Haworth 1873).

The point of the young men's experiences is not that colonialism was easy to subvert and therefore not so bad. Nothing less than the tribe's survival hung in the balance because the pressures on the Kiowa people at this time were enormous. Drought, a buffalo slaughter of incomprehensible proportion, a military policy bent on cutting the Kiowas and Comanches off from Texas, New Mexico, and Colorado—all traditional lands, and a federal policy designed to break down the old southern Plains economy together created an odd conspiracy of weather and American politics against the Kiowa people. The exchange of horses and mules for rations countered a federal policy of starvation to force Native compliance. It was not a game; it was a matter of life and death.

American government authorities saw trade with the Indians as a means to break down Native culture and, eventually, clear the pathway for Indian assimilation into the mainstream culture. While at first inept at interactions with the new economy, Natives, American policymakers, reformers, and missionaries hoped, would follow a pathway to a civilized state through their forced acculturation into the American economy and society. Hence, federal bureaucrats and reformers of various stripes emphasized a need to introduce Native people to white notions of work, individualistic profit seeking, earned wages, and the ideology of producerism associated with the yeoman farmer ideal. Subsequently, the conventional scholarly wisdom has been that Native peoples became quickly dependent on superior foreign goods but lost indigenous production knowledge and, as a direct result of their dependency, became ensnared in Western market forces. The result was loss of Native culture, but without the hoped-for uplifting result. Rather, tribal economies were decimated without benefit of Western market values filling the void.

However, the very structure of the reservation was predicated on a plan not to build local economies but to exert control over western tribes such as the Kiowas by depriving them of resources that the tribe required to maintain political autonomy. Government-distributed rations and trade cloth replaced the quickly diminishing buffalo and other game; annuity goods such as farming implements replaced the horse as a means of production; and per capita payments and indebtedness to licensed Indian traders replaced the indigenous trade system. Land became a resource targeted for exploitation through farming and grazing of livestock. All well and good, but rations were withheld, annuity goods and payments were inferior and inadequate, and indebtedness became more or less permanent. In addition to a lack of knowledge about farming and grazing, and profiting from either, Kiowas were doomed to fail in a region where rainfall was irregular and insufficient for farming. Confinement to the land within reservation boundaries interrupted organized band raids, hunts, and trade practices. The reservation did not fail because of Indian inferiority or misguided policy. Rather, the federal policy succeeded in creating and superimposing an artificial economy on a small-scale society in order to destroy its political autonomy. Uplift might have existed in the minds of some as a desirable outcome, but for the most part it served to merely rationalize American hegemonic aspirations.

The trade of horses and mules for rations challenged the American government's project on three fronts. The reservation opened up an additional outlet for Kiowa goods, not only during the administration of the corrupt Agent Leavenworth but during subsequent administrations when rations continued to be inferior, inadequate in volume, and irregularly delivered. Quaker successors to Leavenworth were ill equipped to impose control on the outside bands, evidenced in the ongoing conflict between Kiowas, Comanches, Texas settlers, and state and federal authorities that lasted to 1875. Second, the exchange of Kiowa horses and mules for rations attests to the stability of social relations among Kiowa leaders and young men. Despite strenuous efforts on the part of military and Texas authorities to cut the tribes off from the Staked Plains in west Texas, drought, and buffalo losses, all of which represented enormous threats to Kiowa subsistence and autonomy, the Kiowas, evidenced by the ration trade, did not descend into chaos. Rather, social relations held across generations and among reservation and nonreservation bands. Finally, the combination of stable social relations and continued exploitation of resources through raiding and trading outside the reservation bridged the economic past and present.

COMMERCE AND CULTURE: KIOWA WOMEN'S BEADWORK AND THE RESERVATION ECONOMY

The material world of Kiowa women offers other possibilities for understanding the reservation and postreservation economy and its implications for Kiowa society. Kiowa women figure most prominently in prereservation trade relations as tanners of buffalo hides. For the Kiowas, buffalo hides were perhaps second only to horses and mules as high-value trade items. Hide preparation was laborious, averaging some two to three days of labor per hide (Weist 1980). The skill of individual women increased the value of hides and the stature of women. The decimation of the buffalo eliminated this area of work and trade, but women continued to make significant economic contributions.

In the post-1875 world of the reservation, Kiowa women's production was consistent with their prereservation period roles as material and cultural providers for their families. Despite the disappearance of the buffalo and the limitations of a reservation economy that turned on distributions of rations, annuity goods, and payments, continuities are evident. Most obviously, Kiowa women's domestic roles in childrearing, food production, and management of home life continued, albeit in the context of daunting poverty and deprivation. Kiowa women also took up the informal exchange of their beadwork for cash and credit at the local licensed Indian trade store. While trade store records merely suggest the existence of this important component of the reservation economy, local museum collections, such as the Museum of the Great Plains in Lawton, Oklahoma, attest that Kiowa women were actively engaged in bead-work production in the reservation period. Women's output followed two tracks: tourist arts and beadwork for community or family utilization (Schnei-der 1980).

On the Kiowa reservation, the licensed Indian trader played a pivotal role in the circulation of women's tourist beadwork. The 1905 records of the Red Store in Lawton, Indian Territory, document in some detail a trade in beaded moccasins, bags, and other items that was practiced in southwestern Indian Territory, if not documented, throughout the last quarter of the 19th century (Sneed 1957; Sneed 1886).[5] Traders received the goods in return for cash or credit to the individual's account and sent them out on consignment to a vari-ety of small shops throughout the United States. The trader's role was more than economic. He was the communications gatekeeper between Kiowa women and the world of small American businesses, providing a kind of cul-tural interpretation, particularly for the curio shop owners. Shop owners learned from the Indian trader that Kiowa women did not produce to specifica-tion, ever. Women controlled their production pace and aesthetic decisions. The trader positioned himself as guarantor of authenticity, which he used to in-crease the value of his "genuine" Indian goods (Lawrence 1908).

It is not clear at all that Kiowa women were concerned about shop owners or consumers' tastes. They made minor production adjustments in obvious re-sponse to the American market. In the late 19th century, beaded watch fobs be-came very popular, for example. Beaded fobs typified the kind of amusing adaptation in beadwork that continues to the present, evidenced in beaded sneakers, baseball caps, and key chains. Such adaptations were very limited in the 19th century.

Claims for economic significance of tourist art production and exchange can only be cautious ones. In fact, the records are so scant and irregular that it is difficult to arrive at any aggregate figures such as totality of output. Rather, it is the richness of museum collections that demonstrates that Native women were producing steadily through the worst of times, perhaps driven by necessity, perhaps lured by opportunity. However, the production of tourist art appar-ently did not divert Indian women entirely from more traditional areas of artis-tic output. Ceremonial garb and regalia from the period also fill museum collections. And it is only the combination of both tourist art and ceremonial goods that might possibly account for the documented large quantities of beads and findings that traders were purchasing for their Indian customers on the KCA reservation. The beadwork trade was important enough to the traders to invest in quite large inventories of manufactured Indian goods, and to invest time in marketing the goods to individual shop owners in the United States.

In this period, women's beadwork production was an important source of resistance to federal government efforts to destroy tribal cultures. The policy of the time aimed to eliminate Sun Dance, traditional dress, and other observable vestiges of Kiowa culture.[6] Kiowa women's successful preservation of their arts under a regime dedicated to the deracination of their people did not go unnoticed by government officials, who sought to inculcate in them white American notions of domesticity.[7] Once again, an entrepreneurial spirit, this time of the local licensed Indian trader, colluded in the subversion of the civilization project promulgated by distant Washington policymakers and reformers.

CONCLUSION

Kiowa women and young men are perhaps most visible in the reservation period in this politically loaded realm of exchange. Their experiences give evidence that Native people engaged with colonialism variously with significant consequences for the preservation of Kiowa cultural autonomy, if not political autonomy. The experiences of Kiowa women and young men also reveal the disorder of the reservation and American hegemony and the inventiveness that emerged out of the common realm of daily life. Kiowa women and young men formed important economic and social relationships with the dominant society that transcended an externally constructed segregation. They breached the social wall that many policymakers viewed as key to the ideology of acculturation and assimilation. Native people were expected to embark on the journey to cultural transformation. Separation from community, from relatives, from the past was critical to the success of this first phase, and to the ultimate outcome: Indian absorption into American society. Exchange has been viewed as an effective means of acculturation among indigenous peoples. Cultures believed to be static and authentic only in some undisturbed form from earlier times are vulnerable to Western goods. But in this case, the inventiveness that arose in daily life, without necessarily intending to subvert this process, did so.

Exchange affirms that colonial projects, as Thomas suggests, are never precise, never completely successful. Kiowa women and young men exploited breaks in the boundaries that surrounded them through which they negotiated their own relationships with the hegemonic society. And there they located and experienced colonialism in other domains, and contested it on very different terms. They waged a war of trade and material production that was as significant as the battles fought between reservation leaders and the United States government.

Colonialism, multifronted and not content merely to subdue militarily, is drawn to every sign of vitality and autonomy with a view to asserting its control over those threatening life pulses. The culture must, too, be subdued. But Americans, like other colonizers, had their own conflicting motivations and goals. By the late 19th century, twin desires to showcase American progress by way of comparison with the primitiveness of its first peoples and to preserve a chapter of the national heritage—the conquered indigenous—blended with the ever-present acquisitiveness. Taking possession of land and other valuable resources was not enough; the Americans turned their eyes upon the material culture, the Indian goods. Entrepreneurs exploited Indian goods for profit in the rising curiosities trade and other commercial realms. Scholars made careers in the nascent professional field of ethnology. Whether for scientific inquiry or for personal possession or for turning profit, American acquisition of American Indian material culture continued steadily throughout this period of imposed Indian segregation. Native things were appropriated by various means and channeled into the tourist trade, collecting circles, and public cultural institutions, such as the National Museum in Washington, D.C., and the Georg Gustav Heye Foundation in New York City.

The ironies of this story are present reservation history of the Kiowa people, although there are many similar examples. At a time when the goal of the United States government and American society generally was to reduce contact with Native people through segregation and anticipate their eventual disappearance through absorption into Anglo society, they provided the means for Kiowas to perpetuate themselves in exploiting American desires for Indian goods. This is no small irony for a history that attributes Native decline to Indian dependence on European goods.

The author thanks Jeff Anderson, Colby College; Robert Nye, Oregon State University; Fred Hoxie, University of Illinois at Champaign-Urbana; and Johanna Schoen, University of Iowa for their criticisms and suggestions. Also, a note of appreciation for the intellectual company of the University of Iowa material culture reading group whose members include Rudi Colloredo-Mansfield, Mark Peterson, Ben Kaplan, Laura Rigal, Julie Hockstrasser, Bruce Scherting, Vicki Rovine, and Paul Greenough.

NOTES

1. The standard for the periodization of American Indian history in the colonial and American eras is found in Prucha (1986).

2. Historians' treatment of 19th-century Kiowa history typify the stark before-and-after effect of the reservation on Native people. See Nye (1968:178), Mayhall (1962:316–317).

3. The presentation of gifts to Native tribal representatives is addressed in the Trade and Intercourse Act of 1802, which formalized the practice of gift-giving as a means of stabilizing Indian relations with the United States government, counteracting settler violence on the "frontier," which undermined that stability, and preventing war with the tribes. Act of Mar. 20, 1802, ch. 13, 2 Stat. 139.

4. "Kiowa Field Notes," box 9, folder 10, Alice L. Marriott Papers, Western History Collection, University of Oklahoma.

5. Archives of the Museum of the Great Plains, Lawton, Oklahoma.

6. In 1883, the Department of Interior created the Court of Indian Offenses, which established reservation courts on which sat male tribal representatives, and which criminalized many aspects of Native cultural practices, including dancing, Native marriage practices, and traditional medicine. The language of the act, however, suggests a broader assault on tribal cultures as a necessary first step to civilizing the Indians (Hagan 1966:107–108).

7. The subversive potential of beadwork is attested to in numerous letters between Washington and the local Indian agent. Even reformers who promoted Indian civilization worried about the ill effects of beadwork. As the president of the American Medical Association noted in his annual address, reservation family members were in the practice of sending goods to their relatives at the Hampton Institute, where some of the Fort Marion prisoners boarded after their release from incarceration. The students, apparently, sold the goods to tourists and collectors of Indian goods for pocket money. This practice, warned the physician, would only undermine efforts to make the students self-sufficient (*Southern Workman* 8, no. 2 [February 1879]:15).

REFERENCES

Anderson, Gary

1999   The Indian Southwest, 1580–1830. Norman: University of Oklahoma Press.

Appadurai, Arjun, ed.

1986   The Social Life of Things. Cambridge: Cambridge University Press.

Asher, Brad
    1999   Beyond the Reservation: Indians, Settlers, and the Law in Washington Terri-
            tory, 1853–1889. Norman: University of Oklahoma Press.

Beede, Cyrus
    1873   Letter to Enoch Hoag, April 4, 1873. Letters Received, Office of Indian Af-
            fairs, National Archives Microfilm, ser. 234, roll 378.

Cumming, A.
    1856   Annual Report of the Commissioner of Indian Affairs.

Di Leonardo, Micaela
    1998   Exotics at Home. Chicago: University of Chicago Press.

Flores, Dan
    1991   Bison Ecology and Bison Diplomacy: The Southern Plains from 1800 to
            1850. The Journal of American History 78: 465–485.

Foster, Morris W.
    1991   Being Comanche: A Social History of an American Indian Community. Tuc-
            son: University of Arizona Press.

Hagan, William T.
    1966   Indian Police and Judges: Experiments in Acculturation and Control. Lincoln:
            University of Nebraska Press.

Haworth, J. M.
    1873   Letter to Cyrus Beede, May 8, 1873. Letters Received, Office of Indian Af-
            fairs, National Archives Microfilm, ser. 234, roll 378.

Horse Back
    1870   Statement by Horse Back, July 22, 1870. Letters Received, Office of Indian
            Affairs, National Archives Microfilm, ser. 234, roll 376.

Hoxie, Frederick E.
    1995   Parading through History: The Making of the Crow Nation in America,
            1805–1935. Cambridge: Cambridge University Press.

Kappler, Charles J.
    1972   Indian Treaties, 1778–1883. New York: Interland.

Kavanagh, Thomas W.
    1996   Comanche Political History: An Ethnohistorical Perspective, 1706–1875.
            Lincoln: University of Nebraska Press.

Kracht, Benjamin R.
    1989   Kiowa Religion: An Ethnohistorical Analysis of Ritual Symbolism,
            1832–1987. Ph.D. dissertation, Southern Methodist University, Dallas.

Lawrence, A. D.
    1908   Letter to A. F. Hatfield, June 10, 1908; Letter to M. Loeb, June 15, 1908.
            Correspondence Files, Lawrence Collection, Museum of the Great Plains,
            Lawton, Oklahoma.

Manypenny, George W.
    1856   Annual Report of the Commissioner of Indian Affairs.

Mayhall, Mildred P.
    1962   The Kiowas. Norman: University of Oklahoma Press.
    1963   Indian Wars of Texas. Waco: Texian Press.

McCusker, Philip
    1868   Letter to Commissioner of Indian Affairs, June 5, 1868. Letters Received, Of-
            fice of Indian Affairs, National Archives Microfilm, ser. 234, roll 375.
Meadows, William C.
    1999   Kiowa, Apache, and Comanche Military Societies: Enduring Veterans, 1800
            to the Present. Austin: University of Texas Press.
Miller, Robert C.
    1857   Annual Report of the Commissioner of Indian Affairs.
    1858   Annual Report of the Commissioner of Indian Affairs.
Mishkin, Bernard
    1992   Rank and Warfare among Great Plains Indians. Nebraska: University of Ne-
            braska Press. Originally published by American Ethnological Society Mono-
            graph, 3. New York: J. J. Augustin.
Mooney, James
    1979   Calendar History of the Kiowa Indians. Washington, DC: Smithsonian Insti-
            tution Press.
Nye, W. S.
    1968   Plains Indian Raiders. Norman: University of Oklahoma Press.
Prucha, Francis Paul
    1986   The Great Father: The United States Government and the American Indian.
            Abridged edition. Lincoln: University of Nebraska Press.
Schneider, Mary Jane
    1980   Plains Indian Art. In Anthropology on the Great Plains, W. Raymond Wood
            and Margot Liberty, eds. Lincoln: University of Nebraska Press.
Sheridan, Philip
    1872   Letter to Commissioner of Indian Affairs possibly, December 9, 1872. Letters
            Received, Office of Indian Affairs, National Archives Microfilm, ser. 234, roll
            377.
Sneed, L. B.
    1957   As I Remember. Chronicles of Comanche County. Autumn:67–75.
Sneed, R. A.
    1886   Red Store Ledger, 1886. Museum of the Great Plains, Lawton, Oklahoma.
Stanton, Edwin
    1967   Letter to Commissioner of Indian Affairs, June 8, 1867. Letters Received, Of-
            fice of Indian Affairs. National Archives Microfilm, ser. 234, roll 375.
Tatum, Lawrie
    1870   Letter to Ely Parker. Letters Received, Office of Indian Affairs, National
            Archives Microfilm, ser. 234, roll 376.
Thomas, Nicholas
    1994   Colonialism's Culture: Anthropology, Travel and Government. Princeton:
            Princeton University Press.
Weist, Katherine M.
    1980   Plains Indian Women: An Assessment. In Anthropology on the Great Plains.
            W. Raymond Wood and Margot Liberty, eds. Lincoln: University of Nebraska
            Press.

Tribal Histories,
Indigenous Histories

Keep Your Thoughts Above the Trees: Ideas on Developing and Presenting Tribal Histories

Craig Howe

American Indian history is a conflation of at least two distinct avenues of inquiry concerning the pasts of indigenous peoples of North America. The majority of inquiries examine the interactions on this land between indigenous peoples and immigrants from foreign places, usually following the immigrants and their descendants as they systematically explore this continent's vast landscapes. As these histories progress through time, they focus on the immigrants' encounters with Native "others" and often on the subsequent policies that were implemented to regulate future relationships between "immigrants" and "Indians." This is Indian history. It implicitly defines *Indian* as a collective term for all indigenous peoples and *history* as an objective, chronological narrative that has a temporal dimension beginning with the appearance of immigrants on these lands and an analytical model requiring the presence of both Natives and non-Natives.

A smaller number of inquiries seek to examine the remembered pasts of particular groups of indigenous peoples. These are tribal histories,[1] of which there are two dominant perspectives. The conventional academic perspective on tribal histories is linear, or sequential, in that it is written. Western European languages are read left to right, top to bottom, beginning to end. The result is a "beginning-top-left" to "ending-bottom-right" narrative predicated upon the written word. This sequentiality generally causes these histories to be organized temporally, though sometimes authors use nonchronological devices, such as flashbacks or dreams, to organize their narratives. Typically, the author's intent is for the reader to begin at one point in time and end at another point, say, from 1750 to 1890. Similar to Indian history, this perspective also tends to be organized around abstract themes that guide readers through the vast amount of historical data along a carefully defined and tightly controlled pathway.

The indigenous tribal perspective on tribal histories, on the other hand, is more likely to be recited in relationship to specific landscapes, waterscapes, and skyscapes. This perspective is event-centered: here something happened and a particular person or being was present. The trigger for the recollection of traditional oral narratives might be a place in the landscape, or a particular word, or someone's name, even a song or a picture. Often, as the storyteller is reciting an account of an event, another trigger is tripped and another narrative begins. Narrators—rather than an abstract theme or predetermined sequence—stand at the center of these histories. The narrators make connections between narratives on the spot. Instead of following a fixed sequentiality, they use their imaginations and creative abilities to produce oral histories that are full of "permutations, additives, chance, and mortalities" (Vizenor 1984:27, quoted in Albers 1994). In addition to transmitting their accounts orally, tribal historians also employ another system of communication to recall past events: drawing. So whereas the conventional academic perspective on tribal histories is grounded in the written word, the indigenous tribal perspective is grounded in two interrelated systems of communication that predate the written word: drawing and speaking.

> Imagine: somewhere in the prehistoric distance a man holds up in his hand a crude instrument—a brand, perhaps, or something like a daub or a broom bearing pigment—and fixes the wonderful image in his mind's eye to a wall or rock. . . . In our modern, sophisticated terms, he is primitive and preliterate, and in the long reach of time he is utterly without distinction, except: he draws. And his contribution to posterity is inestimable; he makes a profound difference in our lives who succeed him by millennia. For all the stories of all the world proceed from the moment in which he makes his mark. [Momaday 1988:5]

In this imaginative reconstruction, N. Scott Momaday—the quintessential "man-made-of-words"[2]—suggests that before the word—whether it was written or spoken—was the picture. In so doing, he draws our attention to the possibility that pictures constitute a system of communication independent from words. But whereas drawings can communicate to countless communities spanning centuries and continents, a community's oral tradition is far more specific as a communication system. Oral tradition is "the cornerstone of every tribal society," according to Michael Dorris, and is "the vehicle through which wisdom is passed from one generation to the next and by which sense is made of a confusing world. It is responsible in large part for the education, entertainment, and inspiration of the community" (Dorris 1979:156–57). As part of their function of "making sense of the world," the oral traditions of tribal communities focus on events that are important within their cultural contexts.

> For most Native Americans time is marked by events, and these events are more than the temporary surface disturbances that French social historians disdainfully dismiss. Occurrences that take place in myths, in folk narratives, and in native historical traditions are often what I term epitomizing events. Epitomizing events bring several forces together in dramatic combination; they condense various subtle changes into a single transformative act. Whether such events actually took place or not is immaterial; they are explanatory mnemonics of the mind and emotional engrams of the heart and, as such, are "real" for members of the culture. [Fogelson 1984:84]

Communities, then, made sense of their worlds by recounting events that in some fundamental sense related them to their surroundings—to other humans, to plants and animals, to landmarks and constellations. Such narratives recognized and reinforced webs of relationships that connected all entities of a community's spatial domain, and then related that domain to their cosmos.

During the 17th century, at least five peoples of the Great Plains—Blackfeet, Kiowas, Mandans, Poncas, and Lakotas—developed unique documents that organized drawings of important events experienced by their communities.[3] An event that was experienced within a given duration (most commonly a year) was chosen by each community as its name for that period of time, and an individual respected for his wisdom and artistic abilities was charged with recording the event in pictographic form on a tanned hide document. Those individuals were tribal historians, and the documents they created recorded events that embodied the values of their tribes and imbued the lives of community members with meaning and purpose. Following a prescribed schedule and a conventional pattern, each historian added a new event-pictograph to the sequence of pictographs that he and previous historians had drawn on the document. The historians also memorized the name for that year (or other period of time) and the story associated with the event.

At appropriate times, a historian would unwrap the document and invite his community to gather and see it. On these occasions, he enlivened the drawings by recounting the stories of the events they represented. Using a complex calculus that considered community values and situational circumstance, the historian began by reciting an account of a selected event-pictograph. Combining oratorical prowess and creativity, the historian would then jump to accounts depicted by other event-pictographs, weaving together diverse narratives into a discourse performance tailored to the "education, entertainment, and inspiration"—to use the words of Dorris above—of his audience.

TRIBAL HISTORIES

Event-centered histories that aspire to achieve an indigenous tribal perspective must be composed of at least four dimensions—spatial, social, spiritual, and experiential—that conceptually define tribalism[4] from its origins in the American Indian Old World to its resurgence in the American Indian New World of today.[5]

The spatial dimension of tribalism encompasses an implicit hierarchy whereby the land has primacy over human beings; but at the same time it recognizes that peoples and lands are intimately interconnected. Though the earth predates the presence of people on its surface, its substance is in part composed of the dust of the bones of generations of peoples. Tribal lands, therefore, are not perceived as distant and objectified, but rather immediate and personal: "The story of my people, and the story of this place, are one single story. No man can think of us without also thinking of this place. We are always joined together" (Rollins 1992). In discussing the connection between tribal peoples and their lands, Vine Deloria Jr. states that "every location within [each tribe's] original homelands has a multitude of stories that recount the migrations, revelations, and particular historical incidents that cumulatively produced the tribe in its current condition" (Deloria 1994:122). Tribal lands are thus enriched by accounts that link events to places rather than to a chronological narrative. "American Indians," continued Deloria, "hold their lands—places—as having the highest possible meaning, and all their statements are made with this reference point in mind." He contrasted this tribal perspective with that of Western European immigrants who "review the movement of their ancestors across the [North American] continent as a steady progression of basically good events and experiences, thereby placing history—time—in the best possible light" (Deloria 1994:62). Events take place in space, and event-centered tribal histories are centrally concerned with those events experienced by community members within their known geographic universe. These ethnogeographies extend far beyond the political boundaries of contemporary reservations and often beyond the conceptual limits of environmental ecosystems. A community's known geographic universe, then, is the spatial domain of its members' historical experiences.

The social dimension of tribalism relates land and identity to the concept of "peoplehood," a unique community identity differentiated from other tribes and from individual Indian persons. The relationship between a specific people and a particular landscape is not a relationship between an individual and the land or between "Indians" and the land. Instead, it is a relationship between a distinct community and their remembered landscape, a relationship often encoded in stories about particular past events that their ancestors experienced. The multitudes of communities collectively labeled "Indian" by Europeans each have their own history—their tribal histories.[6] Event-centered tribal histories are based on the idea that "Identity is a conception of and feelings about the events which a people have lived. It is the meaning of events in which one's ancestors took part, in ways that make one proud, which differentiate people into ethnic groups" (Sawyer 1976:203). The distinctive identity of each tribal community is fundamental to tribalism. A focus on "the people," as opposed to individuals, all Indians, or abstract themes, recognizes that tribal histories are community-based and tribally specific. Therefore, tribal histories from an indigenous tribal perspective focus on historical experiences that are meaningful to each community as a whole and on the places where a community's epitomizing events occurred. Furthermore, the communication of these experiences rests firmly on the foundation of oral tradition in general, and specific tribal languages in particular.

The relationships between tribal peoples and their lands are guided by the spiritual dimension of tribalism. According to Deloria (1984:8):

> The idea of the people is primarily a religious conception, and with most American Indian tribes it begins somewhere in the primordial mists. In that time the people were gathered together but did not yet see themselves as a distinct people. A holy man had a dream or a vision; quasi-mythological figures of cosmic importance revealed themselves, or in some other manner the people were instructed. They were given ceremonies and rituals that enabled them to find their place on the continent.

We see in this statement the important interrelationship between the spatial, social, and spiritual dimensions of tribalism. Deloria goes on to say, "When lands and peoples are both chosen and matched together in a cosmic plan, the attachment to the land by the people becomes something extraordinary and involves a sense of identity and corresponding feeling of responsibility" (Deloria 1992:31–32). Viewed in this light, tribal communities are guided by spiritual instructions that embody the moral and ethical standards by which tribal members conduct their interactions not only with the land but also with each other and with outsiders. Within these communities, individuals have differential access to special powers and esoteric knowledge. The social transmission of morally sanctioned tribal knowledge is performed by respected tribal members at particular places, or during certain times, or to properly prepared persons. Because tribal histories encompass the historical experiences of a community's members, such histories necessarily begin at least as early as the earliest appearance of a community's ancestors on this earth. As long as community members exist, such histories are ongoing. Furthermore, if a community is aware of future events—perhaps through prophecy or ceremony—then their historical experience extends beyond the past and present. Tribal histories thus minimally stretch the temporal duration of "history" from the origin of a people to their disappearance from this earth. As such, tribal histories are inextricably linked to spiritual traditions.

Lastly, the experiential dimension of tribalism recognizes that tribal communities perpetuate ongoing relationships with their higher spiritual powers. These relationships are based not on what the people believe to be true but rather on what they experience as being true. The experiences of each tribal community are unique and are "primarily a matter of participation in terms of the real factors of existence—living on the land, living within a specific community, and having religious people with special powers within that community" (Deloria 1994:291). Here we see the coalescence of all four dimensions of tribalism. Tribal historians traditionally created multisensory settings within which they presented their tribal history performances. According to the Lakota historian and spiritual leader Black Elk, "Mostly the history tellers were medicine men. They have the power and they know . . . The medicine men were the learned class, the scholars of the tribe" (quoted in DeMallie 1984:334). Of primary importance were their memories and the pictographic documents, both of which they drew from to educate, entertain, and inspire members of their communities. The pictographic documents are similar to Paleolithic art that "is the residue of what was a planned multimedia event designed to impose upon individuals unforgettable patterns of tribally essential knowledge and explanation" (Dissanayake 1988:154). Communal activities such as eating, drinking, smoking, singing, and dancing frequently accompanied tribal history performances. Community members were not merely hearing and seeing these performances; they were also smelling and tasting and feeling them. By incorporating multisensory sensations, tribal historians facilitated the transmission and retention of tribally essential knowledge through multimedia performances during which community members participated experientially.

Tribalism thus includes spatial, social, spiritual, and experiential dimensions that must be incorporated into those event-centered histories that aspire to achieve an indigenous tribal perspective. Can written histories fulfill this requirement? No. History from an indigenous tribal perspective cannot be presented solely through the written word. Though it is possible to write histories that integrate spatial, social, and spiritual dimensions, it is impossible for written histories to be "read" nonsequentially or for "readers" to experience them using multiple senses. Therefore, histories from an indigenous tribal perspective must be presented in a format that can accommodate multimedia data and structure it in a nonsequential order. Two such formats are digital hypermedia applications and museum exhibitions. An indigenous tribal perspective, however, is not inherent in either; each merely possesses the potential to incorporate the four dimensions of tribalism.

PRESENTING TRIBAL HISTORIES

Since the release of HyperCard in 1987 it has been possible for tribal histories from an indigenous tribal perspective to be created outside of community settings and to be presented in digital format on personal computers. This early and widely available computer program was "an implementation of a concept originally christened *hypertext* and more recently expanded in scope and dubbed *hypermedia*" (Vaughan 1988:23). Both terms refer to electronic texts that can combine visual, aural, and textual media and that can be "read" in a variety of ways. Hypertext is writing that "provides the ability to link related concepts and jump from place to place as information needs warrant" (Vaughan 1988:30), whereas hypermedia extends "hypertext's nonsequential concept to include all forms of stored information—graphic, films, video, music, etc. as well as the written word" (Vaughan 1988:25). The technical capabilities of pioneering computer products such as HyperCard were quickly surpassed by newer and faster hypermedia applications, including the ubiquitous web browsers that enable users to access hypermedia information on the Internet. Whether the hypermedia information is stored on a personal computer or an Internet server that is accessible to many different digital devices simultaneously, two central attributes remain the capacity to store data in multiple media and to provide access to that data in sequences determined by individual "readers."

Museum gallery exhibitions similarly incorporate multiple media that may be accessed in a nearly infinite variety of sequences. They feature a broad spectrum of media that visitors access primarily through their sensory organs. For instance, museum visitors are in the physical presence of "real" objects. They are aware of scents. Air temperature, humidity, and movement can be felt, as can surface textures and whether or not a floor plane is flat and level. The primary method visitors use to access these forms of stored information is to move from one point to another. In other words, they determine their sequence by where they move and stop. We see, then, that both hypermedia applications and museum exhibitions have the potential to store multimedia information and to provide access to that information in sequences that are not predetermined.

But there is a difference in how a hypermedia application (hereafter referred to as "the digital project") and a museum exhibition (hereafter referred to as "the gallery exhibition") incorporate the four dimensions of tribalism in their presentations of tribal histories from an indigenous tribal perspective.[7] In both the digital project and the gallery exhibition, the spatial dimension provides the initial entry portal to a number of event-centered tribal histories. In the digital project, a spatial domain defined by geographic features demarcates an area within which tribal histories are mapped; for example, an area bounded on the west by the Rocky Mountains, on the north by the Saskatchewan River, on the east by the Mississippi River, and on the south by the Red River. Though this geographic area, on the surface, falls within the conventional anthropological construct called the "Plains culture area," from the perspective of the digital project, it is quite different. Culture areas are used to organize and reference "information about contiguous groups that are or were similar in culture and history" (Washburn 1988:viii). Implicit in culture areas is the concept of environmental determinism: the notion that tribal peoples' histories and cultures are determined by their surrounding environments. The geographic area of the digital project, however, simply provides a common ground for mapping tribal histories. Whereas culture areas are concerned with the temporal and cultural similarities of tribal peoples who are conceptualized as statically located in space, the digital project maps the locations of epitomizing events in the historical journeys through space and time of specific communities.

The gallery exhibition, on the other hand, focuses on a distinct geographic location, such as the headwaters or mouth of a river, a small island or lake, a freshwater spring, or a prominent landmark. The distinctiveness of that place is represented in the gallery exhibition, but not as experienced at one particular time. Instead, the ambience of that place during various hours of the day and night, and throughout the course of a year, is evoked experientially in a constantly changing setting employing a variety of media. The flora and fauna indigenous to that place are presented, as are its geological and archaeological histories. Whereas the spatial dimension of the digital project encompasses a vast geographic area (e.g., the northern Plains), the spatial dimension of the gallery exhibition is one particular place in the landscape (e.g., headwaters of the Yellowstone River).

What differentiates the social dimension of the digital project from that of the gallery exhibition are the criteria for selecting tribes whose histories may be presented. In the digital project, the geographic area of the base map establishes the spatial domain within which event locations are mapped. Therefore, only those tribes whose epitomizing events all occurred within the geographic area and whose tribally controlled lands are still within that area may be included. The distinct geographic place in the gallery exhibition, on the other hand, represents a particular place in indigenous ethnogeographies. As such, only those tribes whose known landscapes encompassed that place at some time in their histories may be included. Whether or not the tribes are similar in culture or history or currently occupy that area is irrelevant—just so long as that particular place was known at some time in each of their histories, even if it was not simultaneous.

It is fitting that of the four dimensions of tribalism, only the spiritual dimension is the same for the digital project and the gallery exhibition. For both formats the temporal span of tribal histories extends from the beginning of time to the end of time—two temporal poles that are grounded in the spiritual traditions of specific communities. The capacity to encompass this extensive temporal dimension is inherent in both formats.

The two formats once again differ considerably with regard to the experiential dimension. Though both are in some sense multimedia, the digital project can only present information digitally. At present, the technological capabilities of hypermedia applications are limited to digitized images, sounds, and written texts. In the digital project, multimedia information pertaining to epitomizing events for the tribes is digitized, then linked to events whose locations are marked on a common base map where "buttons" are placed over them. By clicking on an event location button, information that pertains to that place and the event that happened there is made accessible. Since the event location buttons may be clicked in any sequence a "reader" chooses, and the information about the event may likewise be "read" in any order, the project positions the "reader" at the center of historical inquiry. As such, "readers" become the creative decision makers as they weave their way through the web of information, linking to digitized information in a sequence they determine. The gallery exhibition, on the other hand, incorporates images, sounds, and written texts in their original formats. Moreover, visitors to the gallery exhibition may experience smells, tastes, and textures, none of which are possible in the digital project. Although all of this multimedia information is still linked to epitomizing events, in the exhibition each event occupies its own spatial location within the gallery. So whereas "readers" navigate the digital project by manipulating a cursor on a computer screen, "visitors" make their way through the gallery exhibition by literally moving on the museum floor from one event display to another, and from one tribal history space to another. Though "readers" and "visitors" seemingly simulate the role of tribal historians, their individual, nonsequential inquiries are conceptually unrelated to the communal responsibilities and nonsequential performances of the historian.

The digital project and the museum exhibition are both composed of three types of modular components that are hierarchically nested. At the highest level is the spatial component. Within the spatial component are tribal components. And then within each tribal component are event components. Each epitomizing event is represented in the project/exhibition by an event component. A set of event components constitutes a tribal history component or module. Though the digital project and gallery exhibition share this module design, the cumulative and ongoing aspect of the experiential dimension is different in the two formats. If digital storage space is sufficient, it is relatively easy to add new data to the digital project. These data may relate to an existing event presented in the project, it may be a new event and related information in the history of one of the tribes presented in the project, a new tribal history module may be incorporated into the project, or an entirely new geographic area module may be developed. The gallery exhibition is cumulative and ongoing as well, but in a different way. Because the floor space available for a gallery exhibition is fixed, the inclusion of additional materials must be facilitated by rotating out existing materials. These rotating materials may relate to one of the events presented in the exhibition, an entire tribal history module may be rotated out, and the geographic place module itself may rotate out. This is the built-in changeability of the gallery. Tribal history modules may be developed ahead of their appearance on the exhibition floor, yet still be available digitally, both in the museum and throughout the world, before and after they are on exhibition. They may also function as traveling exhibitions, again either before or after they are incorporated into a museum exhibition.

DEVELOPING TRIBAL HISTORIES

The above discussion of tribal histories from an indigenous tribal perspective advocates a reorientation in the presentation of tribal histories and a reevaluation in the process of developing them. The development of tribal histories should be undertaken in a good way, a respectful way, a way that acknowledges the inherent expertise, value, and rights of tribal communities. Such histories are about living peoples and ongoing communities. They are complex and require considerable thought to develop and present in a respectful and meaningful manner.

The conceptual-methodological process for developing tribal histories outlined below is not necessarily new or unique, but it has been used with some success in developing digital projects and gallery exhibitions that incorporate more than one tribal history. Its underlying premise is that the process is a collaborative effort on the part of numerous partners, each with its own expertise, value, and rights. Moreover, each partner brings something of benefit both to the process and to its collaborators. One set of partners is the tribal communities. Each community has its own indigenous framework for structuring its past, and organizes and presents its tribally specific history according to unique principles. Putting these unique tribal histories together in a coherent framework and presenting them to the nontribal public is the goal of the remaining partner. This partner, for lack of a better term, will be referred to as "the mainstream institution." A partnership of tribal communities and a mainstream institution undertakes this process, not tribal and nontribal individuals acting independently. Benefits accrue to the partners, and commitments and responsibilities extend beyond the particular individuals participating in the process at any given moment.

On the basis of the spatial dimension criteria mentioned above, the mainstream institution identifies a list of tribal communities that fit those criteria and then selects from that list the tribes it will approach to develop tribal histories. For each tribe, the institution conducts background research on tribal history, develops a preliminary list of epitomizing events, compiles a tribal bibliography and an inventory of institutional resources from or relating to the tribe, and identifies an academic scholar. The academic scholar is someone who has conducted extensive research pertaining to the history of that tribe, knows the location and general holdings of repositories with tribal materials, and has personal contact with tribal members. The academic scholar reviews the materials the mainstream institution has produced, and recommends a number of individuals who might serve as the tribal liaison for the tribal history module.

The tribal liaison is a tribal member who lives in the community, speaks both the tribal language and English, is knowledgeable of community protocol, and is comfortable taking on a leadership role in developing the tribal history module.

Once formal contact between the head authorities of the mainstream institution and a partner community is established and agreement has been reached to proceed, a five-phase iterative process is set in motion. The five phases are characterized by an important meeting between representatives from both the tribal community and the mainstream institution. These meetings punctuate the continuous process of fieldwork and research that goes into developing a tribal history and represent moments of decision making and work review. The locations of these meetings alternate between the two partners; the first, third, and fifth are in the community, the second and fourth are at the institution.

In phase one, mainstream institution staff travel to the tribal community and in a public meeting, organized by the tribal liaison, present the concept of the project/exhibition and invite the community to participate in the process of developing and presenting their community's history module. It is critical that the event-centered concept is clearly articulated at this meeting and that everyone participating consents to work within that framework. Equally important is that the process of developing and presenting the tribal history is explained. Subsequent to the meeting, a small number of community members are selected who will serve as community representatives throughout the developmental process. These individuals, along with the tribal liaison, are primarily responsible for choosing their community's epitomizing events and for selecting the objects, photographs, and other media through which the events will be presented. They also assist in gathering oral narratives, or community accounts, of those events from knowledgeable tribal members. These representatives, along with the tribal liaison, travel to the mainstream institution for the phase two meeting.

The phase two meeting might more appropriately be described as an extended workshop lasting three or four days. The community representatives and tribal liaison travel to the mainstream institution where they are afforded the opportunity to see all of the materials from and about their community that are in the possession of that institution. These are the primary materials from which they will select to illustrate their chosen epitomizing events. Before returning to their community, the representatives and liaison meet with the digital project programmer or gallery exhibition designer to discuss the epitomizing events, the selected materials, and ideas for presenting their tribal history. On the basis of these conversations, the programmer/designer begins to design the tribal history module for that community.

When the tribal history module is at a preliminary stage—schematic drawings of the gallery exhibition or an alpha version of the digital project—institution staff return to the community and present it at a public meeting. At this phase three meeting community members see the results of the phase two workshop attended by their representatives and liaison, and have an opportunity to comment on that work and to suggest revisions. Feedback from this meeting is incorporated into the evolving design of the tribal history module.

The phase four meeting is held at the mainstream institution and lasts one or two days. Tribal liaisons from each of the tribes associated with a spatial module attend this meeting, thereby having an opportunity to meet their peers from other tribes and to see how those tribal histories are being presented. Furthermore, they also see how their tribal histories are linked to the spatial module. By this point in the process, the programmer/designer has completed work on the spatial module (e.g., the northern Plains, or headwaters of the Yellowstone River). The tribal history modules also are highly refined by this meeting, but not to such a degree that recommendations, substitutions, deletions, or additions from the tribal liaisons cannot be incorporated.

After implementing the tribal liaison's suggestions, a final design of the tribal history module is produced by the programmer/designer. This design is rendered as completely and accurately as possible, and then taken to the community for the phase five meeting. At this public meeting, to which the entire community is invited, the tribal history module is presented and the community is asked for their approval. Upon approval, the design of the module is set. Should changes to the module be undertaken by the mainstream institution, staff members return again to the community for another approval. In other words, when community members sign off on the design, they should experience no surprises when they eventually have the opportunity to use the final computer program or visit the museum exhibition.

Again, this is not necessarily a new or unique developmental process. Many individuals and institutions conceive of the work they do with Indians and tribal communities along similar lines. This process does, however, clearly articulate the functions of the collaborating partners. The institution is responsible for developing the overall conceptual framework for the digital project or gallery exhibition, and for funding the processes of developing and presenting each tribal history. Though the conceptual framework of an indigenous tribal perspective on tribal history is grounded in the four dimensions of tribalism, it transcends the idiosyncratic organizing principles of any single tribal community. The framework is, however, void of content. Working within that framework, each community has the responsibility to make their tribal history module uniquely theirs. In other words, to share those important events that they and their ancestors alone experienced.

COLLABORATING ISSUES

There are a number of issues that arise when tribal communities and main-stream institutions set in motion the iterative process of developing and pre-senting tribal histories. One is that a moral and ethical relationship is established between tribal communities and the mainstream institution. It has been my experience that almost without exception, community members find the iterative process exciting. This is due in part to the fact that it respects their knowledge and decision-making abilities, but also, one suspects, because it sets up an ongoing relationship between their community and the main-stream institution. The institution is not just coming into their community once and appropriating what it needs and then going away and doing with that information what it wants. Rather, the institution is committing itself to an on-going collaboration with community members, a partnership wherein commu-nities exert a considerable amount of decision-making authority with regard to their tribal histories. Working within the overall framework of either the digital project or the gallery exhibition, community members decide which events to present, what information to share about each event, who within their commu-nity will share the information, which objects and images to use to illustrate the events, and in the case of the gallery exhibition, even the shape and design of the space within which their history is exhibited. They are telling their own histories from their own perspectives using their own words, instead of being studied by nonmembers who then tell an outsider's version of their history. This level of community involvement and authority is rare.

It is a very potent experience for community members to revisit many of the important events presented in their tribal histories. In some instances, they are sharing their experiences and stories with outsiders for the first time. And their stories are properly their intellectual property. They do not want to invest their time, efforts, and emotions if the process is not going to be done right or if the final product is not going to be good in their eyes. So the mainstream in-stitution has moral and ethical commitments to the communities with whom it works. And that's the issue: Are the commitments going to be honored? Or are they going to be like so many other promises made by outsiders that are cast aside when the institution finds it convenient to do so? The history of relations between tribal communities and outside institutions suggests to community members that they judge the mainstream institution on its actions instead of its words. History is replete with good intentions from institutions gone awry. Therefore, the process is necessarily iterative, takes place over a period of time, and considerably decenters the traditional authority of the mainstream institution.

Another issue that arises from the developmental process is that related processes are set in motion within the communities themselves. Though these intracommunity processes result from the developmental process, they operate independently from the mainstream institution. In many instances, the public meetings to which the entire community is invited are the first times that community members have gathered together to discuss tribal history. Aside from the political machinations that often accompany such gatherings, deep-seated issues within the communities are brought into these discussions. Questions concerning authority to speak, personal character, information dissemination, and loss of tribal knowledge are not uncommon. A recurring theme is that knowledge of the "old ways" passed on with the last of the generation who were educated by the community instead of by formal schools. With a deep sense of loss, community members repeatedly say that these projects are too late, that the old men and women who knew the stories have all passed on. Ironically, after having said this, tribal members are identified who do know the stories. And this is one of the benefits of the process that accrues solely to the community: the collective knowledge of the community is recognized. In discussing their tribal history in public formats, individuals share stories and opinions that other community members are keenly interested in hearing. One outcome of this is that the communities themselves wish to retain copies of all the information gathered during the developmental process, and to make it available to community members.

The developmental process described earlier outlines a different way for institution staff to work with community members. The community people involved are not the usual "Rolodex" Indians; they may not be widely known in the institutional world, or even beyond their own communities in some cases. Most of the people participating in this process are embedded in the day-to-day lives of their communities and often have limited experience working with mainstream institutions. They become deeply invested in the process. They were born and raised in their communities, and they live there now and they will remain living there until their time on this earth is up, at which point they most likely will be interred in their homelands. Many of their ancestors played prominent roles in their community's history, and most of the participants today play leadership roles of one sort or another: political official, spiritual leader, artist, elder, or apprentice. Their reputations are on the line. Similarly, institution staff begin working intensively with community members whom they had not previously known and working with them in new ways. The relationships between staff and community members develop in both the community setting and the institution's urban milieu. During the community-based phases, the relationship resembles somewhat that between ethnographer and ethnographic "subject." During the institution-based phases, however, the relationship more closely resembles that between inside professional and outside consultant. Both of these types of relationships entail obligations and responsibilities that require a lot of time and commitment to maintain.

A fourth, but certainly not the final, issue is that the developmental process requires people to have good thoughts. This is a concern that may be easily overlooked in the institutional world. It tends to sound a little new-agey, but I believe it is essential to successfully developing and presenting tribal histories in a respectful manner. These tribal histories are not merely histories of tribes. They are intimately bound up with the indigenous spiritual traditions of their tribe: tribal history and spiritual tradition are inseparable. To tell the history of their tribe, community members inevitably begin with the appearance of their ancestors on this earth. And some share what the end of time on this earth will be like for their people. So tribal history in this context stretches from the beginning of time to the end of time. And the stories about those two points of time rest firmly within what many people would categorize as spiritual tradition.

When dealing with things spiritual, one is usually admonished to have good thoughts and to conduct oneself in a good way. This is often stated as having a good mind and a good heart. It may also be referred to as keeping one's thoughts above the trees.[8] When dealing with an important matter—which characterizes the developing and presenting of tribal histories—individuals frequently ask for guidance and protection, give thanks, and cleanse themselves. Therefore, prayer and ritual are integral parts of the process. And if we acknowledged that tribal spiritual traditions are ongoing and that they are efficacious, then it seems imperative that the work of developing and presenting tribal histories be conducted in a respectful manner, that it be done in a good way. Not only because it is proper but also because there is a relationship between thoughts and actions, on the one hand, and the quality of completed projects and exhibitions, on the other.

It is evident that even though digital projects and gallery exhibitions have the capacity to incorporate an indigenous tribal perspective on tribal histories, neither replicates the fundamental function of those histories. This chasm is further widened when those histories are presented outside of the tribal communities by mainstream institutions. Whereas tribal histories were intended for the "education, entertainment, and inspiration" of community members, histories presented at mainstream institutions are overwhelming "read" and "visited" by nontribal members. That is their primary audience. But that does not mean that those histories are better organized into a mainstream "Indian history" or a conventional academic perspective on tribal history. Quite the contrary: the organizing principle for tribal histories should be an indigenous tribal perspective. Though the function of the histories has changed, it is possible—by keeping our thoughts above the trees—for mainstream institutions and tribal communities to collaboratively develop and present tribal histories from an indigenous tribal perspective.

NOTES

1. Harvey Markowitz has been a collaborator in the development of these ideas for a number of years. His highly developed theoretical orientations and extensive fieldwork experiences are indispensable in our efforts to articulate the inherent qualities of tribal histories and to develop tribal histories in collaboration with tribal communities. Special thanks to him for commenting on this paper.

2. Not only is N. Scott Momaday a preeminent author and winner of the Pulitzer Prize, he also wrote a wonderful essay touching on the longevity and frailty of oral traditions titled "Man Made of Words," reprinted in *The Remembered Earth* (Hobson 1990).

3. These visually distinctive documents are commonly called "winter counts." One of the earliest articles on winter counts appeared as chapter 10 in *Picture-Writing of the American Indians* (Mallery 1972 [1893]:265–328). *The British Museum Winter Count* (Howard 1979) provides a good overview of winter counts and also includes an appendix of published and unpublished winter counts.

4. As used herein, tribalism refers to the inherent sovereignty of tribal communities, a sovereignty that predated the arrival of non-Indians by millennia. This sovereignty is intimately bound up with tribal spiritual traditions and will continue to exist as long as those traditions survive. Nationalism, on the other hand, refers to a political sovereignty that is recognized as such by treaty negotiations and Supreme Court decisions.

5. "American Indian Old World" refers to the collective land base of tribal communities before nontribal interventions. Essentially it is the Western Hemisphere. The "American Indian New World," on the other hand, is based on control of decision-making opportunities within a land base and is therefore not a static domain. As land passed out of control of tribal communities, the American Indian New World likewise contracted. Today, tribally controlled lands represent the American Indian New World: essentially federally recognized Indian reservations.

6. Though writing about Indian literature, Michael Dorris illustrates how the term

"Indian" negates the concept of "peoplehood": "If there had been a North American language called 'Indian,' the mode of communication within a society called 'Indian,' then there would undoubtedly be something appropriately labeled 'Indian literature'" (Dorris 1979:147). Similarly, "Indian history" is a generalizing and homogenizing term, one that obfuscates the particularities of individual tribal histories.

7. This discussion is based in part on experiences during the process of conceptualizing and developing the Hypermedia Tribal Histories project at the University of Michigan and at the Newberry Library's D'Arcy McNickle Center for American Indian History, and the "Our Peoples" tribal histories exhibition at the Smithsonian Institution's National Museum of the American Indian.

8. Thanks to Mr. Jerry Wolfe for suggesting this phrase.

REFERENCES

Albers, Patricia C.
  1994   Thoughts Have Power, Words Have Privilege: Some Reflections on Social Scientific Observations and Categories of the Ojibwe People. Occasional Papers in the Curriculum Series, 16. Teaching and Writing Local History: Lac Courte Oreilles. D'Arcy McNickle Center for American Indian History, Newberry Library, Chicago.
Deloria, Vine, Jr.
  1978   A Conversation with Vine Deloria, Jr. 29-min. videorecording. Words & Place Series. Tucson: University of Arizona Radio-TV-Film Bureau.
  1992   American Indians. In Multiculturalism in the United States, J. D. Buenker and L. A. Ratner, eds. Pp. 31–52. New York: Greenwood Press.
  1994   God is Red: A Native View of Religion. Golden, CO: Fulcrum.
Deloria, Vine, Jr., and Clifford M. Lytle, eds.
  1984   The Nations Within: The Past and Future of American Indian Sovereignty. New York: Pantheon Books.
DeMallie, Raymond, ed.
  1984   The Sixth Grandfather: Black Elk's Teachings Given to John G. Neihardt. Lincoln: University of Nebraska Press.
Dissanayake, E.
  1988   What Is Art For? Seattle: University of Washington Press.
Dorris, Michael
  1979   Native American Literature in an Ethnohistorical Context. College English 41, no. 2 (October):147–162.
Fogelson, Raymond
  1984   Night Thoughts on Native American Social History. Occasional Papers in the Curriculum Series, 3. The Impact of Indian History on the Teaching of U.S. History. D'Arcy McNickle Center for American Indian History, Newberry Library, Chicago. Pp. 67–89.
Hobson, Geary, ed.
  1990   The Remembered Earth. Albuquerque: University of New Mexico Press.

Howard, James H.
    1979   The British Museum Winter Count. London: British Museum.
Mallery, Garrick M.
    1972   Picture-Writing of the American Indians. New York: Dover.
Momaday, N. Scott
    1988   The Native Voice. *In* Columbia Literary History of the United States. Pp.
            5–15. New York: Columbia University Press.
Rollins, Njemile, producer
    1992   America's Heritage: Preserving Our History. *In* Spirits of the Present: The
            Legacy from Native America. Radio Smithsonian at the Smithsonian Institu-
            tion, Washington, DC, and the Native American Public Broadcasting Consor-
            tium, Lincoln, Nebraska.
Sawyer, Thomas E.
    1976   Assimilation versus Self-Identity: A Modern Native American Perspective. *In*
            Contemporary Native American Address. John R. Maestas, ed. Pp. 197–205.
            Provo, UT: Brigham Young University.
Vaughan, Tay
    1988   Using HyperCard. Carmel, IN: Que Corporation.
Washburn, Wilcomb, ed.
    1988   History of Indian-White Relations, volume 4. Handbook of North American
            Indians. Washington, DC: Smithsonian Institution Press.

Life Proceeds From the Name: Indigenous Peoples and the Predicament of Hybridity

James F. Brooks

> My name is Tsoai-talee. I am, therefore, Tsoai-talee; therefore I am.
> The storyteller Pohd-lohk [Old Wolf] gave me the name Tsoai-talee.
> He believed that a man's life proceeds from his name, in the way
> that a river proceeds from its source.

The Kiowa novelist, poet, and painter N. Scott Momaday begins his memoir *The Names* (1976) with these spare sentences. In a single name we see woven ascription, acceptance, being, narrative, force, and constraint—the logic of operation that gives names their extraordinary salience in life and memory. Yet we also see in Momaday's memoir the way in which names and naming foreshorten and refashion the complexity of history in the process of identity creation. His work revisits five generations of family history through their names, migrations, and places. We come to know that Momaday, the Kiowa, Tsoai-talee embodies a genealogy that includes Cherokee, French, Scots, Anglo, Mexican, and Kiowa progenitors, a densely entangled vine of individual lives and identities that stretch from the mountains of North Carolina to "the knobs" of Kentucky, from the dry sierra of northern Mexico to the plains of Oklahoma, and, finally, to the sand-rock canyon of the Jémez River, where today he writes and paints in the adobe home once owned by his parents.

This centurylong migration of names and places, a toponymic narrative etched with the strands of life's strange detours and unified by the organizing power of kinship and culture, condenses in the power of the story to the single, sacred designation of a name for an infant boy in the summer of 1934. His parents—of Cherokee, French, Scots, Anglo, Mexican, and Kiowa descent—had taken him to the very center of the Kiowa cultural universe, the chimney of volcanic rock rising on the north slopes of the Black Hills of Wyoming, to be held before the "Tsoai" (Rock-tree) of the *Kwuda* (the people coming out). At Devil's Tower, "Pohd-lohk affirmed the whole life of the child in a name, saying: Now you are, Tsoai-talee [Rock-tree Boy]." And yet to accomplish this act of naming, of establishing a course for the river that stirred inside the boy, Pohd-lohk "spoke, as if telling a story, of the coming-out people, of their long journey. He spoke of how it was when everything began, of Tsoai, and of the stars falling or holding fast in the sky." In making a name for the infant cradled in his arms, Old Wolf began his story in a time before names (57).

Thus names and places find union in the people who link them, and in the linkage one kind of history comes into conversation with another. Keith Basso elucidated similar phenomena in his acclaimed *Wisdom Sits in Places: Landscape and Language among the Western Apache* (1996a). When Apache men and women "drink" from places through their place-names, names derived either from a mythic past or from specific historical events, Basso writes that "like their ancestors before them, they display by word and deed that beyond the visible reality of place lies a moral reality which they themselves have come to embody" (Basso 1996b). Compressed into dynamic metaphors, Apache toponyms prescribe specific behavioral solutions for individuals in moral crisis. Yet in summoning one moment from the past while letting others lie unspoken, Apache place-names are themselves acts of voice and silence, of narrative assertion and omission, of inclusion or exclusion in the interest of indigenous identity maintenance. The effectiveness of the place-name resides almost entirely in the linguistic and cultural fluency of the listener: outsiders by birth, generation, or diaspora may find themselves beyond the constituting power of the metaphor. The name becomes, in the words of the critical theorist Charlie Shepherdson, "productive, as having effects within history itself" (Shepherdson 1999:17).

But names and history are also very different things, however much they may be intertwined and mutually constitutive. Momaday's sensitive and elegant family history lies centrally within the question I address in this essay: How might attention to names and naming, powerful acts of assumption and ascription alike, provide one point of entry into the complexity of representing the pasts of indigenous peoples in North America and other regions of the world as native societies engaged with the Western imperial world? Extending this even further, how does "naming the past" in the form of assumed, ascribed, and discovered historical narratives continue to shape the lives and identities of Native peoples today (Cornell 2000)?

My specific interest is with peoples who, like Momaday's progenitors, found themselves by force or volition biologically and culturally mixed with the agents of intrusive imperial powers, yet worked their identity narratives to retain or claim an indigenous stance. I look at peoples of mixed descent who occupied 19th-century pastoral borderlands in the American Southwest, the Russian Caucasus, the Canadian West, and Southern Africa, for across these vast spaces profound socioeconomic change proceeded only lightly mediated by state-level institutions like schools, churches, modern armies, and labor systems, the apparati by which names came to be sedimented in popular imagination and scholarly praxis. Thus the names they gave themselves, and the names by which they were known to intruders, worked with a degree of autonomy absent in the 20th-century world, yet one that I argue is forcefully reasserting itself in the 21st century. The indigenous and imperial peoples who shared common landscapes prior to the formation of 19th-century nation-states sorted themselves internally and interactively into names meant to define, in some sense, the nature of their relationships. For a good portion of the 19th century in each of these regions Native and intrusive peoples inhabited nondominant frontiers, volatile cultural borderlands in which no one group could assert a monopoly of power. This uncertainty in the nature of power found reflection in an uncertainty of names. Group survival often meant the creation of a flexible cultural matrix by which sameness and difference were interwoven in processes of inclusion and exclusion, often violent, yet always conditioned by the need to maintain some form of socioeconomic interdependency. By the late 19th century the formative states in which these mixed-descent peoples lived began to gain the capacity to dominate on-the-ground relations and narrative production, with diverse and unexpected consequences for these borderland peoples. The ability of names to straddle constraint and opportunity began to slip away (cf. Adelman and Aron 1999).

The 20th century saw this flexibility largely lost—however much local peoples worked to hide or disguise their alternative and oppositional transcripts, modern nations like the United States, the Soviet Union, Canada, and South Africa all crafted political hegemonies by gaining monopolies on violence and historical production (Watson 1994; Scott 1999). In this essay, however I proceed on the assumption that our long century just ended has become, for the 21st century, an analytical obstacle. Stable national borders, homogeneous national populations, monopolies of violence, cultural and political hegemonies—all seem to be vanishing in the solvent of global capitalism. And yet the sociopolitical handmaiden of our new capitalism, a neoliberalism meant to emancipate individual subjects from national, tribal, or ethnic passions, seems to have inspired the very opposite. As Peter Geschiere and Francis Nymanjoh have recently argued for Africa, in an insight nearly universal to the 21st-century world, "democratization seems to trigger a general obsession with autochthony and ethnic citizenship invariably defined against 'strangers'—that is, against all who 'do not really belong'" (2000:423). The capacity to claim an indigenous social and moral priority, even if one's descent is largely hybrid, has become hugely more powerful in a world in which the sociological and moral justifications beneath Western imperialism and nation-states lie in ruins. This "dialectic of flow and closure" cannot be entirely resolved by the stories that follow, but might be illuminated by them. My method is to set aside the 20th century and look back to the 19th, when notions like Natives and newcomers, indigenes and imperialists, or nations, tribes, and colors were as yet in the process of evolution. I offer several stories about names that place the tensions between 19th-century identity narratives and those emerging in the 21st century in high relief, and, for the most part, let the consonance and incongruity among them do the work of creating a wider critical vision.

This approach entails an experiment in narrative strategy. I wish first to propose that borderland stories speak in several ways—as histories complete within themselves, as historical dialogues with the potential for mutual enlightenment, and as forecasts for phenomena yet to come. I therefore employ a historical poetics invoking metonym and metaphor. Like Western Apache place-names, metonymic stories pack tremendous richness of detail into dense packages that expand in the listener's mind to stand for even more complex narratives. Lest they stand entirely alone, however, I ask these metonymic tales to engage with their neighbors in a metaphoric relation. By this I mean that metaphors should do more than simply suggest comparison. They ought to work by analogy toward linking domains in unexpected and creative ways and allow a radical shift in perspective through which one particular reality appears wholly different when approached from different angles. I place stories from 19th-century cultural borderlands in discontinuous dialogue with those from our own time and await what Kenneth Burke (1954:90) once called the "glimpse of incongruity—hitherto unsuspected connectives which we . . . note in the progressions of a dream . . . [connections that] exemplify relationships between objects which our customary rational vocabulary has ignored." Crafting dreamlike progressions of incongruity in the interests of analytical insight is a far cry from the conventional approach to comparative history, but just might yield a depth-of-field heretofore lacking in our efforts.

The risk is obvious. Whether or not the strategy succeeds is—like the efficacy of the Apache place-name—entirely up to the audience. But we can only know by trying. Let us consider a series of stories organized around names—of individuals, families, and communities. We can begin with one name, or more precisely, two names that have become so conflated in the popular minds that they pretend to engage in explanation by simple proximity.

INDIVIDUALS

Many of us spent the winter months of the turning century transfixed as the ghastly battle for control of the city of Grozny in Chechnya unfolded. Amid the images of blackened armored personnel carriers, of young men displaying listless bravado or wounded and weeping for their mothers, and the blasted buildings and leaden faces of Grozny itself, two names found constant, symmetrical mention: Shamil Basayev and Shamil, the imam of Daghestan. Shamil Basayev, of course, was the leader of the Chechen forces besieged in Grozny, the strategic culmination of his ten-year career as a Chechen nationalist and military commander. His travels had taken him from Abkhazia to Karabakh to Afghanistan and back to Chechnya for a key role in the first war that brought the two sides to a temporary truce in 1996. It was his decision to export revolution to neighboring Daghestan in the fall of last year that resulted in the Russian siege of Grozny. That action ended in February with the Chechens' nightmarish retreat from the city, in which Basayev had the front half of his foot blown away by a butterfly mine. In a different register the conflict continues today.

Hardly a news report went by that did not find some way to mention that Shamil Basayev shared a name with the Imam Shamil, leader of "the tribes of the north Caucasus" in their first holy war against Russian expansion. Their jihad lasted from 1834 to 1859, when Shamil surrendered himself and his forces at a fortress near Vedeno, Chechnya—Shamil Basayev's birthplace. The master narrative in this evocation of names wished to convince us of the undying and irredeemable hostility between Russians and Chechens and the inscrutable depth of Chechens' ethnoreligious commitment to tribal, if not national, autonomy. In some cases, Western reportage even set aside religion as a causal variable and dwelt instead on the martial culture of Chechens, presumably traceable from the dawn of time through the imam to Basayev without interruption. For example, the American strategy journal *Military Review* offered this assessment:

> The Chechens are a warrior people, one of a number of fiercely independent tribes within the mountainous regions of the Caucasus. Living

along an invasion route between Europe and Asia, a deep and enduring warrior tradition evolved among these peoples. The Chechens gained the reputation of doggedly resisting any foreign domination. Whether it was the Mongols in the 13th, the Turks in the 16th, or the Russians in the 19th and 20th centuries, the Chechens have never accepted foreign rule. Though the Russians managed in the 19th century, after more than thirty years of fighting, to seize most of the Chechen territory, they were never able to fully incorporate the Chechen people into the Russian Empire. [Finch 1997:33]

No student of American Indian history would find the foregoing "warrior race" trope unfamiliar to the ear, nor the way in which such discourse elides the presence of stable and enduring civil societies within "martial peoples" (Enloe 1979).

For his part, Shamil Basayev (2000) does not shy away from the associations, noting on his website that he "honors the memory of the Imam." Unlike the Western emphasis on primordial military culture, however, his explanation for the war in Chechnya is entirely religious: "It is the Islam of the Chechens that fanned the flames of hatred among the Czarists, the Bolsheviks, and the Communists . . . anyone who wants to know about the truth should study history to find out how long the Russians have been taking revenge against the Muslims of Chechnya."

What happens if we take this call for a resort to history seriously and look at the savagery of 21st-century Chechnya from the perspective of the 19th? Doing so casts both Western and local interpretations into some doubt. Indeed, the Russian Empire and the peoples of the Caucasus did engage in protracted violence for the better part of the 19th century, a conflict that ended formally with the imam's surrender in 1859 and the wholesale deportation of holdout Circassians to Turkey in 1864. Unlike the Interior Ministry troops that prosecute the current war, however, the 19th-century Russian advance was spearheaded by local militaries, generally known as the Terek Cossacks, after the Terek River that bisects Chechnya just north of Grozny. In the Russian imagination, these and other Cossacks represented the inexorable advance of Russian civilization through the process of the "gathering of the peoples (nardony)"—a cultural construct that allowed any peoples of Slavic descent and peasant lifestyle to exemplify the essence of Russianness however distant they lived from Muscovy (Barrett 1994, 1995; Barrett in Brower and Lazzerini 1997; Barrett 1999).

But in actuality the Terek Cossacks fell far from the cultural hearth of Russia. Instead, they emerged out of a conglomeration of refugees and brigands from backgrounds as various as Caspian pirates, Kuban princes, Circassian nomads, Okochesnkii Tartars (either Chechens or Ingushi), and migratory Georgians. Thus the "intrusive" agents of Russian expansion were drawn in part from indigenous peoples. Their confessional status seems equally diverse: Old Believers whose primitive gnosticism saw greater danger in the secularizing thrust of the Russian Orthodox Church than in Islam and who managed to live side by side with no small number of Muslim Cossacks; or Orthodox Russian colonists whose commitment to Christianity was more instrumental than heartfelt, adjacent to nomadic "idol-worshippers" who quietly ignored the conversion efforts of Christians and Muslims alike. What they shared was a landscape of grassy foothills and timbered mountains well suited to transhumant pastoralism, a willingness to pledge nominal allegiance to the Russian Empire when doing so met local ends, and an even greater willingness to ignore or subvert Russia's attempts to create cultural quarantines around their regional identity. Indeed, the very gradualness of the Russian conquest may have been due as much to local inertia as to the ferocity of the "hill tribes." For every pitched battle fought between Terek Cossacks and the mountaineers of the Caucasus there took place dozens of face to face negotiations in which products of the steppes were exchanged for those of the mountains. In fact, Thomas Barrett has argued that "trade relations between the Cossacks of the Terek and the peoples of the Caucasus did not diminish [with Russian expansion], but were vital to the Cossack economy into the 19th century, even during the period of the most intense warfare of Russian against Chechen" (Barrett 1997:228). And however many fleet horses were bartered for Circassian cloaks and sheepskin caps, the enduring glue in this borderland's exchange economy lay in human beings.

We can never know the numbers of captives, slaves, fugitives, and deserters who passed from Cossack *stanitsi* into the *auls* of the hill peoples (or vise versa), but their presence in anecdotal sources and Russian literary production suggests a degree of ethnic mixture that today seems staggering. Forcible cross-cultural marriage unions certainly drove the initial phase of exchange—the gender balance in Cossack communities first censused in the late 18th century stood at three men to every one woman, where by the mid-19th century the sexes were equally represented. Russian cossackification policies placed high emphasis on the need for men to marry and raise families, in part to root their loyalties more firmly in their homes but also because in Cossack settlements women farmers produced virtually all of the wheat and wine that provided their economic mainstay. Russia occasionally exported women convicts from the Russian interior to the Caucasus, and Cossacks had first claim on female prisoners taken in military campaigns. State sponsored bride theft even included Russian authorities turning a blind eye to Cossack wife-stealing raids into the Russian provinces of Penza, Samara, and Voronezh. But non-Christian women of the mountains presented the preferred targets for both local men and authorities in Moscow, who offered 45 silver rubles to any Terek Cossack who would convert and marry a captive woman. For Muscovites, such a marriage represented the triumph of Christianity over Islam. For the Cossack husband, however, a captive wife from a hill tribe brought with her the cultural repertoire of language, custom, kinship, and religion that would allow her husband (and family) to tap into resources otherwise beyond their reach (Barrett 1999:129–145). For the question at hand, such captures and assimilations disrupt any easy designation of the Terek Cossacks as allochthons or "outsiders" to the cultural world of the north Caucasus.

This violent and vital system of cross-cultural exogamy did not reside solely with the Cossacks. In addition to extensive intermarriage among the several score of Muslim "ethnic" groups in Daghestan and Chechnya, through which the imam worked to substantiate a shared future for his inclusive Islamic republic, Imam Shamil used marriages to create kin-linkages across the Christian-Muslim divide of the Caucasus Line (Gammar 1994). Cossack and Russian deserters found brides awaiting them in Shamil's camps, since he had issued a regulation that abolished punishments for local girls convicted of premarital sex if they would marry a converted Russian fugitive (Barrett 1999:132). Shamil himself was a practitioner of the trade. His favorite wife, Shuanet, had begun her life as Anna Ulykhanova in the city of Mozdok. Abducted as a teenager, she refused several ransom attempts by her brothers. Twelve years later she played the gracious hostess to two Georgian princesses held captive in Shamil's household, whose published account of their captivity became wildly popular in Moscow. Thus the imam's domestic arrangements reflected outward into his broad, multiethnic vision of an Islamic republic that would unite Daghestan and Chechnya. As objects of Russian literary imagination and as tangible threats to Russian control in the Caucasus, captives and fugitives who "crossed over" (and often back again, several times in a single life) do much to unsettle the essentializing and distancing discourse we see in Western and Chechen accounts of the region's history (Layton 1994:81–99; 1997, 175 ff).

When Shamil Basayev claims to "honor the memory" of his predecessor, we might also wonder what portion of that memory he intends? Indeed, the imam did on several occasions defeat Cossack and Russian armies, sometimes resoundingly. He did at times also torture and execute his prisoners. But his surrender in 1859 hardly proved a humiliation, since he (and Shuanet) became the toast of Moscow, were feted by the tsar, painted and photographed endlessly, and received the gift of an estate in Kaluga. During his 12 years in Russian hands he worked tirelessly to defuse the conflict in his homeland, and helped to negotiate several local truces. In 1870, his captors even permitted him a pilgrimage to Mecca, where he remained until his death in 1871 (Barrett 1994). For his part, Shamil Basayev might do well to place the imam's more complex history next to his own. Basayev, the bearded lion of Chechen nationalism, was in Moscow when the Berlin Wall fell, pursuing a lackluster career as a computer salesman. He first took up arms not to free Chechnya from the Soviet embrace but to defend Boris Yeltsin in the Parliament Building against the army coup of August 1991. It was only with the declaration of Chechen independence later that year that he returned home to organize his elite "Abkhaz Battalion." Even today he admits that he maintains no plans toward "the establishment of a Chechen state that fulfills legal and financial aspirations," beyond a call for the Islamic world to provide "massive financial support and the presence of Islamic scholars" (Basayev 2000). In retrospect, the 19th-century imam of Daghestan seems much more the modern nation builder, and Basayev more the opportunistic tribalist. Further vexing to the exclusivist indigenous stance taken by Basayev and other ethnic nationalists in the Caucasus is the ongoing effort—sanctioned by the Russian Federation since 1990—by descendants of the Terek Cossacks to assert themselves as an indigenous "nationality" within the new federation (Holquist 1988). Among the new identity symbols they flourish is the slogan—of tortured logic given their diverse origins—KAZACHEMU RODU NYET PEREVODU (The Cossack bloodline will never perish). As Cossack ataman Vladimir Shevtsov, founder of the volunteer Yermolov Battalion formed to fight Basayev's Chechens in 1996, recently told a visiting journalist, "You can use names in many ways" (Karny 2000:38, 49).

What are we to make of this story of the two Shamils? It certainly falls in line with the ongoing work of progressive scholars to undercut narratives of "primordial hatreds" and "blood politics" throughout the 21st-century world (cf. Bringa 1995; Daniel 1996; Karakasidou 1997; Besteman 1999). It does much to point a causative finger toward the role of 20th-century states like the Soviet Union in creating ethnically defined political blocs that were vulnerable to ethnonational entrepreneurs like Basayev and Slobodan Milosevic after the collapses of 1991. But it also casts unsettling light on local identity dynamics where assertions of autochthony may be manipulative and instrumental, thereby tainting the authenticity of more just claims. My goal in looking backward to 19th-century patterns of interethnic conflict and accommodation, of names and naming, is to also seek meaningful commonalties and divergences in those relationships, to take the shape-shifting essence of names in the borderlands as a place of entry into more complex levels of analysis. In this case (and those to come), the question of names leads us directly into the realm of gendered power.

I have written elsewhere about the peculiar structures of constraint and opportunity that some women found in the captive-exchange system of the Southwest borderlands, wherein Indian and colonizing men vied to seize and assimilate each other's women and children in a broadly shared contest over patriarchal prestige and community honor. This issue lies at the center of my monograph *Captives and Cousins: Slavery, Kinship, and Community in the Southwest Borderlands* (2001), where I looked at several centuries of interaction between indigenous and Euro-American peoples in the American Southwest. I argue there that a "borderland political economy" organized much of interethnic life across that region, wherein through the seizure and exchange of human captives and livestock Indian groups and Euro-American settlers came to share an understanding of the production and distribution of wealth as conditioned by social relations of power. This mutual understanding depended much on the ability of colonizing and indigenous men to agree that their women and children were at once their most cherished relations *and* their most contestable of resources. This gendered universe of emotional, cultural, and material exchange produced a history by which the peoples of the Southwest—Comanches, Kiowas, Apaches, Utes, Navajos, Pueblos, and Spaniards—were drawn, in the words of the poet A. D. Hope, "closer and closer apart" (1986:20–21).

Valorized as objects of contestation, yes, but more than a few such captives found their multilingual and multicultural skills valued and respected in their "host" societies. Some attained through their victimization social status and economic autonomy they might never have dreamed possible in their natal homes. María Rosa Villalpando crossed from Comanche captivity through Pawnee slavery to marriage with the French fur trader Jean Salé, after whose return to Europe she became Marie Rose Salé, the matriarch of a prosperous mixed-blood mercantile family in St. Louis. Juana Hurtado Galván crossed from Spanish servitude through Navajo captivity to a freehold near Zia Pueblo, where she amassed a small fortune in the Indian trade and resisted all efforts by Spanish padres to reform her free-wheeling conjugal lifestyle (Brooks 1996). Others remained with their captors. Ten-year-old Andrés Martínez became Andele, fully accepted and thrice married among the Kiowas (Methven 1997 [1899]). And Momaday's great-great-grandmother, her Mexican name unknown, moved through captivity and slavery to marriage with the Kiowa Ah-kgoo-ahu, and in doing so gained her enduring name, Kau-au-ointy. Many other women and children simply settled into the kinship nexus of their capturing society, whether Indian or Spanish, and in time achieved full cultural enfranchisement. Their names, or course, changed with their movements across cultures, are nearly lost to us today.

I caution in that work, however, that their stories must always be viewed in the context of a highly militarized and masculinized borderlands economy that rested on what Maria Mies has termed a "predatory mode of appropriation" (1988). The obvious extension here is to current cases of interethnic conflict in which women and children remain objects of male contestation, but brutally so, in that "kin-building violence" of forcible adoption and exogamy is replaced with "exclusionary violence" of rape and murder. The successful 1998 prosecution of Rwandan Hutu rapists under UN genocide codes—and movement toward the same in the former Yugoslavia—is an important breakthrough in humanitarian law but does not solve the analytical challenge. As in Veena Das's (1990, 1998) work on the gendered violence of Hindu-Muslim conflict along the Indo-Pakistani border, I wish to grasp the particular sets of historical forces and circumstance that account for transpositions in these two faces of the patriarchal construction and preservation of local communities. Answers lie in careful contextual study of cases in which transformations in cultural meanings of patrimony, property, citizenship, and territoriality become manifest.

The Southwest borderlands suggest at least one story. I argue that certain families and communities found prosperity amid this constellation of predatory and appropriative exchanges. Operating within a political economy of mutually held respect for patriarchal honor and pastoral wealth, poor or landless Spanish colonists and neighboring Indian groups like Utes, Navajos, Kiowas, and Comanches elaborated a captive-and-livestock raiding economy that brought real power to both sides as they plundered resources from each other's societies.

They did not do so gently. Driven by parallel desires for emotional retribution and economic redistribution, settlers and their indigenous neighbors waged two hundred years of what contemporary observers termed a "ceaseless and predatory war" but that in actuality may be better encompassed by Clifford Geertz's phrase "a low-intensity peace" (2000:260). The real bloodshed and dislocation occurred in the process of American "pacification" of the Southwest. Military conquest, civilizing missions, and ethnological systemization disrupted a flexible and locally negotiated social formation. Conquest imposed in its stead new categories of racialized and second-class citizenship for mestizo New Mexicans and "tribal" membership for Indians, both of which were "exclusive identities" whose security lay all too heavily in dependence on a none-too-sympathetic state (Brooks 1999, 2000).

One key to the earlier pattern of long-term, agonizing "peace" lay in the forceful assimilation of women and children from the other society, an exercise of "community as violence" that whatever its amorality, must be analyzed as constitutive of enduring social formations. Shared codes of patriarchal and pastoral honor were probably crucial to the creation of widespread communities of violence that—while they terrorized and alienated women and children— seldom raped or killed them. This seems congruent with studies in other cultural borderlands, like David Nirenberg's (1996) work on early modern Spain, Deborah Poole's (1988, 1994) on the Peruvian Andes, and Steven Caton's (1990; 1998) work with the poetics of gendered power among Yemeni tribesmen. Each suggests communitywide understandings of the role of culturally sanctioned violence in producing social stability, a "sensible violence" rendered insensible to us from our particular frames of reference today.

Other elements were necessary as well. Seasonal coresidence on hunting and grazing lands created a spacious middle ground whereon "identity-as-territoriality" was seldom invoked, a no-man's-land that was in fact all-men's-land. (And I do mean men.) Populations damaged by epidemic disease nurtured a customary cultural openness to the creation of cross-cultural affinal and fictive kin ties. And the presence of "portable" wealth like stolen sheep, horses, and cattle provided ample opportunities for "communities of interest" to form irrespective of their "ethnic antagonisms." In this latter aspect the imam Shamil's mixed racial and ethnic "republic" in the Caucasus stands as anomalous only in its size and durability. Many similar raiding bands roamed other borderlands, lesser in size and at a greater distance from intrusive state power. Even when severe hostility or judgment might be directed against any specific act on their part, the unfolding fabric of violent interaction "produced a shifting but coherent reality" that liberated some peoples from class, gender, and racial subjugation (Calhoun 1998). Others, both innocent and complicit, it punished. It seems clear that like their 19th-century counterparts, 21st-century borderlands redirect social patterns of flow and obstruction in unexpected and sometimes opportunistic ways for peoples formerly fixed in the lower strata of a given society. While borderlands are often places of terror, they are places of possibility as well.

FAMILIES

If the tale of two individuals bound by a single name leads us to one perspective on the intricacies of indigenous identity across the centuries, another story, this time of one family and their experience in the borderlands of western Canada, leads us to quite another. A less dramatic story, yet for its protagonists just as emotionally complex and politically confounding. We can take it up simply enough, in a letter from James Douglas to his youngest daughter, Martha, attending boarding school in England in the 1850s. "I have no objection," he wrote, "to your telling old stories about 'Hyass,' but pray do not tell the world they are Mamma's" (Van Kirk 1980:237).

In certain respects Martha's mother, Amelia Connolly, is a mirror image of Anna Ulykhanova (or Shuanet), yet in a far more humble and less celebrated form. Like hundreds of other mixed-descent children in Canada, she was born around 1810 of a marriage *à la façon du pays* between William Connolly, chief factor of the Hudson's Bay trading post at New Caledonia, and a Cree woman, Suzanne Pas-de-Nom (I need not point out the awful silence in her "name"). Raised in the multilingual, multiethnic society of the Canadian fur trade, Amelia seems to have absorbed the best of the myriad influences surrounding her. In 1828 she married James Douglas, second-in-command to Connolly at the post, again in the fashion of the country (Brown 1980:90–92; 215).

Within months of that union she saved her husband's life through her awareness of local Carrier Indian culture. Douglas had arrested and executed a Carrier man for a murder committed at the Fort George post, after which the Carrier's kinsmen seized and threatened to kill him in compensation. Amelia rushed into the post's warehouse and began throwing trade goods to the angry crowd. Since the "throwing of gifts" was, according to Carrier custom, a mark of deference and submission, the Indians accepted her restitution and departed (Van Kirk 1980:111–113).

James Douglas and Amelia Connolly would move on to the governorship of Vancouver Island, and later, after his elevation to the British nobility, Amelia wore the title Lady Douglas with grace. Yet in their retirement they returned closer to her mother's people's homeland along the shores of James Bay, where Amelia found greater comfort among her Cree kinspeople than she had amid the social scene of the British colonial elite. James too felt more comfortable there, for he had grown bitter about the increasingly racist attitudes that the company (and British Canadians in general) held toward Indian peoples and mixed-descent wives of officers like himself. He had attempted to quiet some of the gossip by inviting Amelia to wed him in 1837 in a Church of England ceremony, but the increasing migration of British women as officers' wives created an atmosphere of constant racial invective. Spurning the example of his own father-in-law, who had repudiated Suzanne Pas-de-Nom in 1832 and quickly married his British cousin, James spoke often in defense of the honor of Indian and mixed-blood women who "lived chastely with husbands of [their] choice, in a state approved by friends and sanctioned by immemorial custom" (Van Kirk

1980:156). But his retreat under the assault of racist ideology is clearly evident in his letter to Martha, a symbolic surrender and conclusion to a long joint effort to "throw" some alternative family conception to a world unwilling to accept the gift.

The Connolly-Douglas family is just one element a larger story I am pursuing across the expanse of the Canadian West. Here I focus on Amelia's Indian kinspeople, known to contemporaries as the Home Guard Cree. Unlike the French-Indian mixed-descent peoples generally referred to as Métis, who have attracted much attention in recent scholarship, the Home Guard Cree remain little understood, perhaps because they represent a maddeningly ambiguous case of borderland community formation. Where the Métis, or at least their famous Red River variant, achieved a cohesive and relatively firm identity as ethnogenetic "New Peoples" by the early years of the 19th century—and would in later years raise two rebellions to retain the right to that autochthonous identity—the Home Guard Cree are hard to pin down. Descended not from French but British fathers and Cree mothers, they were probably every bit as "mixed" as their Métis counterparts, yet they followed various and divergent trajectories across the century. Some, like Amelia, found assimilation into colonial society, despite its many discomforts. Others migrated south to the Red River and took up residence in the Church of England parishes just north of their Métis counterparts. But whereas the Métis elaborated a classically syncretic culture of market-based bison hunting, the Red River Cree settled to become earnest Anglican farmers. Others remained very much Indian despite their mixed blood and became the progenitors of numerous Cree communities in James Bay, Manitoba, and Ontario today (Foster 1975, 1976, 1978, 1985, 1994; Ens 1996).

Their case interests me in that they, more than many such groups, maintained a clear and relatively unproblematic dependency on the Hudson's Bay Company (HBC) and the later British colonial state. While the Terek Cossack "tribe" and Shamil's mixed ethnoreligious "nation" in the Caucasus depended in part for their cohesion on mutual antagonism, the Home Guard Cree seldom rebelled or complained. Even when economic crisis and adjustment within the Hudson's Bay Company shifted their role from that of hunters and couriers to institutionalized "servants" of the firm, the "Country-born" (as they were called to distinguish them from the Métis) adopted the status with relative ease. They developed parallel conceptions of rank and status to their Hudson's Bay Company counterparts and pursued mobility within those ranks in manners similar to the careers of company officers.

Again, it seems that gender and kinship relations provide one important clue to these durable relations of coexistence. The simple fact that European women were absent from the Hudson's Bay trading system prior to the 19th century dictated an impulse toward cross-cultural sexual unions. British men were allowed to consort with Cree women only in the context of Native marriage relationships, however. This constraint quickly led to a locally constructed system of polyandry, in which a Home Guard Cree woman would maintain a Cree husband and children but also wed a British man with whom she might live for varying periods of time. Children born of the latter union, like Amelia Connolly, were raised within the Cree community but had special access to the Hudson's Bay forts and employment therein. From the perspective of the Cree husband, the British husband was a "brother," and a valuable asset to the family and band. In fact, it appears that Cree families engaged in much maneuvering to acquire "brothers" with the best access to HBC storehouses. If their British "brothers" failed to behave and perform within the Cree definitions of reciprocal kin relations, violence was applied to restore proper comportment.

It was only in the 1830s, with significant immigration of British women into Canada and new HBC policies that prohibited mixed marriages *à la façon du pays*, that this remarkable system ran aground on the shoals of institutional racism. The "many tender ties" (to quote Douglas again) that linked British and Cree in a successful borderland negotiation were thereafter sundered, and the divergent paths of the Home Guard Cree noted above would begin to unfold. The Red River community would move in the direction of "whiteness" and assimilation to the British imperial mold, while those who remained in the hinterlands would shade toward "redness"—and treaty recognition in 1980 as "First Nations" within the Canadian national federation—two paths to color and culture that shaped their remaining histories (Flanagan 1999; Niezen 2000).

The kin-and-gender aspects of community formation in the Caucasian and Canadian borderlands seem to affirm Lévi-Straussian notions of exchanges of women as the cauldron of culture, as well as those feminist critiques and extensions offered by theorists like Gayle Rubin and Jane Collier (Lévi-Strauss 1969 [1949]; Rubin 1975; Collier 1988). But to simply dispense with these as yet further examples of how women and children serve as "floating signifiers" in patriarchal negotiations overlooks the unexpected elements of structural opportunity afforded women and children in the cross-cultural event. Jacqueline Peterson (1988) has argued that at least some of the Indian women in mixed Canadian marriages had, in childhood, experienced powerful dreams that set them apart from culturally sanctioned vision roles available to Indian women. Mantled with dream power that in some sense alienated them from their natal communities, they undertook the task of subduing and acculturating dangerous outsiders. A too romantic view? Perhaps. But it confirms our need for deeper and more culturally specific understandings of the gendered experience of transborder exchanges in the creation of cultural mélange amid formative states, as well as the extraordinary risk some women were willing to take when they challenged "primordial divides" in the interests of family, community, and the heart (Carter 1997).

COMMUNITIES

We have now explored two stories of the indigenous experience in 19th-century borderlands—first, the life story of two individuals writ large for the Caucasus, and second, that of the Connolly-Douglas family writ large across western Canada. Let us now consider a third at the more inclusive level of community. Here I draw your mind's eye to the sweet grass of the high veld north of the Orange River in South Africa, where by 1800 a conglomerate community of refugee peoples would soon designate themselves as "Griqua." Over the course of the century they would provide perhaps our best example of a successful plural community, only to serve as a grim illustration of just how vulnerable such an experiment can prove in the long term. From a people with sufficient economic and military power to challenge Trekboer suzerainty in Transorangia, and to buffer the Cape Colony from the regional conflagration of Zulu expansion, they were by century's end landless and had disappeared into the stigmatized status of "Cape Coloureds." Their history is a lengthy and tortuous one, but a glance at one unremarked aspect of that story reveals another contribution border studies may make to questions about the intersections of local and global processes.

Like the mixed communities of the Caucasus and Canada, these too were the product of imperial intrusion. The Dutch colony on the western Cape struck the local Khoikhoin peoples with such force that their pastoral economy and social organization were effectively destroyed. Those who were not enslaved became stockless hunters, gatherers, and cattle raiders in the hills, or took service with Dutch farmers. Their debilitation included forcible capture and concubinage of their women among the invaders, from which unions emerged socially marginal peoples on the fringes of the colony, termed "Bastaard-Hottentots," relegated to bound labor or slavery on colonial farms or squatting as small subsistence farmers along its frontiers (Elphick 1977).

In a sense, however, the concentric waves of disorganization radiating outward from the Cape would be their salvation, especially as imperial wars for control of the colony between 1795 and 1814 destabilized its internal power as well. By the latter quarter of the 18th century a gradual accretion of refugee Khoi and Bastaard peoples commenced along the Berg River under the leadership of a manumitted slave named Adam Kok. Community memory claims that Kok there married "a chief's daughter" among the indigenous Chariguriqua peoples, probably paying the bride-price from the large herd of (stolen) cattle he drove along in his migration. Kok died in 1795, but it seems his Chariguriqua kinspeople accompanied his son, Cornelis, on a long pastoral migration across Namaqualand and into the interior along the Orange River (Marais 1939; Ross 1976:14–17).

This region, known today as Griqualand West, had long been a borderland itself, where the northernmost extension of Khoikhoin peoples met the southernmost expression of Bantu speakers, the Tswana, and the eastern fringes of San hunters and gatherers. Lacking adequate rainfall for settled agriculture without irrigation, it was prime grazing land, and the Kok patriline, with their Bastaard allies, made the most of the opportunity. At the fountains around Klaarwater they established a base that gave them not only control of the regional pastoral economy (and its supply-side variant, cattle raiding) but near-monopoly control of the interior ivory trade as well. Over the next several decades they would add more diverse members to their mixed community. By 1813 it was reckoned that the subjects of Adam Kok II (Cornelis's son) consisted of some 1,200 Chariguriqua and Bastaards, 150 Tswana, 1,300 Kora, and 30 families of Sotho. Even some San peoples found assimilation, but in their case as deracinated servile herders and laborers. Other San became victims of Griqua slavers supplying the ready, if surreptitious, market for slave children south of the Orange River (Legassick 1989).

This last reference sounds a familiar refrain: the willingness of mixed borderland communities to exploit weaker indigenous groups with whom they interacted. No case among the five borderlands I'm studying is without this trait. Even the Home Guard Cree took pleasure in exercising their military advantage over neighboring Assiniboines in the Canadian interior, taking captives or occasionally supplying victims to a regional captive-and-slave trade with Lower Canada. But in all these cases there also existed avenues for adoption and assimilation that enfranchised, if not the first generation of victims, their mixed-blood descendants. In this sense, mixed communities always embodied an egalitarian impulse that pushed against the stratifying tendencies of pastoral patriarchy or colonial emulation.

This paradox provides a place of entry into the last theme developed here: borderland communities as sites where local culture and exogenous force intersect in an imaginative community politics. Across their first several decades these mixed communities had operated under a loose clan structure wherein ties of kinship and clientage remained paramount. Adam Kok II and Berend Berends, his Bastaard ally, wielded classic patriarchal power over their extended kin groups, affirmed from afar when the Cape government recognized them as "joint Kaptyns over the nascent polity" in 1804 (Legassick 1989:380).

But the very success of their borderland adaptation invited instability. As center people in the regional economy, with a virtual monopoly on horses and firearms, they were attractive allies to neighboring indigenous groups and the Cape Colony alike. The colonial government had greater resources with which to entice their alliance (especially gunpowder) but demanded in turn that they supply young men for service in the Cape (Hottentot) Regiment. Kok and Berends saw this as a slap at their hard-won autonomy. A solution lay in pursuing relations with the London Missionary Society, first invited to Klaarwater by Berends in 1801. Missions served as conduits through which Christianity, firearms, colonial citizenship, and collective representation flowed in equal measures. They also acted as magnets for the in-migration of Xhosa and San bands who settled at mission stations as informal dependents of the Kok and Berends clans, thereby swelling the latter's social wealth (Legassick 1989:374ff.).

Commercial power, Christianity, and immigration combined in a volatile matrix of political tensions within and outside of the community. Internal friction sparked in various ways: between junior men of the two principal clans and their patriarchs, especially over the former's wish to continue the traditional commando economy of trading and raiding, as against the elders' plans to develop sheep ranching and commercial farming; between recently arrived peoples who desired full enfranchisement and the foundational clans who wanted subordinate dependents; and between the patriarchs and the missionaries over the political structure of the community in general. External tensions lay in the community's contradictory expectations of colonial citizenship and political independence, both of which had to be mediated by missionaries like William Anderson and John Campbell, themselves viewed as suspicious by authorities in Cape Town.

How could the heterogeneous and contentious community at Klaarwater loosen this Gordian knot of antagonisms? With a creativity of mind equal to the creativity of practice that had brought them there in the first place. In the course of one year (1813–14) these mixed peoples conceived and asserted two interwoven identities, that of a "tribe" and that of a "nation" within an "empire." Casting back to a seemingly minor historical moment, John Campbell reported that "on consulting among themselves they [the peoples at Klaarwater] found a majority were descended from a person of the name of 'Griqua'"– that is, from the nameless Chariguriqua woman whom Adam Kok I had "wed" on his migration toward the Orange River. In a purposeful act of strategic remembering, they renamed her, and themselves, in the interests of community. An act of imagination as well, at least for a great number of its diverse members, but it was effective nonetheless. By "becoming indigenous" they became, however implicitly, culturally autonomous within the world of colonial southern Africa. And in "becoming Griqua" they also shed former indigenous identities like Khoikhoi, San, or Xhosa that bore the stigma of defeat and flight. After centuries of colonial dispersal and denigration, they reinvented themselves as a vital community amid a landscape widespread with devastation and sorrow (Legassick 1989:382–383).

But to have simply "gone native" was only half of the creative act, for they also needed recognition as colonial subjects and citizens to maintain their rights to land, representation, and military resupply. The Griqua now, in collaboration with Campbell, became a "nation" by drafting a formal constitution, which in turn formalized their capacity to negotiate with the Cape Colony as a nominally self-governing state within the colonial sphere. Their constitution also sought to redress some of the community's internal tensions. Adam Kok II and Berend Berends were to remain as "chiefs and kaptyns" (itself a conflation of two cultural categories) and with the missionaries would act as a court of appeal. But the document also called for the open election of nine magistrates responsible for the daily enforcement of its 13 clauses, thus opening the political process to junior men and recent immigrants alike. In doing so, the "indigenous" Griquas simultaneously claimed a "national" identity, modeled on the liberal politics then emerging in the Euro-American world. They seem to have fully expected to receive its associated rights and privileges (Legassick 1989; 384 ff.).

Of course, we know that it did not unfold that way, although the creative moment of 1813–14 would provide the basis for Griqua "democratic oligarchy" under which they functioned for the next two generations. Almost immediately junior men under the leadership of Andries Waterboer, a San-descended Griqua, seized the egalitarian initiative and expelled the Kok and Berends clans from Klaarwater, renaming it Griquatown. The long-term consequence of their rebellion, however, was that the expelled clans would establish new Griqua centers of power at Philippolis in the Orange Free State and Kokstad in Griqualand East, thereby extending their "tribe" and "nation" across some four hundred miles of cultural borderland. But with each successful settlement came undercutting pressures from an expanding "white" settler population moving into the hinterlands, and the funnel toward "Cape Coloured" status became narrower and faster (Ashforth 1990).

Griquas were not alone in finding inventive solutions to complex pressures erupting from colonial expansion across the 19th century. Nor are they helpless in the 21st century. Since the remarkable power reversal of 1994 in South Africa, dozens of indigenous African groups have demanded a place at the political table of that new pluralistic state. So too have some Griqua descendants, as the "Griqua National Conference." The irony here lies in their claim—almost as tortured as that of the Terek Cossacks, but toward which sympathy would extend were it not to erase history so completely—to represent "the last vestige of unbroken and uninterrupted Khoi heritage and identity" (Upham quoted in Morris 1997). Similar predicaments face transborder indigenous peoples today. The Griqua case extends seductively, if not seamlessly, to modern settings where local custom and contention are inextricably enmeshed with global processes. If intergenerational tension, racial politics, market penetration, Protestant evangelism, and immigration were crucial factors in their case, we need only look to Highland Chiapas, the Southern Sudan, or Eastern Europe to see their contemporary influence in midplay. The end game is not in sight, and while we cannot predict from the past, we may certainly find inspiration in its resonance. We can try to cultivate a sensitivity by which particular stories speak to each other, across boundaries, in a poetic, if not an analytical, sense; to find a way by which the distinct is preserved and the shared is enhanced, and to have these stories, at once as hybrid and discrete as their subjects themselves, become mutually embedded metaphors for each other; and to continue the work of names.

REFERENCES

Adelman, Jeremy and Stephen Aron
    1999   From Borderlands to Borders: Empires, Nation-States, and the Peoples in Between in North American History. American Historical Review 104(3):814–841.
Ashforth, Adam
    1990   The Politics of Official Discourse in Twentieth-Century South Africa. Oxford: Clarendon Press.
Barrett, Thomas M.
    1994   The Remaking of the Lion of Dagestan: Shamil in Captivity. The Russian Review 53:353–366.
    1995   Lines of Uncertainty: The Frontiers of the North Caucasus. Slavic Review 54(3):578–601.

1997   Crossing Boundaries: The Trading Frontiers of the Terek Cossacks. *In* Russia's Orient: Imperial Borderlands and Peoples, 1700–1917. Daniel R. Brower and Edward Lazzerini, eds. Pp. 227–248. Bloomington: Indiana University Press.

1999   At the Edge of Empire: The Terek Cossacks and the North Caucasus Frontier, 1700–1860. Boulder, CO, and Oxford: Westview Press.

Basayev, Shamil

2000   An Interview with Shamil Basayev, February 20 2000. www.qoqaz.net.

Basso, Keith

1996a   Wisdom Sits in Places: Landscape and Language among the Western Apache. Albuquerque: University of New Mexico Press.

1996b   Wisdom Sits in Places: Notes on a Western Apache Landscape. *In* Senses of Place. Steven Feld and Keith Basso, eds. Santa Fe: School of American Research Press.

Besteman, Catherine

1999   Unraveling Somalia: Race, Violence and the Legacy of Slavery. Philadelphia: University of Pennsylvania Press.

Bringa, Tone

1995   Being Muslim the Bosnian Way: Identity and Community in a Central Bosnian Village. Princeton: Princeton University Press.

Brooks, James F.

1996   "This Evil Extends Especially . . . to the Feminine Sex": Negotiating Captivity in the New Mexico Borderlands. Feminist Studies 22(2):279–309.

1999   Violence, Justice, and State Power in the New Mexico Borderlands, 1780–1880. *In* Power and Place in the North American West. Richard White and John Findlay, eds. Pp. 28–53. Seattle: University of Washington Press.

2000   Served Well by Plunder: La Gran Ladronería and Producers of History Astride the Río Grande. American Quarterly 52(1):23–58.

2001   Captives and Cousins: Slavery, Kinship, and Community in the Southwest Borderlands. Chapel Hill: University of North Carolina Press.

Brower, Daniel R., and Edward J. Lazzarini, eds.

1997   Russia's Orient: Imperial Borderlands and Peoples, 1700–1917. Bloomington: Indiana University Press.

Brown, Jennifer S. H.

1980   Strangers in Blood: Fur Trade Families in Indian Country. Vancouver: University of British Columbia Press.

Burke, Kenneth

1954   Persistence and Change: An Anatomy of Purpose. Berkeley: University of California Press.

Carter, Sarah A.

1997   Capturing Women: The Manipulation of Cultural Imagery in Canada's Prairie West. Toronto: McGill Queens University Press.

Caton, Steven C.

1990   "Peaks of Yemen I Summon": Poetry as Cultural Practice in a North Yemeni Tribe. Berkeley: University of California Press.

1999   "'Anger Be Now Thy Song': The Anthropology of an Event." Institute for Advanced Study Occasional Papers in the Social Sciences. No. 5.

Collier, Jane Fishburne

1988   Marriage and Inequality in Classless Societies. Stanford: Stanford University Press.

Cornell, Stephen

2000   Discovered Identities and American Indian Supratribalism. In We are a People. Paul Spickard and W. Jerrrey Borroughs, eds. Pp. 98–123.

Daniel, E. Valentine

1996   Charred Lullabies: Chapters in an Anthropography of Violence. Princeton: Princeton University Press.

Das, Veena, ed.

1990   Mirrors of Violence: Communities, Riots, and Survivors in South Asia. Delhi: Oxford University Press.

1998   Official Narratives, Rumour, and the Social Production of Hate. Social Identities 4(1):1–23.

Elphick, Richard

1977   Kraal and Castle: Khoikhoi and the Founding of South Africa. New Haven: Yale University Press.

Enloe, Cynthia

1979   Ethnic Soldiers: State Security in Divided Societies. London: Penguin Books.

Ens, Gerhard J.

1996   Homeland to Hinterland: The Changing World of the Red River Métis in the 19th century. Toronto: University of Toronto Press.

Finch III, Major Raymond C.

1997   A Face of Future Battle: Chechen Fighter Shamil Basayev. Military Review. May–June. Pp. 33–48.

Flanagan, Thomas

1999   Bands, Tribes or Nations? Pimohtewin: The School of Native Studies On-Line Journal. University of Alberta 1(1).

Foster, John E.

1975   The Home Guard Cree and Hudson's Bay Company: The First Hundred Years. In Approaches to Native History. D.A. Muise, ed. Ottawa: National Museums of Canada.

1976   The Origins of the Mixed Bloods in the Canadian West. In Essays on Western History. L.H. Thomas, ed. Edmonton: University of Alberta Press.

1978   The Indian Trader in the Hudson Bay Fur Trade Tradition. In Proceedings of the Second Congress, Canadian Ethnological Society, vol. 2, Ottawa: National Museums of Canada.

1985   Some Questions and Perspectives on the Problem of Métis Roots. In The New Peoples: Being and Becoming Métis. Jacqueline Peterson and Jennifer S. H. Brown, eds. Pp. 73–91. Winnipeg: University of Manitoba Press.

1994   Wintering, the Outsider Adult Male, and the Ethnogenesis of the Western Plains Métis. Prairie Forum 19:1–13.

1999   The Home Guard Cree and Hudson's Bay Company: The First Hundred Years.

In Approaches to Native History. D. A. Muise, ed. Ottowa: National Museums of Canada.

2000   The Origins of the Mixed Bloods in the Canadian West. *In* Essays on Western History. L. H. Thomas, ed. Edmonton: University of Alberta Press.

Gammar, Moshe

1994   Muslim Resistance to the Tsar: Shamil and the Conquest of Chechnia and Daghestan. London: Frank Cass.

Geertz, Clifford

2000   Available Light: Anthropological Reflections on Philosophical Topics. Princeton: Princeton University Press.

Geschiere, Peter, and Francis Nymanjoh

2000   Capitalism and Autochthony: The Seesaw of Mobility and Belonging. Public Culture 12(2):423–452.

Holquist, Peter

1998   From Estate to Ethos: The Changing Naure of Cossack Identity in the Twentieth Century. *In* Russia at a Crossroads: History, Memory, and Political Practice. Nurit Schleifman, ed. London and Portland, OR: Frank Cass.

Hope, Alec Derwent

1986   The Wandering Islands. *In* A. D. Hope: Selected Poems. Manchester, UK:

[1955]   Carcenet Press. Pp. 20–21.

Karakasidou, Anastasia

1997   Fields of Wheat, Hills of Blood: Passages to Nationhood in Greek Macedonia. Chicago: University of Chicago Press.

Karny, Yo'av

2000   Highlanders: A Journey to the Caucasus in Quest of Memory. New York: Farrar, Straus and Giroux.

Layton, Susan

1994   Russian Literature and Empire: Conquest of the Caucasus from Pushkin to Tolstoy. Cambridge: Cambridge University Press.

1997   Nineteenth-Century Russian Mythologies of Caucasian Savagery. *In* Russia's Orient: Imperial Borderlands and Peoples, 1700–1917. Daniel R. Brower and Edward J. Lazzarini, eds. Pp. 80–100.

Legassick, Martin

1989   The Northern Frontier to c. 1840: The Rise and Decline of the Griqua People. *In* The Shaping of South African Society, 1652–1840. Richard Elphick and Herman Giliomee, eds. Pp. 358–420. Middletown: Wesleyan University Press.

Levi-Strauss, Claude

1969   The Elementary Structures of Kinship [1949]. Trans. James H. Bell and John von Strummer. Ed. Rodney Needham. Boston: Beacon Press.

Marais, J. S.

1939   The Cape Coloured People, 1652-1937. London: Longmans, Green.

Methven, J. J.

1997   Andele: The Mexican Kiowa Captive [1899]. With an Introduction by James F. Brooks. Albuquerque: University of New Mexico Press.

Mies, Maria
    1988   Social Origins of the Sexual Division of Labor. *In* Women: The Last Colony. Maria Mies, Veronika Bennholdt-Thompson, and Claudia van Werlhof, eds. Pp. 67–95. London: Zed Books.
Momaday, N. Scott
    1976   The Names. A Memoir. Tucson: University of Arizona Press.
Morris, Alan G.
    1997   The Griqua and the Khoikhoi: Biology, Ethnicity, and the Construction of Identity. Kronos: Journal of Cape History. 24:106–118.
Niezen, Ronald
    2000   Recognizing Indigenism: Canadian Unity and the International Movement of Indigenous Peoples. Comparative Studies in Society and History. 42:1 Pp. 119–148.
Nirenberg, David
    1996   Communities of Violence: Persecution of Minorities in the Middle Ages. Princeton: Princeton University Press.
Peterson, Jacqueline
    1988   Women Dreaming: The Religiopsychology of Indian-White Marriages and the Rise of Métis Culture. *In* Western Women, Their Land, Their Lives. Vicki Ruiz, Sandra Schackel, and Janet Monk, eds. Pp. 49–68. Albuquerque: University of New Mexico Press.
Poole, Deborah
    1988   Landscapes of Power in a Cattle-Rustling Culture of Southern Andean Peru. Dialectical Anthropology 12:367–398.
    1994   Anthropological Perspectives on Violence and Culture—A View from the Peruvian High Provinces. *In* Unruly Order: Violence, Power, and Cultural Identity in the High Provinces of Southern Peru. D. Poole, ed. Pp. 1–30. Boulder, CO: Westview Press.
Ross, Robert
    1976   Adam Kok's Griquas: A Study in the Development of Stratification in South Africa. Cambridge: Cambridge University Press.
Rubin, Gayle
    1977   The Traffic in Women: Notes on the "Political Economy" of Sex. *In* Toward an Anthropology of Women. Rayna Rapp Reiter, ed. New York: Monthly Review Press.
Scott, James S.
    1999   Seeing Like a State: How Certain Schemes to Imporve the Human Condition have Failed. New Haven: Yale University Press.
Shepherdson, Charles
    1999   Comment. *In* James F. Brooks, Nations, Tribes, and Colours: Metaphors Toward a History for the Twenty-First Century. Occasional Papers from the School of Social Science, 3. Institute for Advanced Study, Princeton.
Spickard, Paul, and W. Jeffrey Borroughs, eds.
    2000   We Are a People: Narrative and Multiplicity in Constructing Ethnic Identity. Philadelphia: Temple University Press.

Van Kirk, Sylvia
   1980   Many Tender Ties: Women in Fur Trade Society, 1670–1870. Norman: University of Oklahoma Press.
Watson, Rubie S., ed.
   1994   Memory, History, and Opposition under State Socialism. Santa Fe: School of American Research Press.

NOTES ON CONTRIBUTORS

PATRICIA C. ALBERS, Ph.D. in Anthropology, University of Wisconsin, Madison, is currently chair and professor of the Department of American Indian Studies at the University of Minnesota-Twin Cities. Over the past 30 years, she has published numerous articles in the areas of gender, political economy, intertribal relations, and visual representation. Her most recent publication, "Symbols, Souvenirs and Sentiments: Early Postcard Imagery of Plains Indians," appeared in the book *Delivering Views*, coedited by Christaud Geary and Virginia Webb.

JAMES F. BROOKS is assistant professor of history at the University of California, Santa Barbara. He has held National Endowment for the Humanities Fellowships at the Institute for Advanced Study in Princeton and the School of American Research in Santa Fe. His essays have received the Joan Jensen–Darlis Miller Prize for western women's history (1997) and the Arrell Morgan Gibson Award for Native American history (2000). Most recently, he authored *Captives and Cousins: Slavery, Kinship, and Community in the Southwest Borderlands* (2001) and edited *Confounding the Color Line: Red-Black Relations in Multidisciplinary Perspective* (2001).

JULIE CRUIKSHANK is a professor of anthropology at the University of British Columbia. For more than a decade, she lived in the Yukon Territory, northwestern Canada, where she worked with the elders of Athapaskan and Tlingit ancestry recording oral traditions and life stories. She wrote *Life Lived Like a Story: Life Stories of Three Yukon Native Elders* (1990) in collaboration with Angela Sidney, Kitty Smith, and Annie Ned. Her book *The Social Life of Stories: Narrative and Knowledge in the Yukon Territory* (1998) discusses how changing historical and social circumstances continue to acquire storied meanings.

GUNLÖG FUR, associate professor of history at Växjö University, Sweden, received her Ph.D. from the University of Oklahoma in 1993. Her publications include articles on Saami-Swedish relations, the comparative colonial experiences of Saami and Lenape peoples, and Lenape women's history, the last of which is also the subject of a larger work-in-progress. She has received fellowships and grants from the Sweden-America Foundation, the American Association of University Women, and the HSFR (the Swedish equivalent of the National Endowment of the Humanities).

CRAIG HOWE, an enrolled member of the Oglala Sioux Tribe, is a fellow in American culture studies at Washington University in St. Louis. While deputy assistant director for cultural resources at the National Museum of the American Indian, he conceived and developed the inaugural exhibitions for the Museum on the Mall. Prior to his Smithsonian appointment, he was director of the D'Arcy McNickle Center for American Indian History at the Newberry Library in Chicago, where he initiated an innovative hypermedia tribal histories project. He has taught architecture and Native American studies courses in both the United States and Canada.

LEANNE HOWE is enrolled in the Choctaw Nation of Oklahoma. An author and playwright, her work appears in over a dozen anthologies as well as literary and scholarly publications. Her plays have been performed throughout the United States. In January 2000, she received her M.F.A. in creative writing from Vermont College of Norwich University. She has taught at Carleton College, Grinnell College, and Wake Forest University. She is a mother and grandmother. Her first novel *Shell Shaker* is being published by Aunt Lute Books in 2001.

JACKI THOMPSON RAND is an assistant professor at the University of Iowa with a joint appointment in history and American Indian and Native studies. She earned a Ph.D. in history from the University of Oklahoma in 1998. She is currently working on a book that focuses on connections between Kiowa society, reservation economy, and American hegemony in the late 19th century.

NANCY SHOEMAKER, associate professor of history at the University of Connecticut-Storrs, is the author of *American Indian Population Recovery in the 20th Century* (1999) and editor of *Negotiators of Change: Historical Perspectives on Native American Women* (1995). She has held research fellowships at the Newberry Library and most recently at the Huntington Library. Her current project is a comparison of 18th-century American Indian and European ideas.

INDEX